The Jewish Ethicist
Everyday Ethics for Business and Life

by
Asher Meir

KTAV Publishing House, Inc.

in association with

Business Ethics Center of Jerusalem
JERUSALEM, ISRAEL

Typesetting: Jerusalem Typesetting
Cover design: S. Kim Glassman
Jewish Ethicist cartoon graphic: Yitzhak Attias

Library of Congress Cataloging-in-Publication Data
Meir, Asher, 1961–
The Jewish Ethicist: Everyday Ethics for Business and Life / by Asher Meir
    p. cm.

    ISBN 0-88125-815-6 (hardcover) – ISBN 0-88125-809-1 (paperback)
    1. Jewish ethics. 2. Business ethics. 3. Social ethics. 4. Self-help
techniques. 1. Title.

    BJ1285.M44 2004
    296.3'6–dc22

    MEIR   2004020501

On the occasion of the publication of *The Jewish Ethicist*,
the author and the Business Ethics Center of Jerusalem would like to
express their sincere appreciation to the following devoted friends:

Mr. Paul Baan

Who through his personal encouragement and the
support of the Noaber Foundation advanced the
ethics research which added depth to this work

Mr. Daniel Goldman

Whose foresight and initiative laid the original
foundation for the Jewish Ethicist column

An Anonymous Friend

A loyal supporter who has been an inspiring cheerleader
for all our activities and the sponsor of some of our
most innovative research in Jewish Ethics

Contents

Schoolyard Ethics

Brief Introduction to the Sources

Introduction

As this book goes to press, we are well into the fourth year of the popular weekly syndicated column, "The Jewish Ethicist." The ever-growing number of surfers, subscribers, and print readers testifies to the important need this column fills: the need for advice on everyday ethical dilemmas from a thoughtful Jewish perspective.

From the many hundreds of queries, I know that my readership encompasses old and young, wealthy and poor, Jews and non-Jews. The members of this varied audience share two common denominators:

- They have an intense desire to be ethical in their marketplace relationships, but are not exactly sure how.
- They are convinced that Jewish tradition is an important source of guidance.

The Jewish Ethicist column serves as their "Guide to the Perplexed" through the ethical challenges of today's business environment.

It was only natural that the column would turn into a book. The book format enables me to overcome the limitations of space and present the important ethical insights of the Jewish Ethicist in a more complete manner. It has also enabled me to collect columns on similar topics together and highlight their common themes. Another important consideration is my faith that these discussions, which first appeared in the electronic format of the column, deserve the more permanent expression of print.

Most of all, I hope that the book will make the educational and ethical message of the Jewish Ethicist accessible to a new, broader readership. In this way I hope to continue to do my little bit to move the world toward the ethical perfection expected of mankind by our Creator.

PERPLEXED BUT PERSISTENT

Two generations ago, there were far fewer perplexed individuals. Most people had firmly anchored beliefs about ethical practices, absorbed from their upbringing and from the management culture of their place of work. Furthermore, the business environment was much more stable. The ethical issues of the 1950s were hardly different from those of the 1350s. There were certainly many individuals who did not act ethically, but comparatively few who were uncertain what the ethical course of action really was.

Nowadays, the situation is much different. Today, there are so many competing sources of ethical values that people do not know where to start. Schools and even parents are reluctant to seem authoritarian by giving unambiguous ethical guidelines. Furthermore, today's marketplace is far more complex than that of two generations ago. Ultra-sophisticated accounting tools blur the line separating tax avoidance and tax evasion. Electronic commerce has created an unprecedented degree of anonymity in business. Government regulation has become so extensive that people are confused about the difference between law and ethics.

One thing that has not changed is the fundamental human desire to be ethical. The post-modern maelstrom of values has not, on the whole, generated an attitude of indifference and relativism toward matters of morality; this kind of degeneration is seen only among a small number of "enlightened" academics. By contrast, the average person may be perplexed, but is never disheartened. The proof is in the Jewish Ethicist's inbox, overflowing with the passionate concerns of involved readers who seek guidance in every area of daily conduct. The stubborn determination of Jewish Ethicist readers to clarify and exemplify the ethical course of action in every area of business and everyday life is majestic and inspiring.

Even as I step into the breach and try to clarify the path of integrity, the objective of the Jewish Ethicist is not to act as a substitute for the ethical judgment of the reader by recommending an authoritative guide to action. On the contrary, the columns strive primarily to explain the underlying ethical and educational principles at work, so as to strengthen and cultivate these values in the reader.

THE IMPORTANCE OF JEWISH TRADITION

There are several reasons why the readers of the Jewish Ethicist look to the Jewish tradition as an indispensable source of guidance. One is religious and cultural; most of the readers are Jews with a vibrant commitment to their Jewish identity, and they want, first and foremost, to obtain guidance from their own tradition. But there are two other reasons why Jewish tradition is particularly esteemed as a source of guidance in business ethics, even by non-Jews.

One reason is the remarkable continuity of Jewish tradition. Despite the unbelievable degree of physical dislocation experienced over the millennia by the Jewish people, our legal tradition displays an astonishing degree of continuity and coherence. Any solution arrived at by Jewish law and tradition may fairly be stated to be "tried and true." Most of the ethical insights mentioned in these columns come from the Talmud, a remarkable authoritative corpus of Jewish law and lore compiled over a period of centuries and sealed more than a millennium ago. These same principles have been effectively guiding commerce among the Jewish people for countless generations.

An additional reason why people look to Jewish tradition as a uniquely valuable guide to business ethics is the widespread awareness that the Jewish religious tradition acknowledges the importance and value of the marketplace. Our religion does not condemn business or consider it religiously irrelevant. In fact, the Torah strives to elevate and sanctify business, just as it strives to elevate and sanctify all other areas of human activity. The Torah sanctifies our eating by providing clear criteria for kosher and unkosher foods; it sanctifies our experience of time by fixing times for prayer and, most of all, by requiring us to refrain from weekday activities on the holy Sabbath; and it sanctifies our business life through the myriad commandments that regulate commerce.

Jews have long been known for their prominent role in business, and even many leading religious figures have been involved in business. This includes some of the most famous talmudic sages as well as a number of Hasidic rebbes. At all times these committed Jews have acknowledged the need for their business practices to conform to the standards of Jewish law, which imposes rigid yet realistic standards of ethical behavior.

WHAT IS "JEWISH BUSINESS ETHICS"?

The title "Jewish Ethicist" suggests that there is a uniquely Jewish approach to ethical questions. Our aspiration throughout this book is to present an approach to ethical behavior that is firmly rooted in the Jewish sources. The best way to understand this approach is not to analyze it but to experience it by reading the columns. However, I will say a few words here about the meaning of a Jewish business ethics.

The foremost Jewish source for ethical guidance is, of course, the Torah–the Five Books of Moses, which constitute the original and most authoritative revelation to the Jewish people. Second to the Torah are all the other books of the Hebrew Bible, encompassing God's explicit revelation of His divine plan for humanity through prophecy and divine inspiration. Even a casual reader of the Bible is struck by its passionate concern for integrity and its uncompromising insistence on the equality of all before the Creator.

Another invaluable traditional source is the wisdom of the rabbinic sages of all generations. The Talmud and the midrashic (exegetical) works give us a wealth of ethical maxims as well as instructive examples from the demanding ethical standards of our ancient rabbis.

The Jewish Ethicist makes ample use of these sources, but also draws very heavily on a third source: Jewish law. In our tradition, the main instrument for the elevation and sanctification of daily life is neither prophetic exhortation nor personal example but religious law, the halakhah. The laws of commerce ground the ethical principles in a firm bedrock of immutable mandates. The citations of the halakhah in the columns presented in this book come most often from the great codifications of Jewish law, such as the Mishneh Torah of Maimonides and the Shulhan Arukh of Joseph Caro, but also include the responsa literature and such works as the Sefer ha-Hinnukh.

While the laws of halakhah are obligatory only for Jews, our approach maintains that these *legal* rules express and enunciate eternal and universal *ethical* principles. This idea was given very eloquent expression by the great medieval authority Nachmanides (Rabbi Moses ben Nachman). In his great commentary on the Torah, Nachmanides discusses the commandment "And you shall do what is straight and right"[1]. Here the Torah is commanding us to act in an ethical way, yet the commandment begs the question of how we know what course of action is the ethical one. Nachmanides explains that we are able to deduce general ethical principles from the specific mandates of the many laws of interpersonal behavior, principles that apply even in instances that may be beyond the scope of the law.

> For it is impossible to mention in the Torah all of man's conduct with his neighbors and friends, all his business transactions, and all the institutions of community and national life. Rather, after having mentioned a number of them, such as "Do not go about as a talebearer"[2], "Do not take vengeance or bear a grudge"[3], "Do not stand idly by your neighbor's blood"[4], "Do not curse the deaf"[5], "Stand before the aged"[6], and others like them, [Scripture] goes back to say in a general way that one should do the good and the straight in all matters.

We see that ethical behavior, the good and the straight, is neither independent of fulfillment of the commandments nor synonymous with them; it is an extension and extrapolation of the ethical examples embodied in them. For this reason, the columns never hesitate to draw ethical insights from the rules of Jewish law.

ACKNOWLEDGMENTS

The true father of the Jewish Ethicist column is Rabbi Nechemia Coopersmith of the remarkable Jewish super-site aish.com. Rabbi Coopersmith, an intrepid pioneer of the Jewish Internet, was the first to sense the vast demand for a weekly column that would discuss everyday ethical dilemmas from a Jewish point of view. From the very beginning he defined the tone of a column that would be serious and challenging without being highbrow or overly intellectual. Every column benefited from Rabbi Coopersmith's review and input.

Turning a weekly column into a book of permanence and importance is an involved process. The remarkable success of this transition is due in large measure to the insight and encouragement of the staff of Ktav Publishing House, including the publisher, Bernard Scharfstein, and our dedicated editor, Robert Milch. It is also a privilege to acknowledge the important contribution of my colleagues at the Business Ethics Center of Jerusalem: Rabbi Pinchas Rosenstein, Menny Ben Ady, and in particular the profound insights of Rabbi Yoel Domb. And of course there is the immeasurable debt to my wife, Attara. Our sages say that a man who is without a wife is without Torah; an everyday life shared with a truly upright individual is the best source of guidance and enlightenment in ethical matters.

But without doubt the main acknowledgment is to our tens of thousands of readers. I genuinely feel that reading the questions in this book, and perceiving the ethical sensitivity that informs them, would be no less enlightening than reading the answers. In my personal life, which involves the same ethical dilemmas faced by everyone else, my foremost criterion is: What would my readers and students expect of me in this situation?

In this vein, I close with the statement of the talmudic sage Rabbi Hanina: "I have learned much from my teachers, and even more from my colleagues; but more than from all of these have I learned from my students"[7].

ENDNOTES

1. Deuteronomy 6:18
2. Leviticus 19:16
3. Leviticus 19:18
4. Leviticus 19:16
5. Leviticus 19:14
6. Leviticus 19:32
7. Ta'anit 7a

THE BIG PICTURE

Introduction

Ethical Business

Monopoly on Morals?

The Humane Workplace

Globalization

Biblical Ethics

Gilt Guilt

Introduction

The practice of Judaism, with its emphasis on fulfilling the practical, everyday commandments, trains us to focus our ethical energies mainly at the level of the individual ethical act. The most important way we can improve and perfect the world is for each of us to focus on improving and perfecting our own character and actions.

Yet Jewish tradition, even as it cultivates the individual ethical act, also envisions ethical ideals for society as a whole. We see this most prominently in the tidings of the Jewish prophets of a perfect future world – tidings which continue to inspire all mankind. The harmony between these two levels of ethical insight is highlighted by the Sabbath morning synagogue service. The centerpiece of this service is the reading of the Torah, which is the source of our detailed individual obligations, but this reading is always followed by a reading from the prophetic works (*haftara*) which often gives us a breathtaking glimpse of distant yet attainable human completeness.

This chapter is devoted to studying the big picture: What is the place of business in the divine plan for the world? How can we understand the gigantic currents of change that buffet us, such as the phenomenon of globalization? What is the precise nature of the guidance that Jewish tradition provides for us?

One theme will accompany us consistently throughout this chapter: When the prophets and sages looked at economic systems, their main concern was not efficiency or productive capacity, however important these may be. These men of the spirit directed their attention to the ability of economic systems to promote harmonious and ethical human relationships.

Ethical Business

IS BUSINESS REALLY ETHICAL?

The essence of business is trade: one person trades his goods or services for those of somebody else, for mutual benefit. This very concept of "gains from trade" automatically implies a certain dimension of exploitation: each person is exploiting the possessions and talents of the other for his own advantage. Furthermore, the most successful business people are often managers and traders, who do not engage directly in production at all. This dimension of exploitation and inequality raises ethical questions.

Q The biblical ideal seems to be "each man under his vine and under his fig tree,"[1] with each person engaging in independent productive activity. In light of this, is it ethical to make a living through business and commerce?

A It is true that the blessings of the Torah are usually directed to the individual farmer or herder, not to the trader. Nonetheless, we also find that our tradition greatly esteems the role of commerce. When Jacob arrived in Shechem, the Torah tells us, he "graced" the city.[2] How did he do this? Our sages explain that he established the foundations of commerce by establishing coinage or a marketplace.[3]

In order to understand this approach, we have to understand the role of commerce in human society. Why is commerce necessary to get goods and services to people in the first place? After all, the Creator could easily have arranged the world so that all our needs would be fulfilled without commerce or even without effort, as in the Garden of Eden.

One aspect of the importance of commerce is that it gives people a motivation for cooperation. When every person or every nation is self-sufficient economically, there is a tendency for them to be isolated or even hostile. However, when people see that there is an opportunity for mutual gain through trade, they learn to accommodate each other and get along.

So we see that even the opportunistic Laban, who repeatedly tries to exploit Jacob, learns to get along with him because he needs his help as a hired hand;[4] and when Jacob made his gesture of friendship through commerce with the residents of Shechem, they responded by offering to let his family "live and trade" there.[5]

Of course there is still a special importance to agriculture. The Bible consistently emphasizes that God's blessing is manifest in abundant crops. Rabbi Yair Bachrach explains agriculture's special status as follows: Even though *all* of our earnings are only attained through the blessing of God, the miraculous divine contribution is particularly evident in agriculture.[6] This is because it seems as if we are getting something from nothing, since crops grow from rotting seeds buried in the ground.

Ultimately, however, we have to recognize that earnings from business, no less than those from farming, are a divine blessing, and not just the fruits of luck or of our own cleverness. The Mishnah states, "Wealth and poverty do not come from a profession, for everything is according to merit."[7] From a religious point of view, business is neither more nor less ethical than any other line of work.

"EACH MAN UNDER HIS VINE AND HIS FIG TREE"

We may infer from the preceding discussion that a situation where everyone lived in self-sufficient isolation in his own freehold would actually not be ideal. A fascinating insight from Jewish tradition supports this conclusion.

As the question points out, Scripture tells us, "And Judah and Israel dwelt safely, each man under his vine and his fig tree, from Dan to Beersheba, all the days of Solomon." This sounds idyllic. But the great medieval rabbi Rav Hai Gaon tells us that this very situation caused King Solomon to institute an important legal reform.

Many people are aware that Jewish communities strive to erect an *eruv*, a symbolic enclosure of the neighborhood. Only when an *eruv* is present are observant Jews allowed to carry items from house to house on the Sabbath. Otherwise, each house is considered a separate domain, and carrying from one domain to another is forbidden on Shabbat. The literal meaning of the word *eruv* is "mixture" – all of the different properties are merged together into a single domain. A very ancient tradition records that the requirement for an *eruv* originated in this very same idyllic time of King Solomon.[8]

Rav Hai Gaon explain this as follows: Until the time of Solomon, the Jewish people were in an almost constant state of conflict. The entire country was like one great armed camp. Only in his time did Israel "dwell safely." And in a military camp, there is no need for an *eruv*.[9] We can explain that in time of war, there is an instinctive sense of community and interdependence. There is no need for artificial means to join people together. But the situation of "each man under his vine and his fig tree" carries the danger of isolation and separation; precisely then there is a need to stimulate people to go beyond their private domains and interact with others. One such motivator is mutual economic improvement through trade.

BUSINESS AND BUSINESS ETHICS

This insight into the value of commerce underscores the special importance of business ethics. Jewish tradition is very strict about this aspect of our law, stating that "the punishment for cheating in measures is even greater than the punishment for sexual immorality."[10] If the true purpose of business were to create prosperity, then we could excuse some laxity in business ethics, so long as it did not harm profitability too much. But if the entire purpose of commerce is to create brotherhood and mutual trust, then anything which contradicts this is not only inexcusable in itself, it frustrates the very purpose of commerce.

Business is not only ethical, it is one of the most important ways that God gave us to foster coexistence and understanding among human beings. But this is dependent on business being conducted in an ethical way, in a manner based on cooperation and understanding, not on exploitation.

Monopoly on Morals?

IS THE TORAH THE ONLY GUIDE TO ETHICAL BEHAVIOR?

The idea of "Jewish ethics" is a bit of a paradox. The essence of ethical principles is that they strive for universal validity; yet the designation "Jewish ethics" suggests something uniquely Jewish. The harmonization we strive for in the Jewish Ethicist is to find insights from Jewish tradition on ethical principles that can guide all mankind. But how does this source of ethical understanding fit in with other sources, such as secular ethical thinkers or insights from other cultures?

Q The Jewish Ethicist always gives answers from a Jewish perspective. But does the Torah really have a monopoly on morals? After all, all cultures have ethical ideals, including some that are not given prominence in Jewish tradition.

A The most basic answer to your question is that the Torah does not have a monopoly on morals. All nations have ethical ideals, and valuable moral insights are found in the cultures of every people. Our tradition acknowledges this fact. For example, consider the following passage from the Talmud:[11]

> Rabbi Eliezer was asked, How far does the obligation to honor parents extend? He said, Go and see what a certain non-Jew in Ashkelon, Damma ben Natina, did for his father. [He was offered a massive sum for some precious stones], and the key was under his father's pillow, but he refused to disturb him.

And Maimonides, the foremost Jewish philosopher of the Middle Ages, does not hesitate to cite Aristotle as an authority and example in matters of ethics; he even calls Aristotle "the chief of philosophers."[12]

We obtain a deeper insight into this principle from the prophetic writings. The prophet Isaiah tells the Jewish people that in the future, "Kings will be your tutors."[13] On the one hand, a tutor serves his charge, so this prophecy shows that the honor of the people of Israel will be so great that royalty will serve us. Yet a tutor is someone who provides guidance and instruction; we see that even at the time of the redemption we will still need to learn from the noblest elements of other cultures.

As an example of this prophecy, the Talmud cites the example of the Persian king Yezdegerd, who gave gentle, fatherly advice on dignified deportment to one of the Torah sages who visited him, showing that during the period of our exile we are charged with learning the most elevated elements of the cultures that generously adopt and host our people.[14]

Of course the converse is also true; our sojourn in exile helps to spread the exalted values of our people to other lands and cultures. In the same chapter, the prophet informs us that the Jewish people are to be a "light unto the nations."[15]

It should not be surprising that our tradition sanctions learning moral principles from other cultures. The study of ethics is in large measure a branch of secular wisdom. A person who wants to build a sturdy and attractive house will study the most enlightening works of architecture and construction, without any regard for the nationality or religion of their authors. Likewise, if we want to construct a sturdy and fitting communal life, we are in need of the thoughts and insights of wise individuals of all backgrounds.

However, we must remember that ultimately Torah is not about ethics alone; it is above all about holiness, about drawing near to God. Our sages repeatedly taught that ethical perfection is a necessary *prerequisite* for spiritual elevation; but it is in no way a *substitute*. Consider the following well-known midrash:[16]

> Rabbi Yishmael the son of Rav Nahman stated, Consideration precedes Torah, as it is written: "[He placed at the east of Eden cherubim and the turning sword] to keep the way to the tree of life."[17] "The way" refers to consideration; the Tree of Life is Torah.

It is true that ethical behavior comes first; that is how we set out on the way. But it is only the way – the *goal* is the Tree of Life, which is Torah.

Regarding this distinction, the Midrash tells us: "If you hear that there is wisdom among the nations, believe it. If you hear that there is Torah among the nations, do not believe it."[18] Since ethics is a branch of wisdom, we certainly believe and accept that we can find much of this wisdom in other peoples. Indeed, Jewish law prescribes a special benediction to be recited when one sees a gentile scholar learned in secular wisdom; the benediction praises God "who gave of His wisdom to flesh and blood."[19] If we encounter a scholar with profound insight into the wisdom of human relations and integrity, we not only acknowledge this fact but also thank the Creator for making this wisdom accessible to us through such a person. But we recognize that the ultimate, transcendent wisdom is found only in Torah.

The Jewish tradition is our foremost source of ethical guidance, but not our only one. Wise individuals of every nation and culture can provide insights into ethical principles, and we are obliged to learn from them and to acknowledge our debt to their wisdom. Such knowledge helps us to build a foundation of upright behavior that can serve as the springboard to holiness.

But there is still unique importance in learning ethics from the Torah. First of all, the source of the ethical principles learned from the Torah is revelation, not speculation. Therefore we can be confident that these principles are valid and eternal.

Second, it is true that all valid ethical principles serve as a foundation for moving *toward* holiness. But the principles enunciated in the Torah literature, since they stem from Torah, already *incorporate* an element of holiness.

The Torah does not have a monopoly on morals, which is a branch of wisdom that studies the way to create a human society that embodies integrity and dignity. These qualities, which can be learned from wise people of all backgrounds, are necessary prerequisites for significant growth in holiness, which is achieved through Torah. However, morals learned from the Torah tradition are sure to be a reliable foundation for spiritual growth, and indeed already bear within them a unique spiritual radiance due to their holy source.

The Humane Workplace

CAN AUTHORITY IN THE WORKPLACE EVER BE EXERCISED
FAIRLY?

The Torah contains many commandments that limit the abuse of workplace authority; for example, workers must be paid on time and servants treated humanely. But some people think that detailed regulations such as these will never be enough; what is necessary is an overhaul of the entire system of workplace authority. Let us examine whether the visionary aspect of Judaism identifies with this ambition.

Q How can businesses create new models for a just society? Shouldn't we strive to transform our workplaces from competitive cost-cutters to caring cooperatives?

A There is a very influential movement that wants to create a more just society from the ground up, by remodeling basic institutions. Many people believe that replacing families and firms with communes and cooperatives will lead to a more equitable and compassionate society.

Jewish tradition certainly affirms that the world needs repair, what our tradition calls "*tikun olam*," and that we all need to concern ourselves with advancing the world toward the ultimate perfection of the final redemption, when the righteous Redeemer will "judge the poor with righteousness, and reprove with equity for the meek of the earth."[20] However, we have to consider whether we agree with today's social critics on the ideal way to effect this transformation.

On one point we certainly differ from the anti-authority critics: Jewish tradition cannot condone remaking the family. Our religious tradition has never wavered from the belief that the irreplaceable foundation of a just human society is the nuclear family, with children who acknowledge and honor their parents.

But Judaism presents no fundamental obstacles to remodeling economic institutions. For example, if a group of people want to pool their resources and efforts to create a cooperative – a kibbutz or the like – there is nothing wrong with that. By the same token, Jewish tradition does not condemn equitable government intervention in economic life.

However, we should not fall into the trap of viewing social overhaul as the main way to repair society. It is true that the passion for justice inspired by the prophets has been a driving force behind many revolutionary social movements, but if we read the words of the prophets themselves, we see that they were advocating a different kind of revolution, one that works from the bottom up: a world where each individual takes responsibility to act in a righteous and ethical manner.

Let us examine the words of the prophet Zechariah: "These are the things which you shall do: Speak truth each man to his fellow; judge with truth, justice, and peace in your gates. Don't plot against your fellow in your heart, and do not love false oaths, for all these I hate, says God."[21] The prophet is not demanding that we create revolutionary new social institutions; rather, each individual must strive to act within existing institutions in a true, just, and peaceful way.

Some places of business have cultures that encourage and reward ethical behavior, whereas others have cultures, or subcultures, that make meeting the prophetic standard impossible. So if a manager decides to experiment with a new business structure in the belief that the innovation will empower the individual employee to act honestly, that is praiseworthy.

But if the motivation for tinkering is the belief that it is impossible to act honestly in an ordinary business firm, then the initiative is likely to be counterproductive. The misguided, sanctimonious belief that ordinary business is inherently unethical is one of the main obstacles to motivating business people to conduct themselves in an upright fashion.

REVOLUTION VS. EVOLUTION

Jewish tradition does not deny the importance of great and dramatic acts, but the focus has always been on the silent revolution of individual righteousness. This message is implied in one of the best-known biblical stories, that of the prophet Elijah's encounter in the desert.

As recounted in the eighteenth chapter of First Kings, many of Elijah's countrymen were attracted by the pagan cult of Baal. Elijah decided that the best way to battle this phenomenon was through a dramatic confrontation. To this end, he staged a spectacular showdown with the prophets of Baal on Mount Carmel. Despite the entreaties and the self-mutilation of the hundreds of pagan priests, their offering was not consumed, whereas Elijah's prayer to God was answered with fire which descended from on high and consumed Elijah's offering as well as the wood, even though it had been soaked with water.

This display was so awe-inspiring that the spectators immediately bowed down and proclaimed, "the LORD is God." It seemed as if Elijah had effected a revolutionary change in the people's consciousness.

Yet in the next chapter we discover that Elijah is still a wanted man, and is compelled to flee to the desert. There God told him to stand on a mountain.

> And behold, the LORD passed by, and a great and strong wind rent the mountains and shattered the rocks before the LORD; the LORD was not in the wind. And after the wind was an earthquake; the LORD was not in the earthquake. And after the earthquake a fire; the LORD was not in the fire. And after the fire was a still small voice.

It was in this voice that God spoke to Elijah.

The stirring showdown on Mount Carmel had the visceral impact of a hurricane, or an earthquake, or a great fire. But in the end the voice of God comes to us as something still and small.

Likewise, the tidings of modern social revolutions are powerful and dramatic. Some of them may even be valuable in and of themselves. But ultimately revolution is not a reliable, consistent way of bringing Godliness into our everyday experience.

The biblical prophets were not social revolutionaries in the modern sense. They did not seek to overthrow kings or dispossess the wealthy. Their aim was far more revolutionary: they sought to motivate each of us to fulfill our own individual ethical and charitable obligations. Their vision, which has lost none of its inspirational power over the millennia, remains the main foundation of business ethics.

Globalization

IS GLOBALIZATION A FORCE FOR ETHICAL PROGRESS?

In the past few years we have witnessed a dramatic increase in the scope of international trade and in the power and influence of international business and supra-national economic agencies. This phenomenon presents many ethical dilemmas for the individual and for society as a whole. What are the risks and benefits of a worldwide marketplace?

Q The spread of market institutions worldwide has very powerful supporters and very vocal detractors. What does Jewish tradition tell us about this phenomenon?

A "Globalization" refers to the increasing integration of the economies of virtually all the nations of the world into a more unified global economy, in which market forces are dominant and multinational companies play a major role.

Globalization arouses extreme reactions. Some commentators view it with practically messianic admiration: It brings growth, democracy, peace, and integration of cultures leading to brotherhood.

Others tend to demonize globalization, adopting a pessimistic view of the very same phenomena: It brings despoiling of poor countries, a breakdown of traditional social and authority structures, competition and resentment leading to conflict, and destruction of indigenous cultures resulting in a degraded world culture of the lowest common denominator.

In order to discern the Jewish approach to these questions, we must keep one fundamental insight in mind: the process of globalization is not really a new phenomenon. The great empires of the ancient Near East and the Middle East also united markets and imposed aspects of the conqueror's cosmopolitan culture on a multitude of poorer and tinier kingdoms. The sages of the Talmud experienced this process and had a number of enlightening insights regarding it.

Our ancient rabbis certainly knew how to appreciate the economic benefits of globalization – the ability to enjoy the products of many nations at a reasonable price and with minimal effort. The Talmud[22] relates:

> Ben Zoma…used to say, How much effort Adam had to invest in order to eat bread: he had to plow, sow, gather, heap, thresh, winnow, sort, sift, knead, and bake. Only then could he eat. Yet I wake up and find all of these prepared for me. …All the nations of the world go out of their way and come to my doorstep, and I wake up to find all these before me.

Thus those enamored of globalization can find support for their view in the Jewish tradition.

Other Jewish leaders, however, were keenly aware that economic development can be a tool of domination and moral decay. When Rabbi Yehudah praised the Romans, saying, "They have established marketplaces, built bridges, and made bathhouses," Rabbi Shimon bar Yochai replied cynically: "They have established marketplaces in order to provide a place for prostitutes, bathhouses to indulge themselves, and bridges in order to collect tolls."[23] It seems that the non-governmental organizations that protest the destructive impact of globalization also have a very distinguished precedent.

But it is critically important to note that Rabbi Shimon bar Yochai did not deny the benefits of marketplaces or bathhouses. The opposite is true, as we learn from the continuation of the very same story. The Talmud goes on to relate that when the Roman authorities sought to punish Rabbi Shimon for his words, he hid out with his son for a number of years until the decree was rescinded. As he left the cave where he had been hiding, he decided that he had to do something practical to help mankind. His model, states the Talmud, was the patriarch Jacob. For the Torah tells us that when Jacob reached Shechem, he "graced" the city.[24] Our tradition explains that he graced it with a material benefit of some kind, giving the nearly identical examples of coinage, a marketplace, and a bathhouse!

So we see that markets can be either a mortal enemy that we may risk our lives to protest, or conversely a source of human benefit that we go out of our way to establish. What exactly is the distinction? We need to examine more carefully the differences between the globalization of Jacob, which served as an example for Rabbi Shimon, and the globalization of the Roman Empire, which Rabbi Shimon risked his life to criticize. Let us examine a few.

- *Intent.* Rabbi Shimon states that the intent of the Romans was for self-indulgence and self-aggrandizement. This approach is echoed by a very similar passage elsewhere in the Talmud.[25] By contrast, Jacob's intention was to "grace the city" – to show friendship to the inhabitants.

- *Morality.* The Romans used the marketplace as a site for immorality, such as prostitution. By comparison, the family of Jacob, during their stay in Shechem, were extremely zealous about morality and modesty.

- *Compulsion.* The verse in Genesis states that Jacob graced the *face* of the city. The commentators explain this as meaning that he did not actually enter the city but established his encampment, and his marketplace, on the outskirts. This demonstrates a desire to attract, rather than compel, the residents to take advantage of the benefits of markets, which is rather different from the heavy-handed approach of ancient Rome.

- *Respect for legitimate local leadership.* We see from the Torah that Jacob tried to work with the king and prince of Shechem, who enjoyed the support of the citizens. The Midrash[26] states that he sent gifts to all of the leading officials.

- *Consistency.* One of the complaints against globalization is that the rich countries that impose market institutions in developing countries also try to evade these same institutions by obtaining special political favors. We see that Jacob not only encouraged equitable market institutions for others; he also subjected himself to them by paying full price for his field.[27]

Globalization can be a force for economic and humanistic benefit as long as the powerful groups that spread it and the cultures that adopt it keep it in perspective. Worldwide markets are a good basis for prosperity and understanding, but we need to be careful not to follow the example of Rome, which used them as a bridgehead for immorality and domination. Instead, we need to follow the example of Jacob, who realized that the marketplace is a benefit when it has grace – a sense of proportion and propriety.

Biblical Ethics

WHY DOES THE BIBLE CONDONE ARCHAIC PRACTICES SUCH AS SLAVERY?

The Jewish people, and indeed mankind as a whole, view the Bible as a vibrant source of ethical inspiration. At the same time, some of the institutions described and even condoned in the pages of Scripture do not harmonize with our modern ethical sensibilities. The Torah seems to condone economic institutions that are archaic, to say the least. We need to carefully examine the nature of the ethical insights provided by the prophetic writings.

Q Some of the institutions described in Scripture do not seem very ethical. For instance, we find that slavery is condoned. How then can we view the laws of the Torah as the foremost source of ethical guidance?

A There is unquestionably a certain tension between the ethical values emphasized in Scripture and some of the practices and institutions regulated and accepted by biblical law. In order to understand this paradox, we have to deepen our understanding of how the Torah is meant to lead mankind to an ideal human society.

The central insight in this understanding is that Torah does not dictate exactly how our society should function. The object of the law is not that human beings should be robots and all of their actions inflexibly established by divine decree. The Torah gives *specific laws* that legislate a basic level of ethical behavior together with *exalted values* that guide us in using our own conscience and ethical judgment to build on these values and move mankind forward to the divine ideal.

One source for these ideals is the stories and exhortations in the Torah. For example, the idea of human brotherhood and equality is learned from the creation story. The Talmud states that even though God wanted the world to be filled with many people, He began the human race with a single individual to teach us that all humans are brothers, and no one can boast a lineage more elevated than anyone else's. We all have the same father, Adam, and afterwards Noah.[28]

Another way we can discern the divine ideals is from the laws themselves. Beyond their specific content, each law has a profound inner message. The great medieval rabbi, Nachmanides, writes in his commentary on the Torah:[29]

> It is impossible to mention in the Torah every detail of a person's conduct with his neighbors and friends, all of his business dealings and the policies of towns and countries, but after it [the Torah] mentioned many [individual laws]…it went back to state generally that we should do the right and the good in everything.

In other words, the Torah gives us specific practices to create a foundation and lofty ideals to aspire to.

The next thing we need to understand is how the human race is meant to move forward toward these ideals. The answer is that the process is evolutionary, not a revolutionary one in which our conceptions and institutions are systematically discarded. The Torah does not give us a road map with specific instructions for getting from here to there in a particular place and time. Its main importance is as a compass that provides us with orientation in a specific locale while also pointing us in the proper direction to travel beyond. In other words, the educational vision of the Torah teaches us how to behave properly within current institutions and directs us toward the high road to universal human flourishing.

Let us apply these concepts to the example you mention: slavery. At the time the Torah was given, slavery was a universal economic institution, perhaps a vital one. Since the educational vision of the Torah is not revolutionary, the first step in creating an ethical society is to establish fundamental ethical standards appropriate for the economic institutions that exist at the given time. This is done through the many commandments to ameliorate the status of the slave. Here are some examples: the commandment to give the slave Shabbat rest, through a sense of identification with his plight,[30] the requirement to free slaves if they are subject to physical abuse,[31] the requirement to take care of their basic needs.[32]

At the same time, the Torah contains passages that highlight the human cost of the institution of slavery. For example, the curses the Torah describes as the consequence of sin depict slavery as the ultimate curse; it is mentioned last, after sickness and exile, as the lowest possible rung of human existence.[33] This provides the impetus to create a more humane society in the future, a society in which this outdated institution will no longer have a place.

So we see that the Torah begins by acknowledging the practical state of the human race, including the state that applied in the time when the Torah was given, even as it guides and inspires us to progress beyond our current state. The laws of the Torah contain an outer expression that enables us to maintain an ethical lifestyle according to the material circumstances that exist at any given time, as well as an inner message of human brotherhood that enables the human race to transcend those social institutions, such as slavery, which are ultimately an obstacle to ethical perfection.

THE IDEA OF PROGRESS IN THE TORAH

At the Passover Seder we state that if God had not taken us out of the land of Egypt more than three thousand years ago, then to this very day the children of Israel would be enslaved to Pharaoh. This is a very surprising statement. After all, over a period of thousands of years nations rise and fall, and enslaved nations free themselves, in perfectly natural processes. Certainly we do not know today of any race which has been continuously enslaved for three thousand years.

Rabbi Avraham Yitzchak HaKohen Kook explained this passage by stating that the very idea of historical progress and of a movement toward liberation was inculcated in the human race as a result of the Exodus.[34] The dominant worldview in the ancient world was not one of progress toward a great redemption but a belief in a cyclical, static, or even declining world. The liberation of the Jewish people, and the subsequent giving of the Torah, created a mighty example for all people that human freedom is attainable and worth striving for. This idea has ever since been an important dynamic and progressive factor in human history. And indeed the Exodus is a dominant liberation motif in progressive discourse to this very day.

THE ETHICAL CHALLENGE

A great conundrum in the study of ethics is how to relate to the presence of evil in the world. At one extreme we find ethicists who insist that we must all act in accordance with the ethical dictates of an ideal society, even in a less than ideal situation. For example, many Kantians would say that it is unethical to lie even to save lives, because in an ideal society lying is unethical. At the other extreme we find a belief that realizing a vision of the ideal future justifies any means. Some Marxists believe that any means, no matter how underhanded or brutal, is justified if it helps to bring about a future Communist utopia.

In Jewish tradition as well as in the actual behavior of the Jewish people, we find a unique and effective resolution to this conundrum. The Torah gives us the means to maintain basic standards of decency and ethical behavior according to our imperfect surroundings. But it also provides an inspirational vision of a perfect future world, so that we may simultaneously strive to move beyond these surroundings and continuously work toward human perfection.

Gilt Guilt

IS IT SHAMEFUL TO ENJOY LUXURIES WHILE OTHERS
EXPERIENCE DEPRIVATION?

Lopsided income inequality enables some people to enjoy great luxuries while others lack necessities. To some this seems inherently unethical. Is it immoral to enjoy an extravagant income while others are impoverished? Jewish tradition teaches that the well-off should never forget their responsibility to the deprived, but it also encourages us to enjoy our wealth and be grateful to God for providing it.

Q I work at an interesting job that pays a fantastic salary. I guess I should be grateful, but really I feel guilty for getting paid so much when others are suffering from poverty. Is it wrong to enjoy wealth while others are impoverished?

A The basic approach of Judaism to wealth is that it is a positive thing, which we should enjoy and be grateful for, as long as two conditions are satisfied.

First, we must use our wealth responsibly, always remembering that it is not a reflection of our inner worth but a deposit given us by the Creator. A person who is blessed with material resources is permitted and encouraged to enjoy them. Judaism does not encourage asceticism, and in fact it requires us to recite blessings on all kinds of material enjoyments, including food, drink, and fragrances. The medieval philosopher Rabbi Yehuda HaLevi points out that by taking the time to praise the Creator for these enjoyments, we augment our appreciation of them.[35] At the same time we elevate these enjoyments from being a purely bodily indulgence to a spiritual experience The Talmud tells us that we should recite one hundred blessings each day;[36] a withdrawn ascetic would have trouble fulfilling this obligation.

Second, we must bear in mind that enjoyment is maximized when it is moderated. The main reason for moderation is concern, not for others, but for ourselves. Jewish tradition teaches that when we overindulge our passions, they outstrip our enjoyment; the end result is that we are less satisfied than ever. "One who starves himself is satisfied; one who overindulges is hungry."[37]

In the giving of charity, too, the act is not only for the benefit of the recipient but also for the giver. Enjoyment is maximized when it is shared with others. Maimonides[38] explains how a person is meant to fulfill the commandment to rejoice on holidays:

> And when he eats and drinks, he is obligated to feed "the stranger, the orphan, and the widow," together with other unfortunate poor people. But someone who locks the doors of his yard and eats and drinks, he and his children and his wife, and does not give food and drink to the poor and the embittered, this is not the rejoicing of the commandment but [only] the rejoicing of his belly.

Maimonides does not say that such a person has fulfilled the commandment to rejoice but neglected the commandment to help others; he says that such a person has not experienced the true rejoicing which the Torah commands.

There is never any sense that a wealthy person should feel guilty about enjoying his resources, but only a consciousness that enjoyment is augmented when there is a spirit of moderation and generosity.

When it comes to giving charity, we should be generous but do not need to be profligate. According to Jewish tradition, an average person should strive to give ten percent of his net income to charity; a person of means should aim for twenty percent.[39]

The question mentions that many people "suffer from poverty," but it is also true that many impoverished people are very happy and do not suffer at all. And certainly there are many individuals who suffer from wealth. It is a foundational belief in Judaism that wealth and poverty each have their own challenges. In the Book of Proverbs, we find a prayer in which one asks to be given neither poverty nor riches, "Lest I become sated and deny, saying, 'Who is God?'; or lest I become impoverished and steal, thus profaning the name of my God."[40]

The problem is that a person who has a surfeit of material enjoyments finds it more difficult to remain acutely aware of the guiding hand of God's providence in providing them. Those who have the good fortune to be well-off should be particularly careful to be cheerful and grateful to the Creator for their enjoyments and status. We can illustrate this with what the Talmud tells us about two Torah scholars who possessed legendary wealth.

One of them was Rabbi Eliezer ben Harsom, who had inherited from his father a thousand cities and a thousand trading ships. In order to keep the management of his estate from distracting him from Torah study, he used to wander anonymously from place to place carrying a sack of flour, subsisting on a little bread and devoting himself to study.[41]

The other was Rabbi Judah the Prince, the leader of the Jewish people, redactor of the Mishnah, and one of the most renowned Jewish sages of all time. It was said that his possessions were so vast that the manure from his horses made his stable-keeper wealthier than the king of Persia.[42]

In contrast to the modest sustenance of Rabbi Eliezer ben Harsom, Rabbi Judah did not lead an ascetic life. On the contrary, he lived in such high fashion that prominent Roman nobles and generals were in awe of his wealth and status. Yet of all of our saints and sages, it was specifically Rabbi Judah who was able to swear on his deathbed, "Master of the universe, it is well known to You that I used my ten fingers to exert myself in the Torah, and I did not indulge myself even with one little finger."[43]

Rabbi Judah the Prince's spiritual level was so high that, despite his extravagant lifestyle, during his entire lifetime he consumed nothing for his own enjoyment. Everything was for the glory and honor of the Jewish people and in order to have a greater appreciation of the creation.

Wealth is an opportunity and a challenge. Someone who is blessed with it should enjoy it without guilt, but with a sense of moderation and sharing.

Each of us, whether wealthy or poor, is called upon to serve the Creator from our particular situation. The wealthy run a greater risk of forgetting God's role in providence, but also have a greater opportunity to use their resources to help others and to expand their appreciation of God's loving kindness.

ENDNOTES

1. 1 Kings 5:5
2. Genesis 33:18
3. Shabbat 33b
4. Genesis 29:14–15
5. Genesis 34:10
6. Responsa Havvot Yair 224
7. Kiddushin 4:14
8. Shabbat 14b
9. Cited in Semag, beginning of Hilkhot Eruv
10. Yevamot 21a; Shulhan Arukh, Hoshen Mishpat 331:19
11. Kiddushin 31a
12. See Guide for the Perplexed 1:5
13. Isaiah 49:23
14. Zevahim 19a
15. Isaiah 49:6
16. Leviticus Rabbah 7:11
17. Genesis 3:24
18. Lamentations Rabbah 2:9
19. Shulhan Arukh, Orah Hayyim 224:7
20. Isaiah 11:4
21. Zecharia 8:16–17
22. Berakhot 58a
23. Shabbat 33b
24. Genesis 33:18
25. Avodah Zarah 2b
26. Genesis Rabbah
27. Genesis 33:19
28. Sanhedrin 37a
29. Deuteronomy 6:18
30. Deuteronomy 5:13–14
31. Exodus 21:26–27
32. Leviticus 25:37
33. Deuteronomy chapter 28
34. Cited in a footnote by his son, Rabbi Tzvi Yehuda Kook, in Olat Reiyah II, p. 268
35. Kuzari 2:50, 3:13–17
36. Menahot 43b
37. Sukkah 52b
38. Maimonides Yom Tov 6:18
39. Shulhan Arukh, Yoreh Deah 249:1
40. Proverbs 30:7–9
41. Yoma 35b
42. Shabbat 113b
43. Ketubbot 104a

GOOD CITIZENSHIP

Introduction

Wherever we encounter human interaction, we encounter ethical obligations. We have ethical obligations in our relationships with family members, with neighbors and friends, and with economic contacts such as customers, suppliers, employers, and employees. In addition, all of us are members of a community, a commonwealth, and this implies that we have ethical obligations as citizens.

While the government often seems to be a faceless monolith, at best neutral and at worst hostile, we should recall that the best government is the embodiment of the aspirations of the entire community, and that even the worst government is preferable to anarchy. The Torah commands us not to belittle our leaders: "Do not belittle the judge, and do not deride the prince among your people."[1] Sefer ha-Hinnukh, an important commentary on the Torah, explains: "It is impossible for any settlement of people to exist without one person designated as their head, to perform his commands and carry out his decrees. For the views of people are varied, and they will never be able to completely agree on any issue; as a result, they will end up in inaction and nullity in their actions." The Hinnukh goes on to explain that even though leaders are fallible and will occasionally be wrong, action that is sometimes mistaken is far preferable to inaction.

This principle applies to any society we find ourselves in. Through the prophet Jeremiah, God admonishes the Jews who are on their way to exile in Babylon, "Seek the peace of the city whither I have banished you, and pray on its behalf to the LORD; for in its welfare will be your welfare".[2] This mandate is the basis for the custom of saying a prayer in synagogue each Shabbat on behalf of the monarch, affirming that it is God "Who grants salvation to kings."

The ethical principle of good citizenship found in the Torah and in the prophets is also echoed in the Talmud, which summarizes: "The law of the land is the law."[3] As long as a law is legitimate, equitable, and consistent with Torah values, we have a religious obligation to uphold it.

Is Voting an Ethical Obligation?

HOW IMPORTANT IS VOTING?

It goes without saying that respect for the commonwealth means obeying the law, but it also expresses itself in communal responsibility. One way of showing identification with the democratic process and a sense of responsibility for the community is to take part in elections.

Q Is there an ethical obligation to vote in elections?

A While voting is not an absolute ethical obligation, Jewish tradition educates us in a number of ethical principles that we fulfill when we take part responsibly in participatory democracy.

Participating in elections is a way of showing respect for the government and identifying with it. If we look at Jewish history, we see that appropriate respect and deference toward legitimate authority is an important value. For example, although Moses went through prolonged and trying negotiations with the wicked Pharaoh, he maintained at all times a high degree of respect for Pharaoh's royal status. And despite the bitter enmity of the wicked king Ahab towards the prophet Elijah, Elijah personally ran before the king's carriage to emphasize the honor due the sovereign.[4]

Jewish law prescribes a special blessing to be recited on seeing a king, praising God "Who gave of His glory to flesh and blood." And we are encouraged to see kings so that we may recite this blessing.[5]

It is true that these signs of identification with the sovereign are generally couched in terms of a monarchy, but careful examination shows that they are even more appropriate in a democracy. The commentaries explain that the main reason we have to be so punctilious about preserving the honor of the king is that his honor is the honor of the nation as a whole[6]. In representative government like a democracy, the identification of the government with the people is even greater.

But voting does not merely show our respect for the system of government; it also gives us an opportunity to influence the leaders of the nation or the community. It would be a shame to fail to take advantage of this opportunity to promote the welfare of our own community and the nation as a whole. Voting can be one fulfillment of the prophecy given by God to Jeremiah, who transmitted the following message to the Jewish exiles in Babylonia: "Seek the peace of the city where I have exiled you, and pray for it unto God, for in its peace will you have peace."[7]

Many eminent and outstanding Torah scholars, including Rabbi Moshe Feinstein of New York, made a point of voting in every major election. A surprising number were elected to the legislatures of the countries where they resided. Rabbi Meir Shapira, for instance, was elected to the Polish Sejm in the decades before World War I; later on he was the head of a major yeshiva and the founder of the daily Talmud-learning program, the Daf Yomi.

Voting is a simple and effective way of showing respect for the enlightened system of government that prevails in democratic nations, and gives us a chance to influence public life in a positive direction. While it is not an absolute ethical obligation, it does give us an opportunity to fulfill many ethical ideals. It would be a shame to needlessly neglect this invaluable opportunity.

Paying Taxes

WHEN IS IT CHEATING ON TAXES?

One of the more onerous obligations we face as citizens is the requirement to pay taxes. By the time we are done with federal taxes, state taxes, property taxes, sales taxes, Social Security, user and license fees, and so on, a pretty substantial chunk of our income finds its way to the government. It is hardly surprising that citizens are always looking for ways to minimize their tax burden.

At the same time, today's citizen is, to an unprecedented extent, the *beneficiary* of government expenditures. In most advanced countries we take for granted an extensive system of roads and highways, an efficient legal system, well-planned neighborhoods with sidewalks and green spaces, national defense which gives most people lifetime security, an impressive level of public school education, and generous retirement benefits.

Enjoyment of these benefits implies an ethical obligation to be fair dealers in the tax arena. We are entitled to minimize our tax burden, but we must not engage in or abet tax evasion.

An instructive passage in the Talmud teaches us about the important relationship between the *general* obligation to obey legitimate laws and the *special* legitimacy of taxes that are used for our benefit. "Samuel stated, The law of the land is the law. Rava said, Observe that this must be true. For [the government] fells trees and builds bridges, and we cross them."[8] The passage suggests that if it were illegitimate for the government to appropriate private property through taxes (felling trees), it would be equally illegitimate for us to make use of the stolen property by crossing the bridges.

Let us examine some pressing dilemmas regarding tax evasion.

Q Some of my friends are taking advantage of an innovative and rather elaborate scheme to save taxes. They explained to me that it is based on a novel interpretation of the tax law. Is it ethical for me to take part in this scheme?

A Your confusion is understandable. No less a genius than Albert Einstein is quoted as admitting that "the hardest thing to understand in the world is the income tax."

To begin, we must note the difference between tax avoidance and tax evasion, between exploiting the law and flouting it. It's okay to minimize taxes by taking advantage of legitimate provisions of the tax law, or even by taking a reasonable position on an unresolved question of law. But we cross the line into tax evasion, which is a criminal act, when there is no sincere claim of lawfulness. This is the basic ethical distinction; now let us examine some criteria that will help us evaluate any given scheme.

A good way for the average person to distinguish between a prudent plan to save money and an illegal and immoral scam – which may ultimately be extremely expensive – is to ask a reputable tax adviser. If this professional clearly advises that you need not declare sheltered income, then you may assume that your acts are solidly defensible. But an evasive answer, such as "Nothing will happen to you if you don't report," or "I know that many people employ these methods," is a sign of danger.

Another guide is the degree of secrecy called for. Watch out when ordinary, prudent discretion crosses the line into "cloak and dagger" activities like wiring small amounts repeatedly, moving cash, or using way stations in moving money.

An ordinary person can rely on a reputable accountant, but the accountants themselves cannot just pass the buck. They have to answer to a higher authority – not to mention the Higher Authority. Their obligation to know and conform to generally accepted accounting procedures is legal, ethical, and professional. An accountant who deviates from these principles is in violation of the professional code of conduct and may be subject to prosecution. From a Jewish point of view, the accountant is abetting wrongdoing by the client, as we explain in the next section.

Of course an accountant, like a lawyer, is permitted to interpret the law in a new light – if the interpretation is professional and defensible. But it is unethical to make an audacious claim, based on the hope that the tax authorities won't notice.

Cash-Only Business

CAN I PATRONIZE A "CASH-ONLY" BUSINESS?

Q Some businesses in my area are run on a "cash-only" basis. Can I patronize these businesses, or is this encouraging tax evasion?

A There are three possible answers to your question:

- It's fine; paying taxes is the proprietor's responsibility, not yours.

- It's all right to patronize these businesses, but demand a receipt so that you are not encouraging deceit.

- You should boycott dishonest businesses.

Which answer is correct? All three. It depends on the exact situation.

Jewish law distinguishes three levels of cooperation with wrongdoing and prohibits anything that would abet wrongdoing. The three levels, in decreasing order of gravity, are:

- *Enabling a transgression.* If the transgression could not take place without your participation, you are enabling the wrongdoing to take place. This is categorically forbidden by the biblical injunction, "Do not place a stumbling block before the blind."[9] Our tradition explains that this refers primarily to a spiritual stumbling block, which causes someone to transgress.

- *Abetting a transgression.* This means that you take an active role in the unethical activity, but if you didn't do so, someone else would.

- *Condoning a transgression.* Normally, we are obligated to protest wrongdoing. Whenever we remain silent and even benefit from it, we may seem to be condoning it. The ethical status of condoning depends on the degree of identification we show with our participation as well as our ability to make an effective protest; these factors vary according to the situation.

In short, Jewish tradition urges us to exercise moral leadership and take responsibility for the moral progress of the world. This means that we cannot shirk responsibility when our actions encourage wrongdoing.

But we should not jump to the conclusion that we should immediately boycott or even turn in the suspected tax evader. An equally important principle of Jewish tradition is that we should give others the benefit of the doubt, as the very next verse tells us, "Judge your neighbor favorably."[10] And certainly it is not a mitzvah to be a busybody.

Therefore, Jewish law states that even if someone may seem to be involved in wrongdoing, we do not have to scrutinize his or her activities if a favorable interpretation is reasonable, even if it is less than probable. The example given in the Mishnah is someone who buys an ox during the Sabbatical year.[11] Even though most oxen are used for plowing, which is forbidden during the Sabbatical year, it is not unusual for someone to buy an ox for its meat. So we may give the buyer the benefit of the doubt and sell him the ox.

Thus, if the cash basis of the business has a reasonable explanation besides tax evasion, we do not need to scrutinize the proprietor's motives. Possible examples: a retail business constantly dealing with small amounts of cash, or someone for whom writing receipts would be impractical, such as a peddler. (Practically speaking, we must admit that such examples would be fairly rare nowadays, when even small businesses are generally required to have cash registers and issue receipts.)

However, if a permissible explanation is quite improbable, or if the seller admits right out that he is trying to evade taxes, then we must avoid helping. In this case, explain that you will be able to patronize the business only if you can obtain a proper receipt.

In some cases it would be necessary to avoid the business altogether. This is because of an additional problem called *marit ayin*, or giving the appearance of wrongdoing. If the business in question is well known as one that evades taxes and others can easily see that you are patronizing the business but do not know that you are demanding a receipt, then you could be giving the impression of abetting the seller's subterfuge. In this case it would be proper to find a way to publicize your insistence on a receipt, or to avoid the place of business altogether.

Now You Tell Me!

WHAT DO I DO IF A WORKMAN REFUSES TO GIVE ME A RECEIPT?

A very awkward variant of this question arises when the cash-only demand comes as a surprise. Here is the situation:

Q I agreed to a $500 estimate to have my apartment painted. When the job was done, the painter made a fuss about giving a receipt, claiming he had given me a cash-only estimate. I discovered that other house painters in my area also work on a cash-only basis. Should I agree to a compromise?

A While it is always best to clarify the details of a business deal before work starts, in this case the client can hardly be blamed. Why should a customer routinely consider the possibility that a merchant is engaging in tax fraud? Even so, in a place where cash-only work is common, it is best to specify in advance that you will need a receipt.

There is no question but that the house painter is to blame for the awkward situation. It is his legal and ethical responsibility to pay taxes; if he is trying to evade them, the least he can do is to point out explicitly that his estimate applies only to cash-only jobs.

Still, the ethical approach of Judaism to these situations can be summed up as "Fix the problem, not the blame." Jewish law generally rejects a punitive approach to wrongdoing. When someone acts improperly, Jewish law does not advocate turning the other cheek, but neither does it advocate taking self-righteous advantage of another person's misdeed. Rather, the wrongdoing needs to be acknowledged, and then the sides should do the best they can to negotiate a fair outcome.

For example, one who steals is certainly obligated to return any ill-gotten gains. But Jewish law does not prescribe imprisonment or corporal punishment for stealing[12]. And if a worker fraudulently misleads an employer into agreeing to an unusually high salary by telling him that the higher amount is standard, the employer does not have to pay the higher amount but does have to pay whatever really is accepted.[13]

The devious worker is not rewarded for lying, but he is not penalized either.

The application to your case is that the painter deserves to get a fair price for painting your house, despite his tax-evading machinations. If, in the first place, you would have agreed to have the work done for the price painters normally obtain when they give receipts, this is the price you should pay now. Tell the painter you need a receipt but are willing to pay the price customary for "over the table" work.

If you would have forgone the whole job had you known the true price, then you have, in effect, been misled by the painter. He led you to believe that you were getting a price you could afford. In this case you should settle on some intermediate amount that you would have agreed to in the first place.

This constructive and non-vindictive approach in money matters is a reflection of a profound religious principle in Judaism. Jewish tradition affirms that sin must be rectified; yet this very affirmation also implies that sin *can* be rectified. On the one hand, sin is not forgiven without repentance, which includes acknowledging our transgressions, renouncing them, and confessing them to God. In the case of sins against other people, repentance requires appropriate recompense. We do not believe that God lets us off the hook without proper repentance. But we also do not believe that God is vindictive. Once a person has properly repented, including making appropriate recompense, He freely forgives the penitent. "As I live, says the LORD God, I do not desire the death of the sinner but rather that he should return from his sin and live".[14]

Bribing Public Officials: Grease or Graft?

CAN I PAY A FUNCTIONARY TO "GREASE THE WHEELS" A
BIT?

Bribery, even the petty kind, terribly undermines sound public administration and public trust. It imposes unfair costs on citizens, degrades the level of service by enabling people to get around the law, and leads to a general atmosphere of cynicism and exploitation.

At the same time, a blanket prohibition on giving bribes would make life unlivable in places where this corrupt habit is a way of public life. Let us examine the guidelines Jewish law provides for coping with this destructive phenomenon.

Q "Business as usual" for our construction firm is like this: We have to pay off city hall to get a building permit, compensate the police to let us unload building materials, acknowledge the union official in order to get construction workers, and reward the city engineer to certify the building. Finally, we have to pay the tax examiners to let us declare all these payments as a business expense! Is it ethical for me to continue in this business?

A Judaism's view of bribery is clear: "Do not accept bribes, for bribery blinds [even] the wise and distorts [even] the words of the righteous."[15] Although the verse refers to a judge, the rationale applies to anyone in a position of public trust. A person may rationalize accepting a bribe and convince himself that his judgment will be unaffected, but the Torah tells us that even a wise and righteous person cannot avoid having his point of view influenced by a bribe.

The example of the Jewish sages is to go to the utmost extreme to avoid even the appearance of favoritism. The sage Samuel disqualified himself from judging a litigant who as a simple courtesy gave him a hand as he alighted from a boat; the sage Ameimar disqualified himself from someone who drove away a stray bird who landed on him.[16] The sage Rav disqualified himself from judging someone who had once hosted him in his home; the replacement judge, Rav Kahana, saw that this litigant continued to make an ostentatious show of his "friendship" with Rav, and threatened to ban the litigant for creating even an impression of favoritism.[17]

So *accepting* a bribe can never be tolerated. But what about *giving* a bribe? Here, the key ethical question is: Does my bribe contribute to wrongdoing? If a public official is fulfilling his public trust and someone offers him money to betray it, this is clearly leading him astray, placing a spiritual "stumbling block before the blind."[18] Furthermore, if an official deviates sufficiently from his mandate, the service he performs is effectively unauthorized. This may amount to stealing from the public, which Jewish tradition tells us is the severest kind of theft.[19]

The more complex ethical question arises when an official demands payment to carry out what he is supposed to be doing anyway. This is a perplexing gray area. There is no betrayal of public trust, because instead of inducing him to stumble, we are urging him to do the right thing. Insofar as the demand comes from the official himself, and he has a responsibility to carry out his duty, this situation is closer to extortion than to bribery. Yet even this kind of payment has dangers.

First of all, if everybody becomes reconciled to bribes, it will be impossible to rectify the situation. Open bribery undermines society's moral fiber; condoning it shows a lack of moral leadership.

Second, it is easy to cross the line into criminal activity. The building inspector who charges $1,000 to approve a sound building would probably accept $10,000 to approve an unsound one. In turn, the builder may find that it is an attractive bargain to cut corners and just pay off the inspector.

The same distinction between paying someone to do something he should not and paying him to do something he should is entrenched in American law. The Foreign Corrupt Practices Act prohibits payments "influencing any act or decision of [a] foreign official in his official capacity." But there is an exception to the prohibition for payments to "expedite or to secure the performance of a routine governmental action," such as obtaining permits. These are sometimes known as "grease payments."

Let us apply these insights to your case. Extorted payments for routine things like building permits, getting workers, and obtaining approval are not necessarily unethical if you are fulfilling the legal requirements and not transgressing any laws. City officials are already required to provide these services; any demand for payment clearly constitutes extortion. According to the legal definition we would view these as "grease payments."

Even so, you should do your utmost to avoid giving in to this extortion. Experience shows that businesses can successfully resist extortion through the following steps:

- An inflexible policy not to pay any bribes, which clearly broadcasts the message, "Don't even ask" and tends to forestall demands for graft;

- Meticulous fulfillment of appropriate by-laws, thus making it difficult for an inspector to find a legal excuse to penalize the firm;

- A non-judgmental attitude towards corrupt officials. While threatening exposure or legal action may sometimes be necessary, often a non-threatening attitude is more effective in promoting a livable relationship with officials. Functionaries themselves may find the habit of graft demoralizing, and may be positively relieved to encounter a workplace where more enlightened practices prevail. But they will not find it relieving to sense that they are being judged or condemned.

Paying off the police is very demoralizing for society and is unquestionably much worse. Police are not mere supervisors of specific regulations; they are guardians of the law. Technically speaking, you face extortion, and these payments can be ethically justified if you scrupulously move construction materials and waste in strictest accordance with accepted practice. But this should absolutely be a last resort.

What about payments to the tax officials? These clearly cross the red line. Your firm is paying them to betray their public trust to supervise your accounts; furthermore, you take advantage of this betrayal to gain an illegal tax break. An additional consideration is that one of the reasons bribes are disallowed as deductions is precisely to make it unprofitable to operate in a corrupt manner. This is meant to introduce some accountability into the other public institutions, such as city government. So the bribes to the tax official undermine the law's last bulwark against the cancer of public corruption.

The ethical ideal is to stand up to moral challenges, not to evade them. As the popular saying goes, it's easy to be an angel if nobody ruffles your feathers. It is praiseworthy to strive to continue in your current line of work, while adopting policies which contribute at least incrementally to upright conduct in your industry. But it is true nonetheless that some kinds of business have to be left to scoundrels, and if corruption is deeply entrenched it may be that construction in your city is one of them.

Out of Sight, Out of Mind?

CAN I PAY BRIBES TO HELP ORPHANS IN A BACKWARD
COUNTRY?

The issue discussed in this column is an interesting variation on the
bribery question.

Q I support a charitable organization in a somewhat backward developing country. A local official warned me that any donations are likely to be skimmed by the administrators. I'm thinking of offering this official a small payment to keep an eye on the crooked administration, but I wonder if this kind of bribe is ethical.

A As we have just explained, giving someone an inducement to *fulfill* his professional responsibility does not create a stumbling block. Since public officials are already obliged to prevent skimming and other crimes, the payment you describe should be acceptable.

Even so, immense care is needed before giving someone a bribe even to do something proper. First of all, we need to carefully examine our own motives to see if we are truly impartial. Perhaps we are really seeking some kind of unfair favoritism. Another problem is that making these payments perpetuates the corrupt system whereby people only do their job if they are given inducements.

Careful thought is needed to see if your situation meets all these criteria. If it would be appropriate for this official to prevent the kind of skimming you describe as part of his job, but local ethical norms are so backward that your silent protest by refusing to pay a bribe is really of no relevance, it may be ethically justified to make a payment, especially for such an important objective.

In order to avoid the problem of partiality, a better solution would be to seek a way to motivate this official to keep an eye on *all* contributions in his city, not just yours.

Witness Character

CAN AN EXPERT WITNESS TAILOR TESTIMONY?

The secular justice system is a perplexing amalgamation. The adversary system on which it is based reminds us of the laissez-faire orientation of the marketplace. Each side competes to convince the judges of the superiority of its own claims, just as each competing business tries to convince the consumer of its own superiority. Yet the ultimate objective is to mete out impartial justice, where the weak and the strong have equal standing.

Getting impartial justice out of a competitive process is a daunting challenge, and it demands the highest ethical standards from the participants in the system. Participants must respect the limits of the adversarial aspect of the process, and know when they are called upon to act with impartiality and integrity. This naturally raises the question of whether a hired expert witness has to be impartial.

Q Much of my income as a real estate appraiser comes from testifying as an expert witness. The litigants who hire me expect me to give low appraisals that will help them in court, and if I do not meet their expectations they'll hire someone else who will. Can I tailor my testimony to the needs of my clients?

A In order to answer your question, we have to clarify a critical distinction. There is a big difference between a litigant, or *party* to a trial, and a *witness* in a trial. Everyone understands that the litigants are not impartial, and that their claims may be carefully crafted to help their case in court. But a witness is expected to provide only facts, and to be completely impartial.

Of course, even claims made by litigants must meet basic standards and be reasonable and defensible. The Torah warns the judge to "Distance yourself from falsehood."[20] The Talmud explains that in order to maintain this distance, the parties to a lawsuit must help the judge by making only factual claims, even if a fraudulent claim would be necessary to achieve a just outcome.[21]

Realistically, however, we have to accept that in an adversary system the litigants are permitted to stretch their claims within the limits of what is reasonable and defensible. The job of the litigant is to present his own case in the most favorable light and to highlight weaknesses in the opponent's case. The job of the judge and the jury is to impartially adjudicate these presentations.

We applied this idea above in explaining that an accountant is permitted to make a novel interpretation of a tax law in order to help his client, as long as he believes the interpretation can be defended. The accountant does not have to pretend that he is a judge making an objective determination. He is making a claim, and if the tax authorities disagree, they are welcome to make a counterclaim and let a judge decide. By the same token, if your client wants to *claim* that his property has a low value, you can work as a consultant and prepare documents that tend to support the claim, as long as the documents do not violate the basic standards of your profession.

But a much different standard applies to a witness. A witness is never allowed to distort the truth. Even if a witness is called by one side, he is testifying on behalf of the court, not on behalf of a litigant.

Jewish law is particularly strict on this point. Not only is a witness forbidden to *actually* distort testimony; he is forbidden even to *feign* willingness to serve as a witness in order to intimidate the other litigant into settling. This is true even if the decoy witness is convinced that this will lead to justice being done. The basis for this rule is again the verse, "Distance yourself from untruth."[22] It is not enough merely to *refrain* from injustice; we have to *distance* ourselves from injustice by avoiding distortion of the judicial process.[23]

While the content of testimony should be unaffected by the payment to the expert witness, the hired witness may and should be careful to bring to light those facts which favor the side which hired him. In other words, he does not bias his judgment, but he does want to make sure that his impartial judgments are brought to the attention of the court so that the side which hired him can get a fair hearing.[24]

By the same token, it is understandable if an expert witness is particularly careful to emphasize points favorable to the side which hired him. But this is not the same as making statements that go against your professional judgment and training.

The real problem is with the system. An expert witness is an unfortunate hybrid – engaged and paid by one side yet expected to provide impartial testimony. The ideal situation in cases where expertise is required would be for both sides to agree on an expert. It would be wonderful if judges would instruct litigants to try and agree on an expert in such cases, just as judges sometimes instruct the sides to try to reach a settlement or to engage in mediation. Then there would be a strong incentive for the appraiser to be right on target, since the fairest appraisers would get the most business.

If you develop a strong reputation as an impartial and accurate assessor, perhaps you could get business from disputants who will use you as an arbitrator. They will prefer to take their case to you rather than to court, knowing that they will get a fair judgment at a bargain rate since they do not have to pay lawyers.

Revolving Door

HOW CAN PUBLIC SERVANTS POLICE INDUSTRIES AND THEN JOIN THEM?

When public servants such as regulators leave their jobs, they often go to work for the same companies they used to supervise. This "revolving door" can create severe conflicts of interest as the public servant has an interest in impressing and accommodating his potential future employer.

Q Should public employees go to work for the very same businesses they policed while in government service?

A Before we analyze this problem, we should acknowledge that there are many advantages to this "revolving door" between the public and private sectors.

- *Communication.* When there is turnover between the public and private sectors, the communication and understanding among them is increased. It is hard to regulate an industry effectively if you do not have inside knowledge of how it really works. Conversely, when business people have a deeper understanding of the regulatory process, they can conform to requirements more effectively. Excessive parochialism in each sector leads to suspicion and competition between them.

- *Education.* Each sector absorbs some of the organizational culture of the other. Business organizations focused on the bottom line tend to have more accountability and discipline than public agencies. Public agencies are more affected by political considerations and are attuned to the public interest.

- *Incentive.* It's not always easy to attract talented people to public service. Recruiting is easier when workers feel that the public sector is not a dead end but, on the contrary, can open doors for them in other fields.

A measure of turnover in the governing class is an important characteristic of a functioning democracy. This advantage was known in antiquity. The Mishnah speaks of one member of each family being taken into the king's service for a period of time, and Rashi explains that it was customary to take civil servants in rotation from the various families in the kingdom.[25]

However, we must acknowledge the problem of conflict of interest. It is difficult to police people effectively if at the same time you are trying to find favor in their eyes as a potential employee. A regulator exercises judgment on behalf of the public. In some ways his responsibility is similar to that of a judge. He certainly must avoid the appearance of being beholden to those he regulates.

The Torah states, "Do not take bribes, for bribery blinds the sighted and distorts the words of the righteous."[26] Even a righteous person who intends to judge with integrity will find his judgment distorted by a bribe. Rabbi Yechiel Michal Epstein writes in his Arukh ha-Shulhan.[27]

> One cannot say that the prohibition is directed against taking bribes to distort judgment, for this is already explicitly forbidden in several places. ...Rather, it certainly means that taking bribes is forbidden even to vindicate the party in the right and to condemn the offender. ...And it is not only a judge who is forbidden to take bribes, but anyone appointed to or occupied with a communal responsibility.

Just as bribes can distort judgment, so can the expectation of future benefits, and judges and public officials are equally forbidden to take gifts from litigants after a case has already been judged.[28] For this reason our sages warned that judges need to take special care to avoid being obsequious to the powerful.[29]

How can we enjoy the benefits of cooperation and openness without having our regulators beholden to powerful interests? One way is education – cultivating a public sector with a culture of independence. Another way is to prevent concentrations of power and knowledge. When a single individual exercises too much judgment and controls access to too much information, the temptation and ability to depart from norms is great. Rather, we should adopt norms of teamwork and transparency in regulation. The Jewish tradition is to have a panel of judges, rather than a single judge, in order to balance out any excesses or distortions of judgment; as the Mishnah warns, "Only One can judge alone."[30]

One common solution is to have a "cooling-off" period between roles as regulator and regulated. A reasonable period greatly reduces the appearance and reality of a "quid pro quo." This norm is found in Jewish law regarding the laws of usury. While it is forbidden to pay usury even after the loan is repaid, a gift which is given some time after the loan repayment and doesn't appear connected is permissible. By the same token, a firm can hire a former regulator after a reasonable interval, on the condition that no mention is made of any benefits rendered the employer while the new hire was in the public service.[31]

Conflicts of interest can never be avoided entirely, and efforts to completely prevent such conflicts create a problem of excessive polarization in public life. But these conflicts are an ethical problem, and need to be kept under control through appropriate ethical values and norms of conduct that include patience, teamwork, and transparency.

Confidential Ex-Con

SHOULD I REVEAL A JOB APPLICANT'S CRIMINAL PAST?

Deciding whether to disclose someone's past can be a wrenching process. We need to be fair to a person who has transgressed, especially if he seems to have changed his way of life. Yet we also have a responsibility to protect others from any damage he may be likely to cause. Should one tell a business owner that a job applicant has a criminal record? Jewish tradition adopts a very conservative attitude toward disclosure, on the basis of fairness and also to encourage repentance and rehabilitation.

Q If I know that a job applicant has a criminal record, should I inform the proprietor?

A The case of a former criminal can be examined in two ways. From one standpoint, he is the same as anyone else – he deserves protection from slander, but at the same time others deserve protection from any damage he may be likely to cause. From another perspective, there is a public interest involved in this unique case. We will consider these aspects separately.

The discussion here cannot touch upon the grave and complex considerations that apply if the applicant's past creates a concern that he may be dangerous to others. Here we will examine the concern that the applicant may be dishonest and cause a monetary loss.

PRIVATE CONSIDERATIONS

As we have written many times, Jewish tradition deems revealing someone's defects or shortcomings to be a grave transgression. Even casual or innocent gossip is strictly condemned.

However, in some cases our dismay at speaking up has to give way before our responsibility to protect others from harm. The Torah emphasizes the reciprocal connection between these two duties by combining them in a single verse: "Do not go about as a tale-bearer among your people; do not stand idly by the blood of your neighbor."[32] The first half of the verse forbids gratuitous slander or gossip, while the second half requires us to take active steps to protect our fellow man from harm. Sefer ha-Hinnukh explains: "If we hear someone saying something negative about his fellow, we should not tell the other 'So-and-so said such-and-such about you.'" But then he adds "unless our intention is to prevent damage and to calm a dispute."[33]

Since only gratuitous slander is forbidden, it is permissible to inform if we fulfill a number of conditions, as explained in the classic Hafetz Hayyim by Rabbi Yisrael Meir ha-Kohen.[34] They are arranged below in a mnemonic ABC format:

- *Accuracy*. It is forbidden to exaggerate or embellish.

- *Benefit*. Revealing the information must be the only way to way to obtain some constructive benefit.

- *Certainty*. We must be sure the information is reliable.

- *Desire*. The teller's intention must be constructive, not vindictive.

- *Equity*. The revelation must not cause undeserved damage to the subject. It is not equitable to protect one person at the expense of another.

In order to fulfill the accuracy and certainty conditions, you must make sure that your information is reliable and not based on hearsay, and that you only transmit the basic facts.

In order to fulfill the desire condition, you must examine your motivations and make sure that you are not trying to punish the applicant or get back at him for his past actions, but are only interested in protecting the proprietor.

The benefit and equity conditions require the most careful thought. The fact that someone committed a crime in the past does not automatically mean that he is likely to cause harm in the future. You are only permitted to reveal information if you have a firm basis for believing that this person will cause loss to the proprietor. If all you know is that he has a criminal record, you do not know enough. People can be convicted for many different crimes, and may have committed them for many different reasons; they also go through a variety of rehabilitation processes. Some criminals were never bad employees; others only transgressed because of unique circumstances; still others have found the inner strength to conquer the drives that once led them to crime.

You also need to pay attention to the equity condition. If the proprietor's only reaction to your report will be a sober evaluation of the likelihood that the applicant's past makes him an imprudent hire, then your story is not causing the applicant an inequitable hardship. But if there is a likelihood that your story will cause the owner to reject the application outright, or will further publicize the applicant's past, then you are bringing about a benefit to the owner at the expense of causing harm to the applicant. The laws of slander do not permit such an inequity.

There is also a certain interaction between the certainty and equity conditions. Normally, we may not reveal any information unless we are certain of its accuracy. A rumor that a person has been convicted for embezzlement is not enough. Yet such a rumor is in itself a worrisome sign. Reporting a rumor of this kind depends in large measure on the equity conditions. If you have heard a rumor that someone is dishonest, you certainly may not state that he is dishonest. But you may be able to tell the proprietor that there is such a rumor if you know that he is a fair person who will not take the rumor at face value but will check it to the best of his ability and give the applicant a fair chance.

The ethical course of action here is based on a sense of responsibility. On the one hand, we may not spread irresponsible rumors or surmises. But in the presence of firm evidence that a person is likely to cause harm, it is irresponsible not to provide others with the information they need to protect themselves.

PUBLIC CONSIDERATIONS

There is also a public interest involved in this unique case. Even if the usual factors governing harmful speech would permit some level of disclosure, we should weigh the additional concern that unconsidered application of these factors might make rehabilitation of criminals almost impossible. What could easily result is a vicious cycle: Many released criminals return to a life of crime; therefore no one is willing to hire them; therefore they have no recourse except a life of crime.

Once this vicious cycle is ingrained, anyone who warns an employer is within his rights. After all, the applicant's past does create a significant likelihood that he will cause damage. Yet this likelihood is in itself partially due to the spreading of the information. If people were more circumspect about revealing the past follies of others, it would be easier for those who have erred to overcome their personal history. Perhaps the likelihood of backsliding would then be much reduced.

This way of looking at things does not necessarily conform to certain aspects of modern policy analysis. Many of the most accepted theories in the social sciences encourage a mechanistic view of human nature. According to these theories, by the time we are adults our tendencies are pretty well ingrained. Whether these tendencies are stamped by nature or by nurture, by the time we are grown up they are virtually impossible to change.

Jewish tradition, in contrast, strongly emphasizes our immense potential for change and growth. Our belief is that human beings are fundamentally good, that "God created man straight."[35] The Hebrew word for "repentance" literally means "return" – returning to our genuine, righteous selves, created in God's image. So fundamental is the idea of "return" to our view of humanity that our sages say that repentance was created before the world.[36] Human existence is basically predicated on our free will and our ability to transform ourselves for the better.

It is only natural that our tradition sought ways to encourage this vital process of self-transformation. There are many instances of Jewish authorities amending laws and creating special leniencies in order to make it easier for transgressors to repent. The principle is "Do not lock the door before repentance." For example, the Midrash teaches that we sometimes accept repentance even if it is not completely sincere, so as not to discourage others who fear they will be similarly judged.[37] In some cases, we do not require a person to return money he acquired improperly because of concern that his reluctance to give up the money will prevent him from changing his way of life.[38]

Thus one reason for being more circumspect in the case of a former criminal is that we want to weigh the possible harm to society against the immense importance of encouraging the applicant to adopt a normal lifestyle.

A second, related reason is that to some extent informing on the applicant does not necessarily protect society at all. Even if the applicant is a crook, informing is likely to protect this employer to the detriment of some other employer, with society as a whole no better off.

A well-known passage in the Mishnah conveys a subtle yet profound message of solidarity: one person should not seek to protect himself from danger at the expense of imposing the same danger on others. It is a basic principle of prayer that we do not pray to change the past, that any such request is a "vain prayer." Mishnah Berakhot 9:3 states:

> One who requests about the past, that is a vain prayer. How so?...If he heard a cry arise from a city and prayed, "May it be Your will that those [who are crying] are not members of my household," that is a vain prayer.

This example conveys a profound message of social responsibility. The Mishnah could just as easily have taken the example of one who prays, "May it be Your will that no one has been harmed." Instead, it gives examples of someone who wants to have misfortune fall on others instead of himself. Perhaps the Mishnah is hinting that this, too, is a kind of vanity.

Our joint responsibility to encourage rehabilitation should come into play in borderline cases. If we have firm reason to believe that this applicant will cause loss to the employer, we should pass along our information to be responsibly used; if our concern is based solely on hearsay and surmise, then we should just keep quiet, especially if the anticipated possible loss is not great.

But in borderline cases, we should try and give the former wrongdoer the benefit of the doubt, in order to do our bit to enable his rehabilitation and to encourage him to summon the inner strength needed to adopt a new, more enlightened path in life.

ENDNOTES

1. Exodus 22:27

2. Jeremiah 29:7
3. Gittin 10b
4. 1 Kings 18:46
5. Shulhan Arukh, Orah Hayyim 224:8–9
6. See Ketubbot 17 and the commentary of Maharsha
7. Jeremiah 29:7
8. Bava Kamma 113b
9. Leviticus 19:14
10. Leviticus 19:15
11. Mishnah Sheviit 5:8
12. Shulhan Arukh, Hoshen Mishpat 348:2
13. Shulhan Arukh, Hoshen Mishpat 332:4 in Rema
14. Ezekiel 33:11
15. Exodus 23:8
16. Ketubot 105b
17. Sanhedrin 7b
18. Leviticus 19:14
19. Tosefta, Bava Kamma 10:14
20. Exodus 23:7
21. Shevuot 31a
22. Exodus 23:7
23. Sanhedrin 23a
24. This "inclination" has an interesting parallel in Jewish law. One kind of Jewish legal proceeding is *zabla*, an acronym for *zeh borer lo ehad*, meaning that each litigant chooses one judge, and the two judges together choose a third. The three-judge panel then tries the case. Some commentators explain that each chosen judge will be likely to emphasize the strong points of the case of the litigant who chose him, bringing them to the attention of the other judges. Once all the facts are brought to light, all the judges will, of course, judge impartially. See Shulhan Arukh, Hoshen Mishpat 13:1; Shakh commentary on 75:1.
25. Bava Batra 144b
26. Exodus 23:8
27. Shulhan Arukh, Hoshen Mishpat 9:1
28. Glosses of Rosh on Sanhedrin 27b; Pilpula Charifta commentary
29. Sotah 41b and Rashi's commentary
30. Avot 4:8
31. See Shulhan Arukh Yoreh Deah 160:6 and Shach commentary. The Pilpula Charifta commentary just cited (on the Rosh Sanhedrin 27b) draws a general parallel between delayed interest and delayed bribes.
32. Leviticus 19:16
33. Sefer ha-Hinnukh is referring to one kind of gossip – telling someone that another person has slandered him – but the same principle applies to other kinds of damaging reports.
34. See especially sections 1:10 and 11:10

35. Ecclesiastes 7:29
36. Pesahim 54a
37. See Deuteronomy Rabbah on Deuteronomy 4:25
38. Bava Kamma 94b

FAIR COMPETITION

Introduction

Competition for customers brings out the best in firms, motivating them to provide the best product at the lowest cost. The Talmud states, "Competition among scholars expands wisdom,"[1] and the same principle applies in other fields as well. But competition in the marketplace, like that on the playing field, has to be sportsmanlike. Otherwise, everyone loses.

While the Jewish sources acknowledge the benefits of competition, the approach to this concept is not as extreme as is common today. Contemporary business mores exalt business competition into a sanctified value. This is based partially on a materialistic outlook which holds that the consumer is king; therefore competition, which tends to benefit the consumer, becomes all-important. In addition, there is a strong tendency toward laissez faire, "let it be"; contemporary morality tends to look with suspicion on any interference in private decision-making.

The Jewish approach gives much more emphasis to the human element. First of all, there is a concern for equity as well as efficiency. This means that the economic interests of the sellers are of some importance even if they come at the expense of the consumer.

Attention to the human element also means that we are sensitive to the impact that economic relationships have on our human relationships. Economic competition can lead to social opposition. In fact, the modern Hebrew word for "competition," *taharut*, is used in the ancient Jewish sources in a very negative sense, with a meaning similar to "antagonism" or "animosity." This impact is not inevitable, but we must be alert to the problem.

The insight provided by this etymology can explain some of the differences between the approach to competition in the traditional

Jewish sources and what we are accustomed to in the world at large. For example, today there is a very strong bias against any kind of cartel or monopoly. The talmudic sources also warn of the dangers of cartels, but overall the approach is more balanced, and the rabbinical authorities sanction cartels in some situations, especially when they are subject to public oversight.[2] Transparent agreements among suppliers help their livelihood, even though this may come at the expense of the consumer, and they also help create a positive dynamic of cooperation and association which is of social value. Certainly our tradition rejects a thoroughgoing martial model of business in which the competitor is the enemy and all means are acceptable in trying to overcome him.

The general approach in Judaism is to encourage cooperation and moderation and to believe that in the end God will provide for all. "A person cannot touch what is designated for his fellow…even to a hair's breadth."[3] The fair competitor will do his best to attract customers to the advantages his place of business provides and trust in God that underhanded tactics will avail neither side in wresting from the competitor what the Creator has designated for him.

Competitive Intelligence vs. Intelligent Competition

CAN I TRICK COMPETITORS INTO REVEALING VITAL
INFORMATION?

In many industries, accurate and up-to-date information about the competition is critical to business success. Unfortunately, this sometimes tempts merchants to use unethical methods to obtain the information they need. One of the most common means is to impersonate a neutral figure, such as a customer, supplier, student intern, or government official. Is this a legitimate way to obtain information about a competitor? We need to know where to draw the line between legitimate market research and improper industrial espionage.

Q I'm interested in finding out if I can effectively compete in a certain market. Can I do a surreptitious survey of the level of price and service by pretending to be a potential customer or investor?

A Your desire to help customers by providing better service than they are getting from the existing suppliers is certainly commendable. But this end does not justify the use of deceit to examine existing market conditions. By viewing your suggestion through the prism of Jewish law, we will be able to discern the ethical problems it poses.

DECEIT

The most severe problem here is deceit: the bogus survey is a way of tricking your competitors into revealing information they would like to keep secret. According to Jewish law, this kind of deceit is forbidden even if one does not lie outright. The relevant prohibition is known as *geneivat da'at,* meaning "stealing confidence." Confidence and trust are the foundations of civilized society; it is not justified to breach them just in order to make a few more dollars.

Stealing money by fraudulently offering something in return is scarcely better than breaking and entering. Likewise, stealing information through deceit is scarcely more ethical than breaking into your competitor's safe to extract sensitive documents.

EXPLOITATION

Knowing your competitors' prices will help you to undercut them. But more important, it will give you a picture of the business environment in their industry. Their prices are probably based on a prolonged and expensive process of trial-and-error and learning about the market. Not only do you want to acquire this expensive commodity on the cheap; you also want to use this information to their disadvantage.

The Mishnah[4] tells us that if one person climbs a wild olive tree to shake out the olives, another person is not allowed to go and gather them from the ground. The second person would be taking advantage of the first person's efforts instead of going to the trouble of finding his own tree to harvest. In your case the transgression is compounded, because you would be using the "olives" – in other words, the market information – to the detriment of the person who invested in them. This is truly adding insult to injury.

The practice you ask about resembles stealing a trade secret in order to compete with the inventor. Jewish law tells us that we should not take a free ride on the investments of others. They are entitled to a fair recompense if we appropriate their efforts.

UNTRUTH

Furthermore, your survey letter is an outright lie, yet the Torah commands us, "Distance yourself from every falsehood."[5] Truth is a supreme value, which should not be compromised even if there is no element of deceit or exploitation. According to Jewish law, we should only bend the truth in rare instances to avoid creating embarrassment or hurt feelings.[6] Certainly, it is not permissible in order to fleece our business competitors. Human beings are created in God's image; we should strive to liken ourselves to Him; and as the Talmud states, "The seal of the Holy One is truth."[7]

Business often requires a degree of concealment, and that is why your competitors want to keep their capabilities and prices secret. But the legitimate practice of concealing some private information from your competitor or bargaining counterpart is far removed from a deliberate untruth.

DISAPPOINTMENT

Finally, the Talmud tells us that there is an additional, human dimension here. A businessperson who suggests a deal to a prospective customer has some legitimate hope and expectation of making a sale. The Mishnah states: "Just as it is forbidden to take advantage of others in commerce, so is it forbidden to take advantage of them in discourse. Do not ask [a merchant], 'How much is that item?' when you have no intention of buying."[8] The reason is that you are causing not only unnecessary trouble to the seller but also disappointment.

Of course, merely inquiring about prices or services does not obligate you to buy from a particular merchant, and it is ethically permissible to shop around. But if you inquire about the terms of sale of a vendor, you must intend to give him a fair chance at getting your business. Otherwise, you are guilty of causing the vendor distress and disappointment. A bogus survey improperly raises false hopes.

What options are open to you in your search for market information? Here are a few ideas:

- *Public sources.* You may be able to get important information from public sources. Perhaps the firm publishes a catalogue. Industry newslettters sometimes publish current pricing information. Advertisements occasionally offer special prices. Firms that do business with the government may be required to make the terms public, giving you at least a ballpark figure for private-sector pricing. The reporting requirements for publicly traded firms include the disclosure of accounting information that could be valuable to you. With a little imagination, you will probably find much useful data.

- *Make a deal.* Instead of trying to get information underhandedly and on the cheap, decide that the market data you seek is valuable and worth paying for. Instead of pretending to be an investor, you can enter into a partnership with a current firm if conditions in the industry seem promising. (As assurance that you are not taking advantage of them, you can sign an agreement not to enter this industry on your own for some agreed-upon period.)

Other possible deal partners are the other market players. Current merchants would be harmed by your entry into this market as a competitor, but customers and suppliers would benefit, and they may also have the information you need. Instead of making a fraudulent offer to a merchant, make a genuine offer to a supplier – one that will provide him with some guaranteed business in return for reliable market information. Or else sit down with a customer and suggest a deal that will provide him with special low prices in return for a survey of the market.

However, you have to be careful. If suppliers or customers have agreements with merchants not to reveal pricing information to outsiders (like you), then it is unethical to persuade them to reveal this information. If you induce the customer to contravene his agreement, you violate the biblical mandate "Do not put a stumbling block before the blind"[9] – do not cause someone to stumble spiritually by transgressing.

Another option is to actually decide to make a purchase. Then you may make an honest inquiry of competing businesses. For example, if you are thinking of opening up a haberdashery, you can decide to buy a hat. Then you may go out and do some comparison-shopping.

Even in this case, you have to be careful of the ethical problems we mentioned.

To avoid deceit and unfair disappointment, you should plainly state that you are shopping around for the best deal. Most customers will go to at most two or three shops before deciding. If you are doing a broad survey, let the merchant know, so he can decide whether it is worth his while to invest a lot of effort in selling to you. Likewise, you need to restrict your research to a specific type of item. It is unfair to ask a merchant to take out his entire inventory in order to have a one-in-ten chance of selling one item.

And to maintain truthfulness, you should not make up a cover story – hinting, for example, that you are looking for a birthday present (even if you do intend to give the hat away, that's not your main object).

Of course it is also necessary to actually make the purchase at the end of the day.

Success in business sometimes depends on keeping some of your knowledge concealed. So you do not have to inform your prospective competitors that you are planning to go head-to-head with them. But for this exact reason you need to respect their right to keep their service and price information under wraps and to disclose it only to serious prospective customers.

Copycats

CAN I TRADE IN DESIGNER LOOK-ALIKES?

"Imitation is the sincerest form of flattery," and when one merchant has a successful product, others are sure to follow. But there is an important difference between an imitator and an impostor. Producing and trading in knock-offs of name-brand products poses a number of ethical problems.

Q Since name-brand items are so expensive, many enterprising individuals market look-alikes. Is it ethical to sell or to buy these knock-off products?

A In order to answer this question properly, we have to make clear that there are two quite different kinds of look-alike products:

- *Counterfeits* are designed to fool the buyer into thinking that the product is a genuine name-brand item.

- *Copycats* do not pretend to be the original name-brand, but the similarity in design informs the customer that the copy is designed to function or appear like the original.

It is certainly unethical to sell counterfeit items. This practice violates our duties to both the customer and to the manufacturer. (Generally, selling counterfeits is also illegal.) We can discern these ethical problems in the relevant prohibitions in Jewish law.

First of all, selling counterfeits constitutes fraud toward the customer, which is known in Jewish law as *geneivat da'at*. The Talmud tells us that it is forbidden to sell a lower-quality item if the purchaser has reason to assume that it is the higher-quality type. This is forbidden even if the difference is completely immaterial to the purchaser, and even if the purchaser will never find out. The example in the Talmud is a kosher butcher selling non-kosher meat to a non-Jew. Since the seller is a kosher butcher, the non-Jew has a reasonable basis to assume that he is getting kosher meat, which is more expensive. Even though non-Jews are not commanded to eat kosher meat, and even though it is impossible to distinguish kosher from non-kosher meat, misleading the customer in this way is forbidden.[10] Selling superb counterfeits is an almost exact parallel of the Talmud's example.

Second, this kind of practice constitutes unfair competition toward the original manufacturer. The name-brand invests large sums in associating its name or trademark with quality and desirability; it is unethical for the competitor to take a free ride on this investment. The Mishnah tells us that if one person goes to the trouble of shaking olives out of a tree, it is wrong for someone else to steal his effort by just picking up the olives; he should find his own olive tree to harvest.[11] Likewise, a person should not steal the customers that a competitor has already invested in and attracted by using his own investment against him.

This would also be a violation of encroaching, or *hasagat gevul,* which includes taking business that rightfully belongs to someone else. Of course, what constitutes "unfair competition" depends on the rules of the game. Blocking a competitor's approach to the ball is okay in soccer but forbidden in squash. Likewise, there are varying norms on exactly how far a person may go to convince a competitor's customer to defect.[12] But in this case the counterfeiter is not merely persuading the customer, he is actually misleading him into believing he is buying the original. This is certainly an unwarranted intrusion.

A related problem is that a knock-off of inferior quality will reflect unfairly on the name-brand manufacturer.

What about buying these items? If you are aware that the item is counterfeit, you should refrain from buying it. Patronizing unethical merchants is improper, since it encourages fraud and is part-and-parcel of the debasement of the brand name. Scripture tells us that "one who splits with the thief hates his soul"[13] and this practice is similar.

Copycat items, however, are completely different, and do not present any special ethical problems. The fact that a major brand of cola soft drink uses brown food dye and a red label should not stop others from making a brown-colored cola drink with a red label. Indeed, what right do they have to prevent others from using perfectly standard characteristics for their products? (Trademark laws are designed to deal with this exact question: when is a trademark so distinctive that the merchant has basically created its value, and when is it sufficiently generic that it would be unfair to prevent others from taking advantage of its inherent value?)

As long as it is clear to all that my soft drink is not the name-brand, there's nothing wrong with using some secondary characteristics to help the customer know what kind of product you're trying to compete with.

Indeed, the "Jewish Ethicist" name and logo were chosen to hint at a superficial resemblance to the "Ethicist" column in the *New York Times Magazine*, informing new readers that this feature has a similar format of giving practical answers to everyday ethical dilemmas. This is proper because the differences are as important as the similarities. As hinted by the name "Jewish Ethicist" and by the benevolent, grandfatherly rabbinical figure smiling from the logo, this feature provides answers from a traditional Jewish perspective.

Stealing a Salesman

CAN I HIRE AN EMPLOYEE FROM A COMPETITOR?

Headhunting – the practice of luring employees away from a competitor – is relatively new as a formal industry, but the practice of hiring star employees from other firms is hardly new, and it is widely discussed in the Jewish sources. Let us examine some of the ethical dimensions of this practice.

Q Can I hire a salesman away from a competitor?

A There are many reasons someone might want to hire an employee currently working for a competitor. Some are a lot more ethical than others. Let's take a closer look at some of the motivations for this practice.

THE PRETTY GOOD REASON

You might want to hire this individual because he has excellent qualifications and you believe he has exactly the skills needed to be a valuable asset to your firm. This scenario is the least problematic, since you are not working against your competition but *for* your own benefit. If the worker is truly more valuable to you than to your competitor, then the worker will also benefit.

Even so, there is one ethical issue that needs to be addressed. You should not hire away a key employee if you could easily find a suitable person without raiding your competitor's roster. A general principle of negotiation in Jewish law is that we should not interfere with existing business relationships if we can obtain what we need without doing so. Whether we are looking for a worker or a job, an apartment or a tenant, if someone else is already committed or even involved in serious negotiation, we should not interfere if we can find an equivalent situation somewhere else.[14]

This principle has several justifications. Take the example of the salesman. It is true that you will benefit if you hire your competitor's employee, and so will the employee. Yet the benefit to your firm is minimal if you can find a suitable employee somewhere else, and so is the benefit to the employee, since the improvement in his job situation would come partly at the expense of a change in working environment. At the same time, the damage to your competitor could be very great, since he has to find and train a new worker.

But if you hire someone else who is truly suitable and is looking for work on his own initiative, the benefit to him is immense. His job search shows that he is unsatisfied with his current situation. And the damage to his current employer is avoided.

Another reason mentioned in the Jewish sources that militates against interfering with someone else's situation is the stirring up of antagonism. While your competitor does not own his salesmen, he does feel that he should be able to have some degree of reliance on their continued loyalty. Firms, even competing ones, generally develop a delicate understanding regarding the extent of competition; breaking it can lead to escalating and damaging actions. Sometimes these hires lead to a whole series of raids and counter-raids that can wreak havoc on the involved firms, and this may not be in your best interest. Even the employees who are the supposed beneficiaries of such a hiring war could find their satisfaction decline due to the disruption of workplace routine.

So even when you have a pretty good reason for headhunting, you should inject a measure of thoughtfulness into your calculations.

NOT SO GOOD REASONS

Sometimes a firm recruits key employees from its competitors for malicious reasons. The firm's objective is to hire away someone who is critically important to the competition, whether or not it really needs the new employee. This would definitely be considered unfair competition. Every employer has the right to look for the personnel who best suit his workplace, but it is unfair to take a destructive attitude and try to harm other firms. In some jurisdictions, such recruiting is actually illegal.

Here's another bad reason for recruiting a competitor's employee: as a shortcut to obtain access to his customers or his firm's specialized knowledge. This is a common motivation for recruiting salespeople from rival firms, but it is definitely improper. Not only is the customer list confidential, but even if customers move of their own free will, the relationship which this salesperson developed with the competitor's customers was cultivated on behalf of the employer, not for the salesperson individually. Sometimes such a hire may violate specific agreements the employee has with his current employer, such as a non-compete clause.

If you're convinced that the customers are coming over because of your superior product and your highly qualified new salesperson, try the following test: ask yourself whether the salary you're offering the new hire reflects only his ability to attract "new" customers or also signals a down payment on his ability to deliver his *current* clientele.

In this case, you are not the only one acting unfairly toward the competitor. The salesman is also acting improperly, by taking proprietary information with him when he switches jobs. Now an additional ethical lapse is involved: persuading the salesperson to act with a lack of integrity towards the current employer.

A good rule of thumb in these situations is to ask yourself whether you would make an offer to the same individual, with the same compensation, if he did not work for your competitor but for some unrelated business? If the answer is no, there is good reason to think that the hire may be an instance of unfair competition or of stealing customers.

To sum up, if you want to hire this individual solely because of his qualifications, your motivation is ethical. Before acting, though, you should consider whether you can meet your needs just as well by hiring somebody else. You should also consider whether the hire is likely to cause a wrenching and costly change in the competitive norms in your business.

If your objective is to harm your competitor or obtain access to his hard-earned business assets, then you should definitely refrain from poaching the salesman from your business rival.

Stealing a Business Plan

CAN I COPY A BUSINESS IDEA FROM A SUPPLIER?

Fair competition has to tread a fine line. While it is certainly unfair to steal a rival's idea, it is equally unrealistic to think that one firm should be able to acquire a permanent monopoly on a line of business just because they were there first. In the end, a firm that wants to keep its competitive advantage has the primary responsibility for keeping its advantage alive.

Q I have a consulting business that provides a unique service. When I offered my services to a local firm, they expressed interest and asked me to give details of how I work. A few weeks later I learned that they had decided to enter my business as a competitor. Can I make them pay me for my idea?

A Maybe *you* should pay *them* for the valuable lesson you have learned about the importance of discretion in business dealings. A business that has unique expertise should be extra-careful not to reveal any tricks of the trade when describing its service.

Now let us discuss your question in detail. The basic ethical question here hinges on the issue of whether or not you have a genuine secret or unique specialized knowledge that you disclosed to the potential client. If you approach a developer suggesting that he rent you space to open a fast-food restaurant in a shopping mall, you can hardly claim that he stole your idea if he opens one himself. Even if the idea had never occurred to him before you suggested it, the concept is hardly original.

A similar distinction is found in Jewish law. If someone knows of a unique business opportunity and sends an agent to take advantage of it, it is unethical for the agent to abandon his commission and buy it for himself. But if someone tells a colleague about the opportunity, offering to go in as partners, the prospective partner *is* permitted to decline the offer and take advantage of the opportunity by himself. This would not be unethical, because he never agreed to work together with the "innovator." The proposer has to take a calculated risk if it is worth revealing the information, weighing the benefits of cooperation against the risk that the prospective partner will take advantage of the knowledge.[15]

Basing ourselves on this distinction, we have to ask whether your client ever undertook, explicitly or implicitly, not to take advantage of the business opportunity you revealed to him – the profit potential in your own business. If you did not make a non-compete agreement and did not present your idea as a secret, it seems you have very little recourse.

But if you have a real business secret, and you made it clear to the client that your presentation contained confidential information which you revealed only in order to explain your service and under condition of secrecy, then it would be unethical for him to steal your idea. The Bible tells us, "A talebearer reveals secrets, but a faithful person conceals a thing."[16] It is certainly forbidden to reveal or to take advantage of business secrets disclosed in confidence.[17]

In consumer protection, Jewish law rejects a buyer-beware approach, which relieves the seller of all responsibility, but also a strict-liability approach which relieves the buyer of responsibility. Rather, both sides need to act responsibly in order to ensure that there is a fair transaction.[18] The same is true in negotiations. While the client does bear the responsibility not to steal your idea, you have a responsibility to clarify in advance what you consider to be protected aspects of your presentation and to conceal business secrets that are not essential to your presentation.

Costly Competition

CAN I USE MY COST ADVANTAGE TO DRIVE MY COMPETITORS OUT OF BUSINESS?

Fair competition entails having fair rules and applying them equitably. Ideas about what rules are fair have changed considerably over the generations, but we can still learn a great deal from the ethical sensitivity of Jewish authorities. The case in this column discusses the question of whether one can use a cost advantage to drive a competitor out of business.

Q We have found a way to attain an overwhelming cost advantage over our competitors. Is it ethical for us to lower our prices so much that they are left with almost no business?

A The issue of fair price competition is an ancient one, which is extensively discussed in the Jewish sources.

The most important insight they offer is that fair competition means not only that the rules are fair, but above all that they apply equitably to all players. The Mishnah states: "Rabbi Yehudah says, A storekeeper should not distribute treats to children, because this accustoms them to buy from him; but the sages permit it. And [Rabbi Yehudah also says,] he should not undercut the going price; but the sages said this is praiseworthy." The Talmud explains why the authoritative majority opinion – that of the sages – finds no fault with such inducements: "He can say, I give out nuts, you can give out prunes."[19]

In other words, attracting customers by providing an advantage in merchandise or price is permissible and even praiseworthy, provided the merchant is not exploiting an unfair advantage unavailable to competitors.

In your case, all producers are constantly seeking ways to cut costs, and so you can say to your competitors, "I have saved money on raw materials; you go ahead and save money on payroll." The fundamental ability to compete is common to all sellers in your market.

Nonetheless, many authorities added a caveat to this principle: it is appropriate to draw customers, but not to the extent of depriving a competitor of his entire livelihood.[20] The sages throughout the generations were passionately concerned to maintain the ability of each and every person to support himself at some minimal level.

This approach is not in complete harmony with some modern ideas. Free-market advocates argue that the growth and development of the market necessarily involves business failures, and that ultimately the entire system works more efficiently when there is no interference in the process. There is much truth in this insight, and much to be gained from the action of the "invisible hand" of competition.

But practically speaking, there are some instances where the hardship of a business failure really outweighs the economic benefits to the market. Consider this: Almost any economics professor will tell you that keeping an inefficient business in operation by limiting competition amounts to no more than a tax on consumers. Perhaps the gross income of this inept firm is $1 million a year; ten percent of this is just a de facto subsidy paid by customers in the form of inflated prices for the firm's product. Result: $100,000 of consumer money wasted. This is undoubtedly correct, and as an economics professor myself I teach the same thing.

But sometimes we need to ask ourselves what the alternative is. Perhaps right now there are no employment opportunities in the vicinity of the failing plant. If the company goes out of business, the burden on the dole will be $500,000 a year. Result: wastage of $500,000 of public money instead of $100,000; a tax imposed on all citizens, instead of one that falls only on customers of the firm's product; scores of frustrated and idle unemployed who feel they are not contributing to society, instead of scores of busy workers who are proud of their work, even if they are aware that other, competing firms may do a better job.

Now the fact remains that in today's business environment, drawing the line at driving a competitor out of business is *not* in the "rules of the game," and in most cases people *can* find an alternative livelihood. So in all probability it is not unethical for you to fully exploit your cost advantage, thus providing a substantial benefit to your business, as well as to your workers and to the consumers in your market.

But before you adopt this approach, take a moment to look at the bigger picture. If you can make a similar return with more gentlemanly competition that does not deprive your competitor of his livelihood, this is a praiseworthy and ethical course of action – one you should carefully examine and consider.

ENDNOTES

1. Bava Batra 21a
2. See Shulhan Arukh, Hoshen Mishpat 231:28
3. Yoma 38b
4. Gittin 5:8
5. Exodus 23:7
6. Yevamot 65b, Bava Metzia 23b
7. Shabbat 55a
8. Bava Metzia 4:10
9. Leviticus 19:14
10. Hullin 94b
11. Gittin 5:8
12. See Shulhan Arukh, Hoshen Mishpat 156:6 in Rema, Responsa Hatam Sofer Hoshen Mishpat 79.
13. Proverbs 29:24
14. Shulhan Arukh, Hoshen Mishpat 237:1–2
15. Shulhan Arukh, Hoshen Mishpat 183:2–4
16. Proverbs 11:13
17. Hafetz Hayyim 12:13
18. See Shulhan Arukh, Hoshen Mishpat 228:6
19. Bava Metzia 60a
20. See Bava Batra 21b

DATING ETHICS

Introduction

While the Jewish Ethicist column is primarily focused on marketplace ethics, a few questions have pertained to dating ethics. Including them in this book is certainly not meant to legitimize a cynical view of courtship as a glorified shopping trip and a spouse as a durable appliance. On the contrary, Jewish tradition emphasizes that the process of finding a mate is really just a way of identifying the *beshert*, the person God intended for us all along.

This being said, it must be admitted that there are many parallels between dating and selling, and singles do try to "sell" themselves to their dates. So it is important to emphasize that this "marketplace" is also subject to strict ethical constraints.

The ideal marriage is one based on complete and implicit trust. It should be obvious that two individuals are never going to attain a relationship of trust through a process fraught with deceit. Anyone involved in the "dating game," whether as a participant or as a facilitator, should recognize that this process demands the highest levels of integrity at all stages of the process.

Dating Disclosure

CAN I CONCEAL MY REAL AGE IN DATING?

Shakespeare wrote, "The better part of valor is discretion,"[1] and there is no question but that etiquette requires a refined sense of discretion, of knowing what to conceal. However, building a lasting relationship of trust is a process characterized by respect and openness, not exploitation and deceit. This insight is applied below to the practice of misleading others about age in dating.[2]

Q A single friend of mine in his late forties would like to marry a woman in her thirties, so he pretends to be forty. He has asked me to confirm that he is forty if I am asked. Should I play along?

A It's certainly very important to make a good first impression in dating, and we can well understand why your friend wants to start off the acquaintance with a positive message of youthfulness. However, it is important in all such matters not to cross the fine line between a positive impression and a deceptive one.

Jewish tradition has a lot to say about this issue. Marriage and family are paramount values in Judaism, and our sages, who had a profound understanding of human nature, were aware of the importance of first impressions and adequate discretion. Yet because integrity and truth are the foundation of the Torah, Jewish law long ago delineated appropriate guidelines for disclosure in dating, or what one might call ethical dating.

To a great extent, ethical dating is really a question of ethical salesmanship. In the marketplace, too, the merchant wants to make a positive impression, but needs to avoid deceit.

Beyond the obvious requirement that we may never lie, there are two basic rules of integrity in selling merchandise:

- A common deficiency that many people do not mind need not be disclosed, but it may not be deceitfully hidden.

- A true defect must be honestly disclosed to the purchaser even if he does not ask, but it is permissible and proper to disclose it in a delicate way that won't deter the buyer too much.

For example, someone selling a ten-year-old car does not need to mention that there is a little rust, since that is a normal condition. But it would be improper to use special paint to cover up the rust.

Conversely, if the brakes are deficient, this fact must be mentioned. But the seller does not have to say, "You should know that the car is a death trap." It's enough to clearly but delicately mention that the brakes need some work.

The same basic principle applies in dating. A man does not have to tell prospective dates that he has only a tenth-grade education, since this is not really a deficiency. But he should not go around wearing a college ring.

Conversely, if he has a serious heart condition he should make this known to a prospective spouse, but he does not have to say, "You should know that I'm living on borrowed time."

For most people, a significant age difference falls in the first category. It's not a "defect" that would automatically disqualify a potential partner, but it is an important consideration that needs to be weighed against other, positive characteristics. And for a few individuals, a big difference in age is unqualifiedly unacceptable.

These guidelines tell us *what* needs to be disclosed, but they do not tell us *when*. Part of the balance between discretion and disclosure is achieved by thoughtful timing. Some qualities would put off a date if revealed before the first date, but would be considered acceptable or even insignificant after a warm relationship develops. A significant age difference is a typical example.

So your friend is allowed to be discreet about his age at the beginning of an acquaintanceship, and if a date asks you about this or calls you up before a first or second date to ask his age, it may be better to dodge the question. Example: "I never really pay attention to age." Maybe, after she gets to know him, she won't mind his age; after all, chances are she's not getting any younger herself.

But if your friend keeps his secret even after things get serious, you should reevaluate the situation. If asked, you should be open, though of course delicate. If you tell her that he is a wee bit past forty, she'll get the picture; you do not have to state that he's old enough to be her father. If you suspect that the true age difference may really be worrisome to his date, you may even consider calling her up and initiating the conversation regarding his true age.

It should be self-evident that we may never lie outright about the characteristics of a potential match, such as age. Your friend may not say that he is forty, and if he does you may not back him up. But we also need to be careful not to allow relatively superficial deficiencies to interfere with the cultivation of our deepest human relations.

I wish your friend the best of luck in finding his *beshert* (destined spouse) in the near future!

Dating for Dollars

ARE COMMERCIAL DATING AND MATCHMAKING SERVICES ETHICAL?

Money is a two-edged sword. It can motivate us to do valuable things we would never do without the inducement, but it can also distort our perspective and tempt us into unethical behavior that we would otherwise eschew. Jewish tradition believes that this conflict can be managed, and sanctions paid matchmaking if carried out in an ethical fashion.

Q I have many friends who are using dating services or marriage brokers to help find partners. Sometimes the cost is in the thousands of dollars. Is this practice ethical?

A Helping someone find his or her life's partner is one of the greatest acts of loving-kindness we can perform. In fact, our tradition tells us that the Holy One, blessed be He, is Himself a marriage broker. The Midrash[3] relates that thousands of years ago, a Roman noblewoman asked the sage Rabbi Yosi what God had been doing in the generations since He created the world. The rabbi replied that God was busy as a matchmaker!

The matron scoffed at the idea that the Master of the universe would occupy Himself with such a trifle and asserted that nothing was easier than making matches. To prove her point, in a single night she matched up scores of her slaves. However, the very next day she was besieged with complaints from the disappointed newlyweds and conceded the great wisdom needed for making a match that leads to a happy marriage.

What about taking money for this wonderful kindness? According to the Jewish approach, when an act of kindness is ethical in itself, taking money for it does not make it unethical. We just need to take steps to ensure that the financial motivation is not so great as to dominate the human element. For this reason, paid matchmaking is sanctioned by our tradition. Indeed, the professional marriage broker has been a respected figure in Jewish communities for centuries. Paying a fair price for matchmaking helps ensure that professionals and others are willing to invest efforts commensurate with the great importance of the institution of marriage.

However, money may also lead people to neglect their ethical obligations, and this business does involve a number of ethical pitfalls. Dating services work under a variety of payment schemes, and each one has its own ethical challenges. Let us discuss each approach separately. Practitioners should be careful to avoid these problems, and customers should be on the alert to avoid being victimized by them.

UP-FRONT FEES

Some dating services require payment of a substantial up-front subscription fee, in return for which the service promises to supply a constant supply of suggested suitable matches. This payment scheme is not inherently unethical, and has the advantage that it encourages the customer to maintain an ongoing connection with the service to fine-tune the criteria. A few thousand dollars may sound like a lot, but it is a trifle if it leads to a lifetime of domestic harmony and fulfillment.

Even so, this type of scheme seems to be the most problematic. Many clients complain that this structure encourages overly optimistic promises in advance but gives the service no real incentive to invest effort in creating high-quality matches. Someone who runs this kind of service should be especially careful not to raise unreasonable expectations among customers, and to work hard to try and emulate the Creator in seeking the greatest degree of compatibility among clients. And customers should carefully check the reputation of such a service before paying significant sums.

INTRODUCTION FEES

Many Internet dating services provide free profiles of potential matches, but require payment when contact is actually made. The same often applies to personal ads in newspapers. Since the service leaves all the initiative to the couple, the ethical problems here are mostly on the side of the consumer. Those who use such services should take care to avoid misleading potential dates, keeping in mind the guidelines outlined at the beginning of this chapter.

One kind of deceit pertains to personal qualities: age, looks, income, and so on. Profiles should be reliable guides to these qualities. The previous column gave guidelines for making a positive impression without materially misleading the other side.

Another problem is when a person advertises for a serious relationship but is really looking for something more casual. This is doubly unethical. Judaism disapproves of casual dating; a meaningful romantic relationship can be successful only if based on commitment. At the very least, someone who is not looking for a permanent relationship should be careful not to mislead a potential partner who is seeking something serious.

Even though the ethical problems concern the consumer, the services should not take a hands-off attitude. They have a responsibility to make sure that their service is providing a valuable contact to the customer and not just another fee. And they should keep in mind that they are facilitators, not panderers. These services already carefully comb the ads to ensure that subscribers are not providing information that would enable them to bypass the service and avoid payment. While they're at it, they can examine the ads to make sure they do not contain messages that are inappropriate for a serious dating service which is helping customers find a soul-mate.

PAYING FOR RESULTS

The payment structure most familiar in Jewish life is the marriage broker who gets a fee only when there is an engagement. This guarantees that the matchmaker has the greatest incentive to find the most promising candidates. It also results in satisfied customers, who are asked to pay only when their hopes are fulfilled, and are often more than happy to show their gratitude to the matchmaker.

This arrangement also has pitfalls, however. Some practitioners forget that they are occupied in a holy mitzvah and think only of the bottom line. This may lead them to pressure couples to get engaged before they are ready or even if they are not really compatible. This concern doesn't mean that the *shadchan* (marriage broker) must adopt a hands-off attitude, for the gentle guidance of an experienced matchmaker can be valuable for the couple. It does mean that pressure tactics must be avoided. Ultimately the couple must make their own independent decision.

One ethical challenge common to all matchmaking services is that many customers are in an emotionally vulnerable state. Indeed, such vulnerability is often the reason people turn to special services. Some may face special handicaps in finding a match due to age, health, or similar factors; others may be recovering from a previous failed relationship. Matchmakers must not take advantage of this situation to push services or charge prices that would not interest the client if he or she were in a more balanced state of mind.

Matchmaking is a valuable and respected profession, but precisely because of its immense importance it must be practiced with the highest level of integrity and sensitivity.

ENDNOTES

1. Henry IV Part IV:IV
2. The discussion draws heavily on chapter 3 of Ha-Nisuin ke-Hilkhatam, by Rabbi Binyamin Adler.
3. Genesis Rabbah 68:4

CONSUMER ETHICS

Introduction

Business ethics is usually viewed from the vantage point of the business-person. But every one of us engages in business as a consumer, and the "little guy" also has ethical obligations.

We have previously pointed out that Jewish tradition rejects the extreme of *caveat emptor,* "let the buyer beware," which relieves the seller of responsibility for misleading the consumer. It is equally true that we reject the opposite extreme, which holds that the seller needs to beware and "the customer is always right" even when dishonest or exploitative.

The most pronounced expression of this symmetry is found in the laws of "over-reaching," or taking advantage in commerce. These laws are not unique to Jewish law, and many jurisdictions prohibit sellers from charging exorbitant prices. It is remarkable that Jewish law equally forbids the consumer from obtaining the purchase for an unfairly *low* price.[1]

It is true that the seller usually has a greater opportunity to exploit the customer than the other way around. Customers may have little experience with certain types of products, especially items they purchase infrequently. In addition, the customers for any given product constitute a large and dispersed group, and therefore it would be difficult for them to combine their knowledge and their demands. The sellers, on the other hand, are usually experienced and sophisticated in their business, and they are often large firms with significant market power. Yet there are circumstances where the situation is reversed. In each situation, Jewish law forbids taking advantage of the vulnerable party.

The ultimate insight is that both parties to a transaction have the responsibility to ensure that there is a true and mutually beneficial meeting of the minds. A deal is unethical if either side exploits an advantage in knowledge or power to mislead the other and to draw them into a disadvantageous transaction.

The Talmud[2] teaches us to cultivate a feeling of gratitude toward the merchants who bring us valuable goods and services that we benefit from with a minimum of effort.

> Ben Zoma...used to say, How much effort Adam had to invest in order to eat bread: he had to plow, sow, gather, heap, thresh, winnow, sort, sift, knead, and bake. Only then could he eat. Yet I wake up and find all of these prepared for me. And how much effort Adam had to exert in order to wear clothes: he sheared and bleached and carded and spun and wove, and only then found clothes to wear. Yet I wake up and find all these prepared for me. All the nations of the world go out of their way and come to my doorstep, and I wake up to find all these before me.

This gratitude is part of the basis for our ethical obligations toward merchants.

Is the Seller Taking Advantage of Me?

DO I HAVE TO PAY AN OUTRAGEOUS PRICE FOR AN ORDER?

Business ethics is based on understanding; ethical problems begin when there is misunderstanding. Sometimes misunderstanding arises because of deliberate deception; in other cases it is a result of poor planning and faulty agreements.

When agreements are not carefully understood in advance, one side may seem to have excessive leverage. Sometimes it is our own ethical values that put us at a disadvantage. But there are some basic principles that can help us attain a just outcome even in such awkward situations.

Q I ordered personalized address labels and left a deposit without asking the final cost. When I came to pick up the order, I was scandalized by the seemingly outrageous price and refused to accept them. Now I feel guilty. Do I have to send the storeowner the balance?

A You're certainly in an awkward position. If you pay the full amount, you will feel that the seller is taking advantage of you; if you do not pay, then you will be taking advantage of him. The best advice about these situations is to not let them arise. Whether you are buying or selling, never let work be performed unless it is clear to both sides exactly what is expected and how much it is going to cost.

In cases where there is no explicit agreement, Jewish law is clear: payment for services should be based on the customary amount.[3] The ethical principle underlying this law is that our obligation to pay is ultimately based not only on the principle of agreement, but also on the principle of reciprocity. Since the storekeeper did work on your behalf, you have an obligation to pay him.

The difficulty in your case is deciding what is customary. The storekeeper will claim that by placing an order you agreed to pay what is customary in his establishment. You probably believe that you should pay what is customary in other shops.

So the ethical dilemma is as follows: you have an obligation to pay for the work done on your behalf, but the fact that you did not check up on the price beforehand does not mean that you have to pay any price the seller demands. While a seller can charge a fully informed customer any price he wants, he cannot expect to foist an outrageous price on an unsuspecting shopper.

Let us examine a few factors that may help in resolving this dilemma.

If the store has a clearly displayed policy on these matters, then it is best to follow it. Perhaps store policy states that the deposit is meant to cover exactly these situations, and you do not owe any additional amount. Alternatively, you may find that the prices in the store are clearly posted. If this is the case, the storekeeper may be justified in assuming that you were informed about his policies. Conversely, if he has a hidden and mysterious method for pricing each individual order, then your claim that the pricing is unreasonable seems more convincing.

It is also worthwhile to do research on what similar shops charge for such labels. You may be surprised to discover that the "outrageous" price you were asked is actually about what other, similar stores demand. In this case, that would be considered the customary cost even if mail-order houses charge far less.

What happens if, after you do your homework, you still think the price is unreasonable? Your first step should be to suggest a compromise. Jewish law strongly encourages compromise as a path to conflict resolution. Parties to a conflict are urged to seek a practical solution to their problem, not vindication for their positions, as can be see from the following Talmudic passage:[4]

> Rabbi Yehoshua ben Karcha says, It is a mitzvah to seek a compromise. As it is written, "Truth and peaceful judgment should you judge in your gates."[5] It would seem that where there is judgment there is no peace, and where there is peace there is no judgment. What is the judgment that incorporates peace? Compromise.

This statement teaches a profound message. Compromise does not "compromise" justice. It is, in itself, a form of justice, a unique kind of judgment that takes account of each side's point of view and any special circumstances. This kind of judgment is most likely to lead to peace.

Another recommendation of our sages is to show a willingness to yield. When Rabbi Nehuniah ben ha-Kaneh was asked the secret of his unusual longevity, one of the traits he mentioned was: "I was always willing to yield in monetary matters."[6] If the amount is small, the best idea may be to just pay the money and not make a big fuss simply because you cannot bear the thought that you were taken advantage of.

But ultimately, your obligation to the seller is to reach a fair settlement, not to accept any price the seller demands. You should suggest a compromise; if the seller won't accept one, make it clear that you are willing to cooperate in reaching a settlement through discussion, arbitration, or adjudication.[7]

Make sure your offer does not sound like a threat. The seller should understand that you are genuinely interested in reaching a fair solution, and are not warning that if he doesn't negotiate on your terms he'll be left with nothing.

It is a cardinal principle of the Jewish faith that we cannot obtain atonement from God until we seek forgiveness from those we have wronged.[8] But this does not mean that the wronged party can demand any price for granting forgiveness, and make the wrongdoer a hostage to his demands. It means that we have to be sincerely willing to hear the claims of the injured party and to resolve them in a fair and prompt manner.

Renegotiating a Low Estimate

DOES A CONTRACTOR DESERVE EXTRA PAY FOR A HARDER-
THAN-EXPECTED JOB?

Despite our best efforts to settle on a fair price, life is full of surprises
that can make even the most carefully negotiated agreement seem unfair.
This is well illustrated by the problem of whether a contractor is entitled
to a little extra if the job was more difficult than anticipated.

Q My contractor made an estimate assuming that it would take two
days to clear and paint the wall. But the wall was in unusually
bad condition and it took three days instead. Does he deserve extra
payment?

A When you hire a contractor you are paying for results, even though
the price is usually based on an estimate of the required work. So
the price quote does take into account some normal variation in the
amount of work required.

However, when there is a big surprise, like the bad condition of
your walls, the fairest policy is to offer to make some adjustment. Let
us see why.

Jewish law states that when an employee does more or better work
than anticipated in the face of unexpected conditions, he is justified in
expecting improved treatment, even when he cannot actually compel
the employer to give extra. His extra effort may not be mentioned in
the contract, but it is right and fair to acknowledge it.

We learn this principle from an important passage in the Talmud.
The tractate Bava Metzia discusses a case where the employer agrees to
pay a certain wage, but in the middle of the work period it becomes
possible to obtain workers for much less. The employer is resentful of
the high wage which he is now locked in to. If the workers succeed in
persuading the boss to keep them on, they will get the same pay they
originally bargained for; however, the Talmud states that it is reasonable
for the employer to expect them to work more assiduously than usual.[9]
Likewise, if wages suddenly rise and the workers are resentful of their

low pay, it is reasonable for them to expect the employer to provide better-than-usual working conditions.

It would hardly be surprising if in your case the contractor felt some resentment when he discovered the poor condition of your walls and realized that his original estimate was very disadvantageous. As a result, the fairest policy is to make some adjustment, perhaps by offering an addition to the estimate or by billing separately work that was originally meant to be included.

In some cases you would be obligated to pay extra. One such case is where there is a well-established custom that allows contractors to demand more than the estimate when there are big surprises. In Jewish monetary law, custom is king, and you should abide by the established norm.

You also should definitely make an adjustment if you had reason to suspect that the walls were in bad condition but you didn't notify the contractor. You should not take unfair advantage of the workman's ignorance. The same is true if the walls were in a state completely beyond the normal range, and the contractor had no reason to suspect the problem. In this case it is as if the estimate were given for a different job altogether.[10]

Of course the same thing applies in the opposite direction. If the job takes much less work than anticipated, it is fairest if the contractor offers a discount. From readers' letters I know that many business people adopt this policy.

Our modern economic system is based on the "invisible hand" of the market, the idea that economic incentives result *overall* in economic prosperity, even if in certain individual instances there is a lack of fairness. But belief in God teaches us to supplement this idea with an acknowledgement of another hand: the Hand of Providence, the hand of God, which provides for each person individually. "You open Your hand and satisfy each living creature."[11] Even if sticking stubbornly to the contract does lead to a fair outcome on the whole, we should strive whenever practical to achieve a just result in each individual transaction.

Legitimate Larceny?

CAN I "SETTLE ACCOUNTS" WITH A STORE THAT CHEATED
ME?

We often attribute ethical lapses to greed, but actually it has many complex motivations. The rationale that one is cheating in order to settle accounts is a good example. Jewish tradition provides some valuable insights into understanding and overcoming some of the psychological obstacles to ethical behavior.

Q A store in my neighborhood is always ripping me off: overcharging, giving poor merchandise, and so on. Sometimes I feel that the only way of settling accounts is for me to play the same game–for instance by pocketing a few almonds, or taking a bunch of extra shopping bags. Is this a proper response?

A There's no question that a vindictive reaction is improper. If you think that the store is cheating you, the proper response is to bring any claims you have to their attention; if you feel that they do not handle the claim appropriately, you can initiate legal action of some kind. Of course the best solution is to take your business elsewhere.

Your question is very important, however, because it illustrates an aspect of business ethics that is often neglected. The situation you describe reminds us that there are many reasons why people engage in questionable behavior. We tend to assume that the main motivation for bad morals in the marketplace is plain old-fashioned greed. Yet very often the materialistic dimension in business ethics is relatively minor compared to the human element.

We can learn this from the unique way the Torah describes the prohibition on charging excessive prices, prices far above what is accepted for comparable merchandise in other stores. The verse tells us: "And when you sell something to your fellow or buy from the hand of your fellow, do not oppress each one his brother."[12] The word used for this transgression is *ona'ah*, which does not designate stealing or cheating, but rather oppression or distress. The focus here is not on the monetary aspect but on the human aspect.

A simple example demonstrates that very often this is the dominant problem in overcharging. Imagine that you come home and discover there is a dollar missing from your wallet. You probably wouldn't be overly troubled about such a small amount. Even if you manage to remember where you lost the dollar, you probably wouldn't make much effort to recover it. After all, your time is worth something too.

Now imagine that you come home from the store and discover that you were overcharged one dollar for some item. They charged you two dollars for a pack of gum. Perhaps you are certain that the mistake was intentional. If you're like many people, you will indignantly march back to the store and demand that they correct the mistake. If asked about this seeming paradox, most people will answer honestly and straightforwardly that it's a matter of principle.

Most of us cannot bear to be wronged. Our inner sense of justice is so strong that if we feel the store owner has not given us a fair hearing, we may be tempted to set things right by committing an "offsetting" crime against the store, as if two wrongs make a right.

Interestingly, the Talmud specifically states that stealing is forbidden "even in order to harass."[13] Our tradition recognizes that this can be an important motivation for stealing—and that this motivation cannot justify such behavior.

Ironically, when unethical behavior is motivated by our sense of righteousness, it can be very difficult to overcome. If a person is tempted to act unethically because of a tendency to acquisitiveness, he can usually keep it in check by reminding himself that he would do better to listen to the dictates of his conscience. But when even our conscience convinces us that stealing is ethical, what will keep our behavior under control?

The key to overcoming this kind of temptation is to master our emotions. Do we really want to be subjugated to base emotions like anger and vengefulness? Even if your behavior could be justified, is a handful of almonds worth the feeling that you have lowered yourself to exactly the level of behavior which you condemn?

The Torah's prohibition against overcharging is not only worded in a surprising way, as we have just pointed out; it is also found in a surprising context. It is not included in the chapters immediately following the Ten Commandments in the Book of Exodus, where we find the foundation of the basic monetary regulations of the Torah. Instead it is found in the passage that discusses the freeing of slaves in the Jubilee year. This context seems to hint that the best way to overcome the temptation to act unethically is to free ourselves from enslavement to anger, vindictiveness, and suspicion and to conduct ourselves with generosity and dignity as befits free and noble human beings.

Telemarketing Travails

CAN I SLAM THE RECEIVER ON AN UNWELCOME
TELEMARKETER?

Telemarketing has become a familiar and generally unwelcome part of modern life. Our lives at home are interrupted by a seemingly endless series of unsolicited phone calls offering products or services we usually do not want. The people making the calls are not trying to harass us, however; they are workers trying hard to earn a living. This raises the question of how to deal ethically and humanely with an annoying salesperson making an unsolicited call.

Q If I pick up the phone and hear a telemarketer, do I have to listen? If I am too timid to tell him that I'm not interested, can I just hang up? And what about the salesperson—isn't he guilty of invading my privacy?

A This issue illustrates that many of our everyday dilemmas are not questions of ethics alone, but also of etiquette. There are many norms of considerate behavior that are not really ethical obligations, but we should still strive to fulfill them.

A telemarketer who tries to interest me in a savings plan, or a door-to-door salesperson who wants to sell me cosmetics or cleaning products, has no special right to my attention and resources. I do not have to stay on the phone or open the door. There is no ethical objection to just hanging up, or closing the door.

Even so, remember that everyone has to make a living, and this includes salespeople. Ask yourself how you would want to be treated by prospects if you were in this line of work. You will probably conclude that if the salesperson and the product are not especially offensive, the best course is to be polite and say "Thank you, but I'm not interested" before hanging up or closing the door. If you're not rushed for time, you might try and listen to the pitch for at least a few seconds so as not to discourage the caller.

We can find a hint of this idea in the laws of charity. Jewish tradition emphasizes that giving moral support and encouragement to a poor person is at least as important as giving financial support: "If the poor person asks but you do not have the ability to give, do not rebuke him or raise your voice; speak encouraging words and show him your good will".[14]

Jewish law also states that helping someone to earn a living is the highest form of charity, and is far superior to giving them a handout.[15] Since the average telephone solicitor is probably scraping along, we should not treat them worse then we would treat a beggar. Allowing a marketer a few seconds to make his pitch and responding in a polite and encouraging way can be viewed as an act of genuine piety. Remember that he is ultimately trying to help you.

Of course etiquette is a two-way street. A telemarketer is not allowed to call back after being told not to, so do not hesitate to hang up on someone who harasses you in this way. It goes without saying that there is nothing unmannerly about hanging up on a machine.

Here is another important ethical consideration for telemarketers: A telemarketer or salesperson should not make a call without some minimal expectation that the customer might be interested in the product. We can infer this from the prohibition against coveting, the last of the Ten Commandments. Jewish tradition teaches that this commandment is transgressed when we so covet our neighbor's possessions that we pressure him to sell them. It's not a question of what conditions or what price; rather, these are personal effects that the person doesn't consider for sale at all. Pressuring him to sell them is unwelcome and insensitive. The same censure should apply to the reverse situation: pressuring someone to buy when they are simply not interested in the product.[16]

In many areas there are regulations that protect consumers against unwanted phone solicitations. Several state governments maintain lists of consumers who are not interested in telephone sales pitches, and it is illegal for telemarketers to call them. There is nothing wrong with taking advantage of such protection if you feel that you have little to gain and much to lose from telephone advertising.

Telemarketing harassment is just a new version of an age-old dilemma. The sages of the Talmud discussed the problem of door-to-door salesmen, the "telemarketers" of their day.[17] The rabbis recognized that peddlers provide a valuable service, proffering unique goods and reaching consumers who would might find it hard to reach a store. On the other hand, such salesmen may have an unfair advantage over local merchants, whose expenses are greater because they pay local taxes. Millennia before the Federal Trade Commission, Jewish law regulated such selling so as to balance the benefits salespeople bring and the nuisance they can cause.[18]

Boycotts

CAN I ORGANIZE A BOYCOTT TO COMBAT OVERPRICING?

In the introduction to this section, we pointed out that consumers are often at a disadvantage compared to sellers because they are fragmented. One way they can overcome this handicap is to band together in a boycott, which can be a legitimate means to fight overpricing. However, this power should always be used responsibly.

Q A vital product in our community is sold by two large companies and a number of small ones, all charging similar prices. Recent price increases have been really outrageous. A total boycott of a vital product is not practical, but can we organize a boycott of the large companies that we think are behind the increases?

A Consumer boycotts are similar in many ways to employee strikes; in both cases fragmented stakeholders try to improve their bargaining position against powerful business interests. The approach of Jewish tradition is also similar; the rabbis were sympathetic to the need for "countervailing power", but insisted that it be used in a responsible and accountable fashion.

In the case of worker's organizations, Jewish law gives them authority to regulate rates and working conditions; but this authority is subject to special oversight to make sure that it doesn't contradict the public interest.[19]

A similar approach applies to consumer activism. The Talmud records a number of cases where boycotts were used to bring about lower prices, but as we will see, all of these cases depend on certain justifying factors.

In three distinct cases in the Mishnah and Talmud, we find that sellers were taking advantage of the fact that their Jewish customers were stringent in their performance of commandments and insisted on buying mitzvah objects of the highest quality.[20]

The sellers considered that they had the buyers "over a barrel" (in a vulnerable situation), and exploited this fact to collude to raise prices.

In one instance, for example, the Talmud records that the prices for the best myrtles for the four species used at Sukkot were excessively high.

In each of these cases, a leading rabbi enforced a *de facto* boycott of the overpriced item by making a temporary exemption from the religious need for the good. In the case we mentioned, the authority Samuel ruled that ordinary myrtles were perfectly adequate. In a similar case from the sixteenth century, a leading rabbi instructed his constituents to boycott fish for a period of weeks, although fish is considered an important way of honoring the Sabbath; the reason was that local fish merchants were colluding to raise prices, knowing that Jews would pay an excessive price to observe the Sabbath properly.[21]

These four situations have in common two characteristics that gave the sellers lopsided and unfair bargaining power. First, since the item was a necessity, the sellers had the buyers over a barrel. Second, in each case the sellers joined together in a cartel. Thus, the agreement of consumers to join in a boycott was a necessity in order to create countervailing power.

These elements correspond to two important justifications for labor unions: employers generally do not suffer during short period of low income, whereas the worker is often desperate for his pay (laborers over a barrel); and the relatively small number of employers find it easy to collude, implicitly or otherwise, whereas the large and dispersed community of workers have much more difficulty organizing (cartel).

Let us apply these insights to your question. The first condition is certainly present, since the good in question is a vital one. However, there is some doubt about the second one–cooperation among sellers. Common sense, as well as economic theory, tells us that collusion is not so easy in a market with numerous sellers of varying sizes; someone usually finds it advantageous to defect and sell for low prices, and thus the cartel is dissolved. Perhaps the high prices you witness are just the result of the forces of supply and demand.

The most prudent course of action is to see whether you can find convincing evidence of the collusion you suspect among sellers. If you can present the public with such evidence, your planned boycott will be legitimated, more consumers are likely to join, and thus there will be a better and more realistic opportunity to have an impact on prices.

Avoid or Advise?

SHOULD I TELL A CROOKED MERCHANT WHY
CONGREGATION MEMBERS SHUN HIS ESTABLISHMENT?

When someone's behavior or attitude leads the community to keep its distance from him, maintaining a conspiracy of silence is not the best course of action. Even so, careful thought is needed to determine when communication will be truly constructive.

Q A merchant in our neighborhood is not patronized by members of our congregation because of the many bad experiences we have had with his service. Of course he has noticed this, but whenever he asks the reason for our abstention, we give some pretext. Should we just tell him straight out what bothers us?

A Jewish law offers pretty clear guidance on your situation. On the one hand, the Torah commands us to give guidance and admonishment to others, in order to help them improve. On the other hand, this law is limited by a number of reservations meant to avoid misunderstandings and hurt feelings.

The Torah tells us, "Surely admonish your fellow man, and do not bear sin toward him."[22] This verse tells us that we should strive to inform others of ways they can improve themselves; otherwise, we may build up unnecessary resentment and bear sin toward them. At the same time, this admonishment may not come at the expense of insulting them, which would also be a sin. The very next verse tells us "Love your neighbor as yourself."

Here are three important limitations on the ethical mandate to admonish others:

- The admonishment must be gentle. Harsh and demeaning reproof does not fulfill the commandment.[23]
- Admonishment is only a mitzvah if it is effective. The Talmud tells us, "Just as it is a mitzvah to say something that will be heard, it is a mitzvah not to say something that will not be heard."[24] In

general, the tradition urges us to refrain from unnecessary speech; certainly there is no reason to hurt someone's feelings if there will be no practical advantage.

• Even when it is proper to admonish, it is permissible to refrain if you are afraid that you may be unfairly targeted as a result of the reproof. Many people have an unfortunate tendency to "kill the messenger who bears bad news", and sometimes it is necessary to take this tendency into account.[25]

Here, then, is some prudent advice for your situation. If you think that this merchant will actually be able to improve his service if you clarify the complaints against him, then it is certainly appropriate to gently explain the true reason for his commercial isolation. But if he seems incorrigible, and particularly if you have a well-grounded concern that the storeowner will react in an unpleasant or vindictive way toward you or toward the congregation as a whole, there is no obligation to do so.

Malicious Merchant

SHOULD WE BOYCOTT A HATEFUL MERCHANT?

When we decide to do business with one firm or another, we are mainly concerned with commercial considerations like quality and price. Sometimes, though, it is difficult to ignore the human aspect of our business activities. Jewish tradition encourages us to take this aspect into account, but that does not mean that we should limit our business contacts to a closed clique.

Q A merchant in our area is known for his support of unsavory causes. Is it proper to prefer other establishments?

A In most instances we choose a particular merchant because of the quality and price of his merchandise, and it is certainly valid to make these factors uppermost. But market relationships are also human relationships, and it is neither realistic nor desirable that the cash nexus should be the only bond between buyer and seller.

We learn this from a verse in the Torah: "When you sell something to your fellow, or buy from your fellow, do not oppress each man his brother."[26] This verse prohibits unfairly overcharging the customer, but the Torah uses a surprising term for the prohibited activity; it refers to it as "oppressing," not as "stealing." The emphasis is on the human rather than the economic aspect of dishonesty.

This commandment is quite germane to our question, because as Rashi's commentary notes, the verse also bears an additional, implicit message: When you sell, you should sell to your fellow; when you buy, you should buy from your fellow. Preference should be given to those who share our values.

We can discern two reasons for this preference: One is a desire to help members of our own community by aiding their livelihood. While it is a mitzvah to give aid to any needy person, Jewish tradition emphasizes that we should give precedence to those close to us: family members have precedence over neighbors, neighbors over those who live far away, and so on. In this way close-knit support groups are encouraged.

Adopting this approach, the eminent authority Rabbi Moshe Isserles[27] writes that this preference is an instance of the commandment to provide a livelihood for our fellows, an obligation learned from the verse "And your brother shall live with you."[28]

Another reason is that economic relationships are also human relationships, and thus they inevitably have an important impact on our character. If we do business with someone who has courage and integrity, this will solidify these characteristics in us; if we do business with someone of questionable character, it will tend to have a demoralizing effect on us.

In a similar vein, Maimonides writes: "It is a great mitzvah to cleave to sages and their students in order to learn from their ways;" one of the examples he gives is to do business with them.[29]

Therefore, there is definitely an advantage to rewarding integrity in others, and cultivating it in ourselves, by preferring to do business with individuals of good character and public standing.

Yet paradoxically, the very same principle—the human dimension of market transactions—implies that we should not take this attitude too far. We should not strive for a state where we censor our business contacts and restrict them to a closed clique. The reason is that the very anonymity of the cash nexus makes it a superb bridge to create a human connection between alienated individuals. As we wrote in the very first column of this book, one of the wonderful things about business is that it channels our materialistic desires to consume or to make profits into a motivation to create living human connections with others. Jewish law tells us to help our non-Jewish neighbors to make a living as an expression of "the ways of peace."[30]

So if the merchant in question is really a person of bad character, then it is certainly preferable to give your business to a competitor who will be a more worthy beneficiary of profits as well as a positive example for you. But if he is merely someone with somewhat alien opinions and traits, we need to balance this factor with an opposite consideration: the desire to exploit commercial interests to build constructive bridges between people of diverse backgrounds.

Salad Bar Scandal

SHOULD I ALERT STORE SECURITY TO PETTY SHOPLIFTING?

Calling attention to an illegal act may seem unobjectionable. But in Jewish tradition, any disclosure that harms others is hedged with strict ethical rules, even if the actions concerned are reprehensible.

Q I saw someone at the grocery store salad bar eating as much as she was putting on her plate. Since she would only be paying for what was on the plate, wasn't this shoplifting? Should I mention it to a security guard?

A This is a good time to review the criteria for talking about another person's faults or misdeeds. According to Rabbi Yisrael Meir ha-Kohen of Radin, there are five guidelines.[31] Only if all five are met may we speak negatively of someone. As an aid to memory, we can arrange them according to the letters of the alphabet:

- *Accuracy.* It is forbidden to exaggerate or embellish.

- *Benefit.* Revealing the information must be the only way to obtain some constructive benefit.

- *Certainty.* The information must be reliable.

- *Desire.* The teller's intention must be constructive, not vindictive.

- *Equity.* Revealing the information must not cause undeserved damage to the subject. It is not equitable to protect one person at the expense of another.

Let us see how these apply to your question.

The *accuracy* and *certainty* considerations are easy to apply. You just need to make sure that you limit any report to what you have observed, without introducing inferences or judgments.

The *desire* criterion requires you to scrutinize your motivation. Do you want to protect the store from loss or deter the shopper from continuing her misbehavior? If so, the criterion is fulfilled. But if you have a vindictive desire to see this individual get her comeuppance, you should hold your tongue until you are certain that your motives are pure.

The *equity* criterion requires us to consider the consequences for the shoplifter if you report what she has done. If the store management is likely to consider your report a basis for investigation rather than an absolute proof of wrongdoing, and to take a measured and justified response, such as requesting payment for anything eaten, then the consequence of your reporting would be equitable. But if you are afraid that the store would throw the book at your fellow shopper for her relatively minor infraction, then reporting will cause injustice, not remedy it.

The most problematic consideration in the case you mention is undoubtedly *benefit*. Consider the likely outcome of reporting. Will the store be able to recover its loss? Will the shopper be deterred from snacking in the future? Is there a chance of having an embarrassing altercation? In all probability, you will conclude that it is much more advantageous to give this individual a gentle reminder. Something like "How much are you allowed to taste without paying?" is non-judgmental yet gets the message across. Even asking "How is the salad?" may be enough to remind her that her actions are being observed, but you must say this in a way that doesn't seem to condone the action (Maybe you can ask, "Did you remember to recite a blessing?").

There is always the chance that this won't have any impact (maybe the shopper will even offer you a few morsels). If so, you still have the option of turning to the store management. So the benefit criterion in your case seems to favor turning directly to the shopper before mentioning anything to the store. This has the additional advantage that you have fulfilled the Torah commandment of giving gentle reproof: "Surely reprove your fellow, and do not bear sin toward him."[32]

In your case, someone is taking something relatively inexpensive in an open way. The likelihood that a private comment will be helpful is great. But the case would be greatly altered if someone were surreptitiously shoplifting something of significant value. In that case it is less likely that a private comment would be of any help; at most the person will wait until you have moved on to continue his crime. In addition, such a person is more likely to be dangerous. Furthermore, if you report the shoplifting, the store will be saved from significant loss, unlike the case with already eaten salad, which has a small value that the store will probably never recoup. Now the scales would probably be tipped in *favor* of reporting.

If you do report someone to store management, the equity and certainty criteria are best fulfilled if you do not give any details. Just mention to a clerk or security person, "I think you should keep an eye on so-and-so."

The criteria for mentioning someone's misdeeds are always the same; yet their application differs greatly from case to case. In the salad bar situation, it is likely that turning to store management would not be the most effective way of dealing with the situation.

Deserved Discount

CAN I TAKE ADVANTAGE OF A DISCOUNT IF I'M NOT SURE
I'M ENTITLED?

Sellers are always making special offers in an effort to attract more customers. It's not always completely clear who is entitled to these benefits. The following three columns give some guidelines for deciding when we may take advantage of such offers.

Q My retirement package includes travel discounts, but it doesn't specify from which companies. Whenever I book a flight on a certain airline, I get a 50 percent for my "corporate relationship." How do I know if this is part of my retirement benefits or merely a mistake in my favor? I wouldn't patronize this company without the discount.

A Taking improper advantage of discounts makes us feel clever and virtuous at the same time. We congratulate ourselves on our thrift, and reassure ourselves that we are helping the company by giving it business. After all, as you point out, you wouldn't patronize this company without the discount. Sometimes we're right; perhaps the airline is thrilled that you are filling an otherwise empty seat. On the other hand, perhaps they are fuming at having to turn away a full price customer in order to make good on a promised discount.

The best rule for dealing with these second-guessing situations is, don't guess. If you're not absolutely sure you're doing someone a favor, play by the rules. If this airline decides that it's in their interest to offer you the discount, let them extend it to you.

So you should take steps to make sure you are entitled to this benefit. One way is to send a letter to the airline explaining your situation in detail and suggesting that they verify your status. Make sure that the letter is addressed and worded in such a way that it will reach someone in the company who is properly authorized to carry out such a check. After you have given the company a reasonable amount of time to review your status, perhaps a couple of weeks after the letter arrives, you can go back to taking advantage of the discount if it is still available.

It is not ethical to take advantage of the vendor's mistake; a basic principle in Jewish law holds that "a mistaken waiver is invalid" All our business relations should be based on transparency and full consent.[33]

In this case, you are giving yourself the benefit of the doubt. If the company doesn't respond by opting out, you can continue to use the benefit. This is appropriate in your situation, because you have a reasonable basis for believing that you are entitled to a markdown. After all, you do have a benefits package that entitles you to a similar deal.

The situation is much different if you are offered a discount and you're pretty sure there has been a mistake. In that case, you should not take advantage of the discount until you're convinced that it's legitimate–you should wait for the company to opt in. An example would be asking the company to respond to your letter, or at least to acknowledge receipt.

What about the interim period, when you're waiting for your letter to be processed through either the opt-out or the opt-in procedure? If you take advantage of the discount during this limbo period, you should be prepared to pay the balance of the full price if it turns out that you are obligated to do so.

As the Book of Proverbs tells us, "stolen waters are sweet."[34] This corresponds to the special sense of achievement we sometimes feel when we've gotten away with something. But the same book tells us that "one who hates gifts will live."[35] Life and vitality are our portion when we desire only those gifts which we deserve and which God sends us in a proper fashion.

Promise Predicament

HOW LONG CAN I TAKE ADVANTAGE OF A MONEY-BACK
GUARANTEE?

Q A mail-order clothing company promises: "If you are not completely satisfied with any item you buy from us, at any time during
your use of it, return it and we will refund your full purchase price." Can
I return items that are no longer wearable because of normal conditions
such as stains and fraying?

A The merchant's guarantee sounds very impressive. Yet under Jewish
law, every seller provides an unlimited money-back guarantee. Any
object with a significant deficiency that was hidden from the purchaser
can be returned whenever the deficiency becomes apparent—even after
a period of years. The Shulhan Arukh[36] states: "One who sells to his
fellow…any movable property, and a defect is discovered which was
unknown to the purchaser, [the purchaser] may return it even after
several years, for this is a mistaken purchase." The entire sale is void,
since the purchaser never intended to buy a defective item. This is a
consequence of the insistence that all business relations must be based
on full informed consent.

But the right to return the purchase, like all rights, comes with a
responsibility. As soon as the customer discovers the defect and thereby
learns that the purchase was in error, he must stop using the object.
Thus the Shulhan Arukh continues: "But this is under the condition
that he never used the object after discovering the defect. If he used it
after discovering the defect, he has waived his right and cannot return
the purchase."

This is a direct consequence of the right to void the sale. Since the
customer has concluded that the sale is void, the item does not belong
to him. If the customer uses the item after the defect is discovered, or
could easily have been discovered, this is interpreted to mean that he
does not mind the deficiency.

The mail-order seller you mention goes beyond the letter of the law.

The company doesn't merely promise that the merchandise is free of defects; it guarantees that you will be completely satisfied with it. But the underlying principle is exactly the same: they are guaranteeing that the item you buy, at the time you buy it, is not only suitable for use but also satisfies your demands. This policy is not only good ethics, it can also be good business: it gives consumers confidence to buy without worry or concern and encourages them to buy from this merchant.

The company's promise means that if you discover something that you really do not like about the garment, even after a long time, you can still return it. For instance, if you bought a coat because you mistakenly thought it was waterproof but you do not get caught in the rain with it until months later, you could still return it to the company.

However, a person does not regret buying a garment just because it eventually wears out. At the time you bought it, it was completely satisfactory for you in all respects, including durability. Therefore, you may not return something that gets worn out due to normal use, or anything else that met your demands at the time of purchase.

We should applaud the efforts of the seller to stand behind their merchandise so unconditionally. Our appreciation should certainly motivate us to requite their attitude and display exemplary responsibility as consumers.

By the way, if there *is* a genuine source of dissatisfaction that makes you decide to return the garment, you are, in effect, exercising your right to void the sale. Therefore, you should not use the garment after you decide to return it.

"Fresh or Free"

CAN I SCHEME TO TAKE ADVANTAGE OF A FREE OFFER?

Q A store in our neighborhood advertises, "It's fresh or it's free." If a customer finds food on the shelves that is not fresh, the store will give it to him. Is it ethical to make a special search for these items?

A Let us explore the essence of this generous and unusual store policy.

It is certainly usual for merchants to guarantee, explicitly or implicitly, that their products are fresh. If a customer discovers that merchandise is stale, most stores will readily give a refund or replacement. This policy would be mandated by Jewish law, which states that any fundamental defect in a purchase item voids the sale, since the customer never intended to buy such an item.[37]

However, the store in your neighborhood has gone beyond this guarantee, and instead of giving a refund is willing to actually give you the item. From a commercial point of view, there are two good reasons for such a policy:

The main reason is that it allows the consumer to shop worry-free. Most customers do not want to know that any problem will be taken care of; they want to know that there won't be a problem in the first place. Who has time to go back and get a refund on a pound of tomatoes? The store's magnanimous offer convinces them that the store must have taken great care to clear the shelves of any past-due items.

A closely related reason is that enlightened management wants to maintain quality by being informed of any deficiency in service. One excellent way of doing this is to enlist consumers in the cause. Yet the consumer needs to be provided with an incentive to go the trouble of reporting a defective item. For most people it's just not worth the trouble. Management will never know of the deficiency, and will never be able to correct it; in the meantime, they are losing business because of resentful consumers. Offering the item free is an effective inducement. This is one reason why manufacturers often send free samples to customers who discover and report on defective merchandise.

Now let us see how your suggestion fits in. Scrounging the store for stale produce is not exactly "worry-free" shopping. The store's policy is meant to let you just pluck items off the shelf without examining them; instead, it's inducing you to invest many times your normal shopping effort in order to obtain a freebie. This was certainly not the owner's intention.

On the other hand, this scrounging does have certain value in bringing the store's attention to problematic merchandise—the second objective of the policy. So if you limit your search to items that are prominently displayed, your actions are not exactly inspiring and uplifting, but you are not truly abusing the store's policy.

However, if your search extends even to hard-to-reach nooks and crannies of the store, you are taking advantage of the store's offer in a rather cynical way. The store is providing worry-free shopping and has made sure that any shopper can just pluck items off the shelf with full confidence in their freshness. They are not failing in their responsibility to customers just because someone who really looks can find past-due items. This is pushing the store's enlightened policy a bit far.

A remarkable lesson from the Talmud teaches an occasional exception from this guidance. Giving free merchandise as an inducement is hardly something new; in the time of the Talmud also wine sellers used to give free samples to encourage customers to try and buy their merchandise. Not surprisingly, taking inappropriate advantage of these offers is also not new, and sometimes people would feign interest and tipple free samples without any intention of buying whatsoever.

Rav Nachman bar Isaac states that all subterfuges of this nature are forbidden except for one: Someone who has let blood and is in urgent need of fluid but does not have any money may accept free samples of drinks from sellers even though he has no intention of buying.[38] The free samples are not explicitly conditioned on intent to buy, presumably because of the same consideration that applies today: the desire to free the consumer of all worry and conditions. Sampling without intent is not stealing, it's just a bit cynical. Therefore, even though subterfuge is involved in having a free taste when there is no intention whatsoever to buy, it's permissible in cases of extraordinary need.

Applying this exception to our case, someone truly desperate, for example a stranger in town who has run out of money, could legitimately scrounge the shelves looking for free items which meet the store's criteria.

Sweatshops

IS IT ETHICAL TO BUY FROM LOW-WAGE SUPPLIERS?

Q Many consumer products are made in third world countries in sweatshop conditions. Is buying these products exploiting the workers? Or perhaps it is actually helping them, because it provides them with work and gives them a chance to improve living conditions? What about the effect on local workers?

A The foreign sweatshop debate has raged for generations. Organized labor has traditionally demanded better working conditions not only in the home country, but also abroad; cynics have complained that this demand is really a way of fending off low-cost foreign competition which benefits consumers.

A verse from Leviticus[39] can help focus the debate: "And when you sell something to your fellow, or buy from the hand of your fellow, don't exploit each one his brother."

The simple meaning of the verse is that we shouldn't exploit each other in commerce by charging an unfair price. But Rashi's commentary points out that the verse contains an implicit mandate: when we sell, we should preferably sell to our fellow; when we buy, we should buy from our fellow. In a previous column, we explained that this preference both provides a livelihood for community members and also builds a feeling of connection and solidarity among members of a particular community [See: Malicious Merchant]. Many authorities have stated that we should even pay a premium in order to do business with fellow community members, thus making economic relations complement social ones.[40]

The critical question then becomes: who is my "fellow"? My neighbor? My fellow citizen? Any fellow human being? In past generations this question was easier to answer, because both practically and emotionally mutual awareness and concern could exist only among those who were close by. In the age of globalization, many people believe that it is both practical and obligatory to view all humans as our "fellows"; others worry that this approach carries the danger that existing, functional community relationships will be weakened in favor of a still-hypothetical "community of man," resulting in the loss of all communal concern.

What we need is a concentric set of communal relationships, each one on a suitable scale. It is practical for everyone to be concerned with world ecology and global warming, which are truly global problems; conversely, a free loan society for needy individuals in a small neighborhood is practical, but it would be hard to administer one which serves an entire region.

If you believe that consumers in advanced countries can create genuine empathy and solidarity with sweatshop workers in East Asia, considering these distant individuals our "fellows," then it is definitely appropriate for you to take steps, including consumer activism, to promote better working conditions for these workers. Of course we should take care that our steps don't actually work to their detriment, by destroying their livelihood during a prolonged boycott or pricing their goods out of the market. If you feel that your first concern should be for workers in your own region or country, then you should try when practical to give preference to local manufacturers even if there is a moderate price difference.

In a way, both the stated or cynical understanding of labor groups have relevance. If we do share a sense of community, or worker solidarity, with sweatshop workers in distant countries, then we should be concerned with their working conditions, and not exploit them (as the verse states). If we don't share a sense of community with them, we should try to give precedence to local workers who are our "fellows".

Our aspiration should be for economic relations that harmonize with communal ones; we should engage in buying and selling with our fellows, and avoid exploiting them. When practical, we should either display concern for the workers who make our goods, or buy goods from those workers for whom we can effectively display concern.

Leading by Example

DOES FAVORING LOCAL LABOR DISCRIMINATE AGAINST THE TRULY NEEDY?

Q You wrote that when we can't realistically create solidarity with distant sweatshop workers, it may be better to concentrate on improving conditions for local workers, who are really far better off. Isn>t this evading our responsibility to help the impoverished?

A The previous column discussed the value in Jewish tradition of harmonizing economic and social relations. The conclusion was that consumer activism and power are best concentrated on workers with whom the consumer has some degree of solidarity and identification. Some readers felt it was ironic and unfair to give preference to a local product to save the job of a comparatively wealthy worker in the home country rather than an imported product which could give a new lease on life to an impoverished family in the developing world.

One response to this thoughtful objection is to point out that another solution mentioned is to strive to expand our circle of concern and solidarity and try to create substantive social relations with the distant workers. But as the column pointed out, this is not always practical.

A deeper and subtler response would be based on a remarkable foundation of Jewish faith and tradition: very often the best way to help someone out of distress is not to provide them with aid, but rather to provide them with a worthy example. In our case, one of the best ways we can help undeveloped areas is to provide them with a vivid image of a humane and well-functioning society–one that is willing to make sacrifices to help its weakest members.

History provides many examples of this lesson. A prominent one is Japan's "post-war economic miracle"–post US Civil War, that is. In 1868 Japan was a pre-industrial society; less than 40 years later it was a world power. Japan was not the beneficiary of an outpouring of foreign aid or of foreign sympathy; rather, the Japanese undertook to imitate the attainments of the great powers of Europe and North America.

This insight is one explanation for many of the seemingly insular customs of Judaism, including a preference to do business with co-religionists. Scripture states that God wants the Jewish people to be "a light to the nations"[41]. As a small and scattered nation, we can provide comparatively little direct aid. Very often the best way we can serve as a beacon to others is strive to be an example of a community whose values consistently enable it to attain a high level of spiritual elevation and material well-being even in frequently hostile circumstances. Perceiving the Jewish community in their midst has inspired other groups to emulate customary ways such as high levels of literacy and education, generosity in charitable giving, personal responsibility for the underprivileged, and so on.

The Torah commands us, "Love your neighbor as yourself".[42] Seemingly it would have been enough to command "Love your neighbor"; why "as yourself"? The Torah seems to be telling us that it is impossible to love someone else unless you first love and esteem yourself. Likewise, the love of our neighbor is a pre-requisite for effective love and concern for others beyond my community. A person who recognizes his own worth is capable of loving others; someone who loves and cares for members of his own community is able to push out the envelope and extend that love onward. But if a person starts by deciding that he will love all human beings equally, he will find it difficult to love any human being effectively. Universal love is certainly the ideal, but this love is achieved by cultivating broader and broader concentric circles of concern.

It is important to help undeveloped economies by buying their products. But it's important that the process of international economic development should not turn into a "race to the bottom" whereby advanced economies are compelled to adopt work standards of backward countries. Instead, we want to encourage a general ratcheting up of conditions and standards; very often the best way to achieve this is to concentrate on our neighbors. After all, "charity begins at home".

Outsourcing

Q Many good jobs are now being "outsourced" to foreign firms. Is it ethical to deprive people of their livelihood in this way?

A In the past, it was usually the lowest-wage jobs which were lost to foreign competition. But nowadays North American companies are moving their entire back offices to poorer countries, and also using computer programmers, call-center operators, even radiologists from the far East.

In some ways, this phenomenon is parallel to that of "sweatshops"; cheap foreign workers are displacing the livelihood of our closest neighbors. Yet we should also note that many of the ethical problems we discerned regarding sweatshops are attenuated in the case of "white-collar" outsourcing. Let's review the issues we raised regarding sweatshops and see why outsourcing is not as bad:

One thing we mentioned is that doing business with someone is a way of providing them a livelihood, and "charity begins at home". This creates a preference for doing business with businesses in our home country. Of course this applies to outsourcing as well, but manufacturing workers who lose their jobs to sweatshops are more likely to be poor and vulnerable than the white-collar workers who lose their jobs to outsourcing. Jewish law says that the commandment to support a needy person applies to anyone who is unable to fill his accustomed needs, even a well-off person who has suffered a loss in income; but even so, the truly needy take precedence.

Another critical issue is expanding our circle of concern. We pointed out that instead of giving preference to neighbors over distant foreign workers, we could adopt these foreigners and consider them too as our neighbors and colleagues. At the same time, we acknowledged that there are limits to our practical ability to create genuine solidarity with remote and unfamiliar people. Expanding our circle of empathy to encompass people in the service industries of outsourcing is relatively easier than expanding it to include uneducated sweatshop workers. People are chosen for these jobs exactly because of their ability to fit in with the linguistic and work culture of the customers. When a call center is located in the Philippines, the North American customers actually interact and converse with the operators. So in the case of outsourcing, it's easier to feel that we are actually giving business to a friend.

The other major issue we mentioned was disgraceful working conditions. This problem is rare in white collar service jobs; most of these workers enjoy a work environment which meets the minimum standards familiar to consumers in the more advanced countries.

Globalization presents both a promise and a threat. The promise is not only for greater world prosperity, but also for expanding our horizons and our sense of brotherhood. The threat is the loss of income and of solidarity among those brothers who are closest to us. While both aspects are present in the outsourcing of service jobs, here the promise is greater and the threat less compared to other aspects of expanding world trade.

ENDNOTES

1. Shulhan Arukh, Hoshen Mishpat 227:1
2. Berakhot 58a
3. Pithei Hoshen 8:4; Shulhan Arukh, Hoshen Mishpat 331:2
4. Sanhedrin 6b
5. Zechariah 8:16
6. Megillah 28a
7. Shulhan Arukh, Hoshen Mishpat 4:1, 12:2, 17:5.; Kezot ha-Hoshen 4:1
8. Shulhan Arukh, Orah Hayyim 606:1
9. Bava Metzia 77a
10. See Shulhan Arukh, Hoshen Mishpat 333:5, 334:1; Arukh ha-Shulhan, Hoshen Mishpat 333:27.
11. Psalms 145:16
12. Leviticus 25:14
13. Bava Metzia 61b
14. Shulhan Arukh, Yoreh Deah 249:4
15. Shulhan Arukh, Yoreh Deah 249:6
16. Pitchei Choshen Geneiva veAveida 1:(26).
17. See Bava Batra 22a
18. See Shulchan Arukh Hoshen Mishpat 156:6.
19. Shulhan Arukh Hoshen Mishpat 331:28.
20. The cases are found in Babylonian Talmud Sukkah 34b and Pesahim 30a, and Mishnah Keritot 1:7.
21. Responsa Tzemach Tzedek 28

22. Leviticus 19:17
23. Sefer ha-Hinnukh 239
24. Yevamot 65b
25. Shulhan Arukh, Yoreh Deah 334:48 in Rema
26. Leviticus 25:14
27. Responsa Rema 10
28. Leviticus 25:36
29. Mishneh Torah, De'ot 6:2
30. Shulchan Arukh Yoreh Deah 251:1.
31. Based on Hafetz Hayyim 1:10, 11:10
32. Leviticus 19:17
33. Bava Metzia 67a; Shulhan Arukh, Hoshen Mishpat 241:2 in Rema
34. Proverbs 9:17
35. Proverbs 15:27
36. Hoshen Mishpat 232:3
37. Shulhan Arukh, Hoshen Mishpat 232:3
38. Shabbat 129a
39. Leviticus 25:14
40. Responsa Rema 10.
41. Isaiah 42:6
42. Leviticus 19:18

ETHICS AT THE DOCTOR'S OFFICE

Introduction

The physician is a larger-than-life figure who takes responsibility for the welfare of patients, a responsibility that sometimes involves life-and-death decisions. At the same time, the physician is in business and wants to run his office as efficiently and profitably as possible. While all professionals are entitled to a fair recompense for their special efforts and talents, physicians have a special responsibility to run their offices in an equitable way that reassures patients that they are providing care, and not just a professional service.

The delicacy of this relationship is demonstrated by two of the columns in this chapter. A treatment provider asked if it was possible to charge for no-shows, a frustrating phenomenon for physicians who want their valuable time to be used effectively. This query of the physician who was upset because a late or missing patient cost him minutes of the work day triggered a barrage of complaints from patients upset about the hours they spend in the waiting room. The third column also relates to the proper balance of professional versus business considerations for a treatment provider.

These columns together try to provide useful suggestions for equitable and livable clinic practices, as well as an educational exhortation to try and improve ourselves before we correct others.

Showing Mercy to No-Shows

CAN I CHARGE PATIENTS FOR MISSED APPOINTMENTS?

Jewish tradition teaches us that standing on our rights can be less than ethical and is often counterproductive. This insight has particular importance in caring professions such as medicine, where every business policy, whatever its primary purpose, also conveys a message from practitioner to client. This is especially so in regard to the problem of charging patients who cancel at the last minute.

Q In my medical practice, patients often fail to show up for an appointment, show up too late for a complete treatment to be given, or cancel on very short notice. What am I entitled to do?

A No-shows and late cancellations can be a very frustrating as well as expensive experience for professionals. Yet for ethical as well as practical considerations, it is important not to overreact.

Mix-ups and misunderstandings in the labor market are hardly a new phenomenon. The Talmud provides a detailed explanation of how to resolve situations when a work agreement is not carried out.[1] The talmudic discussion deals with workers who agree to come to do field labor. This agreement can be foiled if either the workers or the employer fail to show up, or if the field is flooded, or by any number of other factors. The ethical resolution depends on a number of factors, including whether the default is caused by the worker or the employer, and whether it is due to negligence or duress. The ethical principles we learn from the talmudic discussion and its commentaries are timeless, and apply equally well to a doctor's office in the twenty-first century.

For instance, it would be wrong to turn a misunderstanding into a source of income. The Talmud states that if a worker is promised work but the employer reneges at the last minute, the worker is entitled to partial payment only if he has already come to the workplace and therefore is no longer able to find day labor elsewhere. The employer's obligation to pay the worker is only meant to compensate him for his lost income. In our case, if a missed appointment does not lead to any lost income, because the physician overbooks or is able to find another patient who can come in on short notice, it would be wrong to "double dip" by also collecting a fee from the no-show.

It is also inappropriate to penalize people for circumstances beyond their control. The Talmud tells us that if the field floods at the last moment, so that the workers are unable to work, the employer does not have to pay them. At the time the agreement was made, the employer had every reason to believe that the work was still necessary; the subsequent flooding was beyond his control. This principle, too, is easily applied to the doctor's office: If a patient makes the same effort as everyone else to arrive on time but is unexpectedly delayed, for instance because of a late train (in an area where the trains are usually on time) or an illness, it is unfair to charge him even if his tardiness causes a loss for the physician.

However, if the workers have no work because of the employer's negligence – for example, if he should have known that the fields were flooded – he has to pay up. But he has to pay less than the full amount, since at any rate the workers have an easy day free of exertion.

By the same token, when patients miss appointments due to negligence, and their absence or tardiness results in lost income, it is permissible to charge them. But even in this case, it is not fair to charge the full amount, because the idle time of the staff is usually exploited in some way. The practitioner and any support staff usually take advantage of "dead time" for paperwork, phone calls, or some much-needed rest, and this should be taken into account. Remember, too, that the poor client did not receive any service. Rabbi Aaron Levine, in his *Case Studies in Jewish Business Ethics*,[2] suggests that charging half the usual fee is an equitable solution in this case.

The same principle applies to a late-show that enables partial completion of the work. If the tardiness is due to negligence and causes a loss of income, then you are entitled to recover some of the loss.

Of course, you should make sure that your clients know that they may be charged for missed appointments. Some clinics announce a uniform fine for any appointment that is missed without giving advance notice. Given the criteria we have just mentioned, such a policy is likely to be unfair, because it will fall on some individuals who don't really deserve a fine.

Consider, too, that charging for no-shows can be problematic not only for ethical reasons but for commercial reasons. This policy can lead to significant ill will and could harm your business. If you apply the policy uniformly, you will inevitably end up alienating some loyal but occasionally careless patients; if you apply it unevenly, you will open yourself up to charges of partiality.

If you must apply sanctions to no-shows, consider non-monetary consequences. Perhaps you could sentence latecomers to less desirable appointment times; or you could offer incentives and discounts to patients with exemplary on-time records. Another solution is to give discounts to patients who are willing to come in on short notice to substitute for a no-show; this could reduce the loss in income due to this phenomenon, especially if a fair number of patients live or work nearby and have flexible schedules.

One more thought: if your practice has an unusual number of cancellations, try and find out the reason. It may be that your patients are ambivalent about the effectiveness of the treatment you provide, or find it unpleasant or painful. Perhaps it is your conduct, and not that of your patients, which requires modification.

Impatient Patients

DOES THE DOCTOR OWE ME FOR WASTED WAITING-ROOM HOURS?

Ethical problems often involve both parties to a dispute. Each side has to learn to concentrate primarily on fixing its own shortcomings. The physician who complained about no-shows was echoed by a large number of patients who complained about long waits; a comprehensive ethical vision helps us find the right balance.

Q I'm often stuck in the doctor's waiting room for hours. Doesn't he owe me something for my wasted time?

A It would be tempting to liken these waits to involuntary imprisonment. And Jewish law teaches that if someone locks us in a room, thus preventing us from working, the offender is liable for our lost time.[3] This is certainly how the patient (or parent) feels – as if he or she is trapped in the doctor's office.

But realistically, a patient is not imprisoned in the waiting room, and it is not really fair to expect the practitioner to compensate you for your time. After all, you're not using it for the doctor's benefit.

Still, it is worthwhile examining how we can deal with this exasperating situation in a dignified way. As in most interpersonal dilemmas, mutual thoughtfulness is the key to curing the waiting-room blues.

Patients should keep in mind that there are many valid reasons for delays. Greed and sadism are not really the only factors at work! For one thing, the problem is sometimes caused by the carelessness of other patients who habitually miss appointments without warning. In order to fully exploit their valuable skills and time in the service of their patients, practitioners are virtually compelled to overbook. When people do show up, long lines are the result. A better on-time record for patients will ultimately mean shorter waits at the doctor's office.

Emergency calls are another reason. As one doctor exclaimed when I asked him about this problem, "How am I supposed to know when some woman is going to come in with chest pains?" We expect the physician to put his regular schedule aside when we have a medical emergency; we need to have patience for the extra wait this imposes on us when the emergency is not ours.

One thing patients can do to shorten waits is to call ahead. If you have a two o'clock appointment, call the receptionist at one. If she says that the doctor is just now taking patients with 11:30 appointments, you know that you do not have to arrive any earlier than 3:15 or so. Of course doctors and receptionists should be forthcoming with this information.

Physicians should do their part, too. If you really care about your patients' time, don't wait for them to call – have the receptionist phone patients and inform them that their appointment is delayed. If possible, let them reschedule. A small extra investment in receptionist hours can save your patients many hours each day.

Practitioners can also adopt more effective scheduling practices. One reader informed me that he has dramatically cut no-shows at his practice by not giving exact times for distant appointments. Instead, the patient is first given a generous advance "window" in which to schedule; a few days beforehand the patient calls to set an exact time. For example, in November the patient is told to call "in two months." Only at the beginning of January does the patient call back and set an exact time.

The best advice of all is take it easy. Learn to take advantage of the waiting time. It is ironic that the harried parent who is chafing at the long line in the pediatrician's office is the same parent who complains that he or she just does not have enough time to spend with the children. And the busy executive who is apoplectic about the wait at the periodontist is the same person who complains that he or she has no time for Torah learning.

A final note: for anyone who thinks that long waits at the doctor are something new, here is an excerpt from a letter written eight hundred years ago by Maimonides, who was not only one of the greatest scholars and leaders in Jewish history but also a prominent physician:

> I do not return to Fostat until the afternoon. Then I am famished, but I find the antechambers filled with people, Jews and Gentiles, nobles and common people, judges and policemen, friends and enemies – a

mixed multitude who await the time of my return. ... [I] entreat them to bear with me while I take some light refreshment, the only meal I eat in twenty-four hours. Then I go to attend to my patients and write prescriptions and directions for their ailments. Patients go in and out until nightfall and sometimes even, as the Torah is my faith, until two hours or more into the night.[4]

Clinic Compulsion

CAN I COMPEL A PATIENT TO COMPLETE A COURSE OF
TREATMENT?

Fair pricing is an important issue in business ethics. Pricing schemes
are often used to build in incentives for use; for example, health clubs
charge large up-front fees that supposedly motivate the client to get
into shape. These schemes can be problematic in regular businesses, and
even more so in the area of medical treatment, which is based on care
and trust. On the other hand, the physician may feel that he or she has
valid medical reasons for wanting to encourage treatment. Thus, some
practitioners employ fee structures that encourage patients to obtain
the treatment they need.

Q Clients at my complementary medicine clinic can get a discount
by signing up for a ten-visit course of treatment. I usually refund
patients for unused visits, but sometimes I am convinced that a client
has a genuine medical need to complete the full course of treatment.
When this happens, can I tell the patient that he cannot get his money
back and has to finish his regimen? After all, I only want to do this when
it is in the patient's medical interest.

A Even though medical practitioners like to think of themselves as
the boss, let us recall that ultimately you are being hired by the
patient for the course of treatment he is interested in. When he does
not want to finish the treatment, this is another way of saying he wants
to fire you.

Jewish law is very protective of the hired worker, and many laws
shield him from being exploited by his employer. For example, the fired
worker does not get paid only *pro rata* according to the amount of work
he does. Sometimes the employer has to pay more: if the interrupted
employment deprived the worker of earning opportunities, then his
compensation must reflect this. It follows that if the patient's termination
harms your income, your refund policy may reflect this. For example,
you may charge for the used visits as if they were single visits, since

this is how you would have booked them if you had known treatment would be interrupted.

But you cannot compel someone to hire you. Even if someone is hired for an agreed-upon period of time, as in the case of your ten-treatment plan, if the employer decides he does not need the work or does not like the worker, he is not locked into the agreement. The employer's only obligation is to make sure the worker gets fair compensation. It is not fair for you to exploit the fact that the money was paid up front to take away the patient's right to choose or decline a treatment program.

There is another consideration in your case. The relationship between the treatment provider and the patient needs to be based on trust. Using monetary sanctions as a way of enforcing your medical opinions is bound to erode your patients' confidence in your professional judgment.

Terminal Transparency

SHOULD I BE FRANK WITH MY SICK RELATIVE ABOUT HER AILMENT?

Behaving ethically usually means being open and honest. But when honesty can be dangerous, we have a profound dilemma. This problem confronts the families and caregivers of seriously ill patients. Should one tell the patient all the details of his condition? Deception may deprive the patient of appropriate medical care and of important experiences; but straightforward honesty can be discouraging or even life-threatening. Jewish tradition provides some profound insights into the ethical conundrums of illness and aging.

Q I have an elderly relative who is terminally ill. Should we be open with her about the details of her condition? I'm afraid she could become discouraged and her condition may worsen.

A The concern you mention is certainly acknowledged in our tradition. One example is the deathbed confession. This declaration is of profound importance and can perfect a person's repentance in his or her last moments. The Shulhan Arukh[5] states:

> When a person is about to die, we tell them to make a confession...
> [saying,] "You may live in the merit of your confession, and anyone
> who confesses has a portion in the World to Come."

The very same ruling goes on to say, however, that we should not mention confession to someone whose spirit is weak. The reason is that mentioning confession will make him realize how serious his illness is, which could break his spirit and worsen his condition.

There are two main lessons here. On the one hand, it is very important for a person to prepare properly for his voyage from this world to the next. Even a few moments of proper preparation can make a difference in our experience in the World of Truth. On the other hand, when a patient's condition is likely to be worsened, this critically important consideration should be put aside.

The Shulhan Arukh also teaches us that when a person is very sick, we should avoid telling him about the death of a relative, since this may worsen his condition.[6] Again, even though mourning is an important mitzvah which benefits both the living and the dead, this mitzvah is subordinated to the vital concern for health and well-being.

It would certainly follow that where there is a well-founded concern that telling the patient about his condition would be discouraging and harmful, it would be proper to keep this information from the ailing patient.

However, great caution is necessary in applying this principle. After all, Jewish law tells us that normally we *should* help a person prepare for death. The person whose spirit is weak is mentioned as the exception to the rule.

The rabbis of the Talmud[7] made a remarkable interpretation of the Torah that emphasizes the importance of awareness of advancing age and proper preparation for death:

> Before Abraham, there was no aging. If someone wanted to speak to Abraham, he would [accidentally] approach Isaac; with Isaac, he would [accidentally] approach Abraham. Abraham came and asked mercy, and aging came, as it is written, "And Abraham was old, developed in years."[8] Before Jacob there was no infirmity. Jacob asked mercy, and infirmity came, as it is said, "And he said to Joseph, behold, your father is infirm."

Jacob's reason for asking for illness was so that he would have the opportunity to prepare for his passing, as he did when he called his sons before him to bless them.[9]

In contrast to the youth-worship that characterizes modern popular culture, our sages are telling us that aging is a blessing, because it distinguishes the old and displays their seniority and experience. Our final infirmity is also a blessing, for it warns us of impending death and enables us to prepare properly, just as Jacob used his last days to instruct and bless his twelve sons.

The lesson of Jewish tradition is that we should view normal manifestations of age and illness not as curses but as invaluable milestones, which inculcate consciousness of our stage of progress in the journey of life. It could be a very serious mistake to deprive others of this special blessing of awareness by misleading them about their true medical condition. Perhaps there are certain things they want to do before death; imagine their frustration and disappointment when they discover that they were prevented forever from realizing their dreams by well-meaning but misguided relatives and caretakers. I heard of one man who, in his last moments, cursed his family for not informing him of his condition, because he was unable to see certain family members and have other experiences he dreamed of completing in his lifetime.

Another insight that should deter us from misleading a patient is that by the time people reach advanced age, they have usually acquired a generous measure of human wisdom. The Talmud[10] teaches this insight through an interesting play on words: the word *zaken* ("elder") can also be read as *ze kanah* ("his person has acquired"):

> And what is it that we acquire with age? Wisdom. *Zaken* [elder] refers only to someone wise, as it is written, "Gather me seventy men of the elders of Israel,"[11] Rabbi Yosi ha-Galili says, *Zaken* refers to one who has acquired wisdom.

There is a tendency to treat old, infirm people as if they were children. This is quite unjustified. We should remember that even if old people are weak in their bodies, they have decades of experience and wisdom, which their children lack. Their understanding and judgment should be respected.

Furthermore, there is a good chance that this same wisdom will enable them to see through any attempted cover-up. This can have a terrible effect on family relations exactly at the time when trust and openness are most necessary. For example, I heard of a case where a man begged his doctor, "Please do not let my family know that I know about my condition. It will break their hearts." Here the patient's condition, the most important concern of the entire family, was known to all. Yet they were prevented from sharing their burdens because of the elaborate charade of supposed ignorance.

Another story concerns an elderly couple who had enjoyed a lifetime of complete trust and openness. The husband complied with the doctor's suggestion to hide the wife's true condition. She sensed that he was keeping something from her, and a lifetime of total trust was put into question, causing profound anguish to the faithful wife.

A further consideration is that lack of information may prevent patients from making informed choices about their treatment. Today, leading medical authorities acknowledge and emphasize the importance of empowering the patient to make such decisions.

In the end, factual considerations have to determine the outcome. While we can find a number of anecdotes opposing disclosure, there are just as many, if not more, supporting it.

Even if we decide that disclosure is the best policy, it is forbidden to be blunt and insensitive. There are horror stories of physicians who think that openness is a license for terrorizing the patient. One can tell a patient that he has a serious and possibly fatal disorder without playing God and predicting that he has only six months to live. This may not be true and is cruel even if it is. The proper course is to present accurate medical information in an encouraging way, pointing out the best opportunities for improvement without resort to misleading and discouraging statistics.

CONCLUSION

There is no unambiguous resolution of this dilemma in Jewish tradition. On the one hand, belief in the next world is a basic premise of Jewish faith, and adequate preparation for death is of paramount importance. Furthermore, sometimes the life of this world can be fully exploited only if we have a clear picture of our opportunities. And obtaining adequate treatment may depend on adequate knowledge. So keeping a patient informed would seem to be an important ethical precept.

Yet the Torah commands us to "choose life," and therefore, if disclosure is dangerous, it should be withheld. So there is a place for keeping up an ill person's spirits by false encouragement.

Given the importance of preparing properly for death, and the wisdom and resilience that generally come with age and suffering, the best policy in most cases is to give the patient accurate medical information presented in as positive and encouraging a light as possible.

Selling Yourself Short

IS IT ETHICAL TO SELL BLOOD PLASMA?

The issue of selling bodily organs or fluids is a very wrenching, and surprisingly ancient, ethical dilemma. More than two hundred years ago, the German philosopher Immanuel Kant discussed the ethics of selling teeth. Today, the debate is more acute than ever. On the one hand, the expanding scope of the market economy creates a great danger that people and their bodies may be exploited and reduced to mere commodities; on the other hand, the life-saving potential for these parts of the human organism is also constantly expanding.

Q I'm really in need of money. I'm tempted to sell my blood plasma to a private company. Is this ethical?

A While it is relatively rare for blood banks to pay for blood donations, sale of plasma is quite widespread. In many places it is possible for healthy individuals to augment their income by going to a center where blood is removed from their body, the plasma is extracted, and the rest of the blood is restored to them. Since the body is able to replace plasma quite rapidly, this can be done several times a month.

Your question about whether such sales are ethical is very apt. Judaism maintains as a basic tenet that we are not the owners of our bodies. God is the owner, and He gives us the responsibility of caring for them during our lifetimes. The renowned Enlightenment-era authority Rav David ben Zimra writes, "A person's life is not his property, but that of the Holy One, blessed be He."[12]

Two important ethical principles limit our rights over our bodies:

- The Torah tells us, "Watch yourself, and watch carefully over your soul."[13] Our sages understood this as meaning that we are commanded to avoid unnecessary danger.

- Our bodies belong to God. They are created in the divine image, and during our lives they are the dwelling place for our divine soul. We need to relate to them with awe and respect. We find this principle in the Torah's prohibition on mutilating the body in any way, including making a tattoo.[14] Even a dead body may not be mutilated or used for personal benefit.[15] Certainly a person should not relate to any part of his body with disdain.

Yet these principles do not exist in a vacuum, and at times they need to be balanced with other values. Although our bodies do not belong to us, the Creator does entrust us with them and gives us the power to make use of them for our own benefit. While we are not allowed to endanger ourselves gratuitously, the Torah recognizes that making a living is a basic necessity and can sometimes be hazardous. Indeed, the reason the Torah gives for having to pay the worker on time is that he "bears his soul" for this pay; in other words, he occasionally has to risk his well-being.[16] Thus an element of danger does not automatically contradict the mandate to take care of our bodies. Likewise, the prohibition against disfigurement is not absolute and inviolable; it, too, can be secondary to other, more important considerations.

Therefore, when considering the question of selling plasma, or blood itself where this is customary, we should pay attention to two things:

- Appropriate standards of safety and hygiene so that the process does not involve unjustifiable risks.

- Appropriate standards of dignity, so that the process of donating precious bodily components is elevating rather than demeaning.

What would be a demeaning use of the blood? It's impossible to set down definite criteria. However, we can cull valuable insights from a variety of instances where Jewish law regulates exchange in order to maintain a certain level of dignity. All of these regulations have two common elements:

- The *exchange itself* should not be solely commercial in nature; the actual use of the item should be the main consideration.

- The *intended use* should be one that dignifies the object.

This pattern is exemplified by the rules governing the produce of the Sabbatical year. Part of the sanctity of this produce is that it can be bought and sold only for need, not traded for profit. Moreover, it may only be used for consumption in its most usual and important way. For example, food usually eaten by people cannot be given to animals.[17]

A similar pattern is found regarding human labor. A Hebrew bondsman is a kind of indentured servant, but the Torah is careful to distinguish his status from that of a slave. The exchange itself may not be commercial in nature; the servant cannot be sold in the marketplace like a chattel slave. And the servant may not be used for demeaning and servile tasks.[18]

Applying these considerations to your situation, we make the following suggestions:

- There is nothing wrong with accepting payment for your time and trouble. But your intention should not be solely commercial; you should have in mind the fact that the plasma you are donating will be used for vital, life-saving treatment and research.

- You should satisfy yourself that such treatment and research is the main use of donated plasma. Using our divine deposit in order to heal others is certainly an appropriate and uplifting use.

Selling your plasma in a purely commercial transaction is not categorically unethical, but it is problematic because it tends to demean our God-given gift of life's blood. Conversely, if you are motivated by a specific intention to advance healing, then there is no ethical objection even though you are paid for your time and trouble, and even though the plasma is purchased by a private company.

In summary, you should take steps to ensure that you are not really "selling" plasma, for this would not uphold the highest level of personal dignity. Make certain you are donating your plasma for a worthy cause. While your main motive may be financial, the benefit you provide others is an important part of your participation, and you should take care to keep this in mind.

Our bodies do not belong to us. They belong to our Creator. Nonetheless, He has given us a broad mandate to use our judgment to employ His deposit in the most productive way for our own benefit and the benefit of mankind.

ENDNOTES

1. Bava Metzia 76a–b
2. Rabbi Aaron Levine, *Case Studies in Jewish Business Ethics*, 2000, p. 271
3. Shulhan Arukh, Hoshen Mishpat 420:11
4. Cited in Fred Rosner, *The Medical Writings of Maimonides*, Maimonides Research Institute Haifa, 1984, p. 2.
5. Shulhan Arukh, Yoreh Deah 338:1
6. Yoreh De'ah 337
7. Bava Metzia 87a
8. Genesis 24
9. Genesis 48–49
10. Kiddushin 32b
11. Numbers 11:16
12. Commentary on Mishneh Torah Laws of Sanhdrin 18:6.
13. Deuteronomy 4:9
14. Leviticus 19:28
15. Avodah Zarah 29b; Shulhan Arukh, Yoreh Deah 349:1
16. Deuteronomy 24:15
17. Maimonides, Shemittah 5:5
18. Leviticus 25:39–42

THE STRANGER, THE WIDOW, AND THE ORPHAN

Introduction

Being ethical does not always mean being impartial. Justice may be blind, but fairness may require taking account of someone's special situation. While the *judge* must be impartial and treat weak and strong alike according to the strict letter of the law, the *individual* is called upon to show special forbearance toward the weak and the downtrodden, and to give them special consideration.

The commandment "Do not show favoritism in judgment; hear the small and the great alike"[1] applies in courts of law, but in our private dealings a different standard applies: "If the [borrower] is poor, do not go to bed without returning his pledge;"[2] "Do not distort the judgment of a stranger or an orphan; do not take a pledge from a widow;"[3] "When you gather in your crop from the field and forget a sheaf in the field, do not go back to take it; let it be for the stranger, the widow, and the orphan."[4] While taking a pledge or taking every last sheaf is not improper in itself, we have to adopt a flexible attitude when dealing with the disadvantaged.

The market, like the law, tends to be majestically impartial. It is exactly this impartiality and mechanistic precision that gives the market so much power, but in order to keep the market from turning into a destructive juggernaut it is necessary for market participants to ask themselves if their actions are truly fair, given the disadvantaged position of others.

In the Talmud,[5] Rabbi Yohanan is quoted as saying that Jerusalem was destroyed in the time of the Romans only because the people judged according to the Torah. The astonished reply is, What kind of judgment should they have applied – that of the sorcerers? The reply: What Rabbi

Yohanan meant was that litigants insisted on strict enforcement of the law and were unwilling to compromise.

Similarly, one could state today that our values are in danger of being trampled by the market system. We may then ask, What system should we adopt instead – an oppressive system of centralized control? The answer is that we do not need an alternative system, but we need to work within the system we have with a measure of understanding and forbearance. The free market is the basis of our economy and our political system, but our society will be undermined if we insist on the strict workings of the market mechanism and are unwilling to make compassionate compromises.

The responsibility for helping the disadvantaged rests on society as a whole, and ethical behavior does not demand that any one sector bear the whole burden of this aid. But that does not mean that a person who encounters the hardship of others can shirk responsibility; this encounter implies a responsibility to be in the forefront of the efforts of the larger community. We find in the Shulhan Arukh that if a needy person comes to our door, we are not personally required to fulfill the Torah commandment of satisfying all his needs; we need to give only to the extent of our ability. But we are called on to display moral leadership and bring his plight to the attention of the community as a whole.[6]

The following three questions show that there can be a wide divergence between a permissible course of action reflecting our rights and a truly exemplary course of action reflecting our responsibility to weaker sectors of the community. There is no doubt that we have a right to fire workers, to evict non-paying tenants, and to accept gifts. But when the affected person is needy or dependent, we must exercise these rights in a thoughtful manner.

Downsizing Dilemma

IS IT ETHICAL TO DOWNSIZE "TO THE BONE"?

Who comes first, the owner or the worker? A work agreement is nominally a contract between equals: the worker provides a service, and the employer provides payment. But practically speaking, the relationship is seldom one of equality, and the Torah urges the employer to keep in mind the dependent and subordinate status of the worker

Q My job is to restructure a bloated company. Should I be trying to fire as many people as possible, or just enough to make the company reasonably profitable?

A A manager is hired to work on behalf of the business owners. And it is a basic principle of Jewish law and tradition that an employee or agent should do his utmost for his employer. A worker "is required to work with all his strength."[7] A fine example is the biblical figure of Joseph, who demonstrated exemplary devotion to the interests of his higher-ups, whether in the house of Potiphar, in the prison, or in the royal palace.

We might assume, then, that the manager should do everything in his power to cut costs, including slashing the number of jobs to the bare minimum, in order to increase value for the owners. But a broader look at the Jewish sources shows that a more balanced approach is called for. The owners have certain ethical responsibilities toward their employees, and these ethical responsibilities of ownership are delegated to the manager just as the commercial responsibilities are.

Jewish tradition gives the employer a special responsibility to consider the welfare of his employees because of their dependent status. For example, he is required to pay them on time: "Give him his pay on the same day, do not let the sun go down on it; for he is poor and his heart is set on it."[8]

In a famous case in the Talmud,[9] some movers accidentally broke a cask of wine belonging to a prominent sage. When the sage wanted to sue them for damages, his teacher admonished him that under the circumstances the fair thing to do was to leave the workers alone and even pay them their wages. The workers toil on behalf of the employer and so the employer has a special responsibility to look after their needs to the extent of his ability.

The Talmud also teaches us that it's spiteful for a manager to bargain workers down to the lowest possible wage if the employer is willing to pay more.[10]

This does not mean that an employer has to hire any particular number of workers or pay any particular wage. On the contrary, the norm in Jewish law is that a worker may be fired for reasonable cause. But it does mean that the welfare of the workers should be one of the many factors that go into making policy; this probably rules out firing "as many people as possible."

There are also excellent business reasons to avoid ruthless job cuts. First of all, experience shows that it is almost impossible to cut the fat without also cutting away some of your organization's muscle. Second, even if you could do away only with superfluous workers, the morale and effectiveness of the remaining workers is invariably damaged by layoffs, due to worry and because their workload is increased as they take on the responsibilities of dismissed colleagues. This is the so-called survivor syndrome. But the impact on morale can be reduced if the remaining workers see that the firings were carried out in a thoughtful, equitable, and rational way.

It is true that the manager is the representative of the owners. But just as he should faithfully represent their economic interests, so should he faithfully represent their ethical interests, including their responsibility to treat employees thoughtfully.

So while laying off workers to increase the firm's earnings is not inherently unethical, you should try and adopt a balanced approach. Remember that Joseph realized that it was ultimately in Pharaoh's own interest to adopt the humane policy of turning Egypt's farmers into independent partners instead of subordinate slaves.[11]

Evicting Indigent Tenants

CAN I EVICT INDIGENT TENANTS?

Some decisions are fair and reasonable from a business point of view but cause substantial hardship. Common examples include downsizing, keeping medications off the market, and evicting indigent tenants. In all of these cases decision-making presents a profound ethical dilemma: How can we acknowledge the economic exigencies that make these decisions necessary without neglecting the human suffering they involve?

Q Is it all right to convert affordable housing into market-price rentals, knowing that the elderly and disabled tenants who now live there will no longer afford it? Is it better to accept government funding and let the needy remain, even if this leads to less profit?

A The mention of evicting needy tenants conjures up visions of the dastardly Snidely Whiplash of cartoon fame. Scripture, too, depicts the hard-hearted approach of some creditors when it describes the pathetic cry of the poor widow who complained to the prophet Elisha, "The creditor is coming to take my two sons to be slaves."[12] But most landlords are not sadists; they only want to get a fair return on their property.

And evicting landlords do have a convincing claim. They probably believe as much as anyone else that society has an obligation to protect the needy and keep them from being cast into the street. But, they argue, it is neither fair nor practical to expect this obligation, which applies to us all, to be borne solely by them.

Jewish tradition acknowledges this claim – up to a point. Jewish law asserts unambiguously, "The judge is not permitted to show mercy to the needy, saying, 'He is poor and the wealthy person is obligated to support him.'...Rather, the two litigants must always be exactly equal in his eyes."[13] Certainly the owner has the right to evict a tenant who cannot afford the rent demanded.

At the same time, it won't do for landlords to stubbornly stand on their rights, insisting that the property is theirs and they have the right to decide who will occupy it and how much they pay. Our sages attributed the destruction of Jerusalem two thousand years ago to the low ethical standards of the residents. In particular, they said, "Jerusalem was destroyed because people insisted on strict justice and were unwilling to compromise."[14]

Tenants and their advocates have to recognize that landlords alone can't bear the burden of the war on homelessness. But the landlords themselves need to acknowledge that they are the ones on the front lines of this battle.

Other groups find themselves in a situation similar to yours. Employers cannot be solely responsible for helping the unemployed, and drug companies cannot be solely responsible for providing medication to the needy, but they are on the front line. We can learn some valuable lessons from the methods used by these other groups. For instance, many downsizing employers invest in outplacement services, helping laid-off workers to find new jobs or to acquire new skills. Some drug companies have tried to form alliances with NGO's (non-governmental organizations) that are working to improve medical care for the needy. And so on.

Following this model, your company might want to set up some kind of service to help tenants find suitable new dwellings. Alternatively, you might want to work with government or community organizations that would help provide them with housing. We explained in the previous column that when a very needy person comes to our door, a single individual does not have to reach into his resources to provide all of the poor person's needs. But the donor *is* called upon to take the initiative and "notify the community of this person's anguish."[15]

The solution that you suggest, of accepting government aid, could also be considered. In cases where you do need to evict, you should try to show flexibility when eviction would cause unusual hardship, for instance, during the winter months.[16]

In ethics, as in many other areas, we often find that "the best is the enemy of the good." The exaggerated demand that landlords take *sole* responsibility for the welfare of poor tenants may lead to the result that they take *no* responsibility. It is both fairer and more realistic to ask them to take advantage of their front-line position to play a leading role in finding a solution which is ultimately the responsibility of all.

Rent Control

IS IT ETHICAL FOR LANDLORDS TO CHARGE ALL THE MARKET WILL BEAR?

What is a fair price for rental housing? When is a rent increase excessive? These questions are among the most emotional, and the most ancient, in business ethics. Even those who favor a free market often believe that the market for housing requires special treatment. Jewish law corroborates this belief, but only to a limited extent.

Q Can I charge the highest rent the market will bear, even if some tenants may be priced out of their homes?

A The tension between landlord and tenant is hardly new. The Torah speaks about charging a fair price for land that will revert to the owner in the Jubilee year, and which is therefore like a rental.[17] And the Talmud gives detailed rules about fair relationships between landlord and tenant. Let us examine the ethical basis of these rules.

Jewish law places no a priori restriction on what rent can be charged. Every location is unique, so it is understandable that real estate is exempt from the general prohibition on overcharging for standard, commonly traded items.[18] However, once a rental relationship has already been formed, our tradition does regulate it to prevent exploitation by either party.

The Mishnah states that a tenant cannot be evicted without reasonable notice: "One who rents out a house in the winter cannot evict him before the Pesach holiday; in the summer, not before giving thirty days notice. And in the city, whether summer or winter, twelve months."[19]

This rule creates a fair balance between the interests of landlord and tenant. The landlord is the owner of the property; he has the right to evict the tenant in order to use the property himself or rent it to someone else. But this right needs to be exercised in an equitable way that will not leave the tenant out on the street without a reasonable opportunity to find suitable new lodgings.

How much time does this require? Our sages recognized that there is no one-size-fits-all answer. Different locales have different realities, which is why the Mishnah gives different answers for different times and places.

The Talmud then adds, "Rav Huna stated, But if he wants to raise the rent, he may." At first glance, this seems fair. The tenant cannot be thrown into the street without adequate notice, but the landlord should at least be able to maintain some control over pricing. On the other hand, this condition seems to nullify the rule of the Mishnah. The rent could be raised so high as to compel the tenant to leave or to pay an extravagant rent to stay, since the short notice puts him over a barrel. The passage in the Talmud then clarifies that "this holds when the price of housing rises."

In other words, it is improper to raise the rent beyond the accepted norm in order to take advantage of the tenant, who is a captive customer. But it is permissible to raise rents in measured response to a general rise in housing (or rental) prices. The landlord is entitled to a fair price for his property, but not to a rate that exploits his special leverage over his tenant.

The problem of exploitation also exists in the opposite direction, although to a lesser extent. Sometimes a tenant may delay paying rent knowing that the landlord's only recourse is an expensive and time-consuming eviction hearing. This, too, is improper. Both sides are entitled to take advantage of other opportunities in the housing market, but they should not exploit the fact that once the tenant is ensconced in the dwelling, it is hard for him to move and hard for the landlord to get him out.

Of course, if the exact terms and rate of the rental are fixed by contract, then both sides are bound by these terms. The rules of the Mishnah and Talmud are meant as fair principles for people who do not want to hammer out terms specific to their situation. Even when there is a contract, tenants very often overstay the original contract period without a new agreement, and then, too, we need to refer to the Talmud's timeless principles of fairness.

Despite this basic leniency, if the tenant is needy and you can afford to keep the rent down, you should think twice before raising the rent to what the market will bear. Remember that the highest form of charity is to help someone through normal market transactions rather than to give him a handout. The most humane and effective way of giving help is to patronize the needy person's business, or give him a business loan, or to do business with him on favorable terms. In this case the landlord has a unique opportunity to fulfill the highest level of helping others.

When Giving Presents Is a Burden

CAN I ACCEPT GIFTS FROM INDIGENT CLIENTS?

Two of the most fundamental principles of ethics are *equity* and *consent*: people should be treated equally and fairly, and they should not be coerced. These principles can be violated in flagrant ways, as when a bribe is given to attain special treatment or when deception or pressure are used to evade true consent. But Jewish tradition sensitizes us to more subtle ways in which these principles can be compromised. These are exemplified by the problem that arises when a grateful but impoverished client gives a gift to a helpful public servant.

Q Clients at our social services agency often show their gratitude by giving presents to the social workers. Is it proper to accept?

A The fact that clients are eager to show their gratitude is a wonderful statement about the ethical climate in the agency. It shows that people are doing their jobs with ability and dedication, and after all, the work ethic is the starting place for workplace ethics. However, these gifts entail two ethical issues that require discussion: equity and expense.

THE IMPORTANCE OF EQUITY

A very serious problem is that gifts can create favoritism. Our tradition tells us that it is almost impossible to maintain objectivity after one accepts a gift. When the Torah prohibits judges from accepting bribes, it does not say that it is wrong to deliberately pervert justice. That is self-evident. Instead the Torah tells us, "For bribery blinds the sighted, and distorts the words of the righteous."[20] Even a wise and righteous person, who fully intends to remain objective despite the gift, will find that his judgment is distorted.

The Talmud educates us to be very sensitive to this consideration. It tells us of important judges who disqualified themselves from judging cases in response to even tiny favors received from one side in the case – favors we might consider routine courtesies. In one case a litigant extended a steadying hand to the judge on a wobbly bridge; in another, the petitioner drove a bird away from the judge's head.[21]

A social worker has to create a working relationship with a client, and exercise a degree of advocacy. He or she can't maintain the same level of detachment that is expected of a judge. But the fundamental psychological insight behind the prohibition of bribes applies in every field. Therefore any gift policy must ensure that all clients are treated equally.

Even if we could prevent gifts from creating inequity, we still need to cope with the *appearance* of favoritism. Some clients will see others giving gifts and will think that they won't get adequate attention unless they do the same. This is a very unfair burden on the agency's impoverished clients.

The need for the appearance of equity is graphically illustrated by a story from the Talmud: One of the greatest sages, known by his title Rav, was approached by a litigant who was sure that Rav would remember and favor him. In fact, Rav barely recognized the man; yet he disqualified himself as a judge in the case because the litigant's behavior conveyed the *impression* that the two of them were on friendly terms. And even the replacement judge, Rav Kahana, warned the litigant to stop cultivating the impression of being favored by Rav.[22]

DURESS

The second possible problem is that accepting gifts may make people feel pressured to give them. This problem can be present even in the case of an ordinary, friendly gift where the question of equity does not arise. For example, in a social situation, we do not mind that a gift may create a feeling of gratitude and commitment; on the contrary, this feeling is one of the lovely things about gifts.

But even in this case there is a problem in accepting a present that is beyond the giver's means. Maimonides writes, "Accepting hospitality from someone who does not have enough for himself verges on stealing. Yet the recipient thinks that he has done nothing wrong, saying, 'Didn't I take only what he offered me?'"[23]

Maimonides awakens us to an important insight: seeming consent can be affected by different kinds of hidden duress. Although the urge to be hospitable is laudable, we should not take excessive advantage of it.

We find the same insight regarding charity. Jewish law tells us that charity collectors need to be careful not to put pressure on people to give beyond their means.[24]

WHEN GIVING IS GETTING

The considerations we have just discussed dictate that any gift policy should ensure that gifts do not affect the judgment of the social workers and do not put a financial burden on clients. Does this mean that gifts should be forbidden altogether? Not necessarily. There is an additional ethical consideration we should keep in mind: the value of expressing gratitude. Allowing some gifts may be an excellent way to give your clients this opportunity. Sometimes accepting is the greatest form of giving.

A blanket prohibition on gifts could prevent the clients from expressing their feelings. This definitely presents a problem. Jewish tradition teaches us that giving is a basic human need. This is most clearly demonstrated by the stipulation in Jewish law that charity recipients, who are entitled to support for their needs, should be given enough so that they are themselves able to give charity from the donations they receive.[25]

One good solution is to adopt a strict policy of not accepting any gifts worth more than some nominal value. Two or three dollars is enough to buy an attractive greeting card or an inexpensive novelty trophy, allowing the clients the satisfaction of expressing their gratitude. But this amount is not so large that it would create an impression of inequity or constitute a real hardship even for a poor person.

Everyday Dealing with Widows and Orphans

DO I NEED TO MAKE EXCEPTIONS FOR WIDOWS IN MY
BUSINESS?

The essence of market relationships is that they are detached and imper-
sonal. They take place through the "cash nexus." But the requirement
to be considerate toward the emotionally vulnerable challenges us to
display human sensitivity even within the framework of our economic
relationships.

Q If I have a customer who is a widow, should I give her a discount?
If she's late paying, am I allowed to use normal collection methods?

A The Torah repeatedly admonishes us to display special consideration
for widows. An examination of these admonitions will lead to an
answer to your question.

One common motif regarding widows is to take account of their
often precarious *economic* circumstances. In at least a half-dozen passages,
the Torah specifically mentions widows as among the needy persons we
should provide for when we give charity, agricultural tithes, and so on.
"When you reap the harvest of your field, and you forget a sheaf in the
field, do not go back to take it; let it be for the stranger, the orphan, and
the widow, so that the LORD your God may bless you in all the work of
your hands."[26] Someone who has enough is always obligated to provide
for those who are needy, but we should pay particular attention to the
widow because of the unusual difficulties she has in supporting herself
and, often, her family.

But the Torah also tells us, "Do not cause anguish to a widow or an
orphan."[27] This commandment relates to any widow, whether rich or
poor. Here special consideration for the widow is called for because of the
likelihood of *emotional* vulnerability. Her memory of her loss together
with the ongoing experience of going it alone mean that the widow is
likely to be more in need of support and encouragement than others.

The first consideration is relevant to your question if the widow is poor. While there is no commandment to give a discount to poor people or to refrain from collecting debts from them, we have often pointed out in our columns that the ideal way of helping the needy is through normal market transactions. If you are in a position to give charity to the poor, then an excellent way of doing so is by giving service to them at special low prices or unusually favorable terms of credit. This would apply particularly to a widow.

The second consideration does not apply solely to economic transactions and holds irrespective of the widow's financial situation. We should be thoughtful and considerate in all our relationships with others, and most especially with someone who is emotionally vulnerable.

These two commandments define two poles: one relates specifically to economic interactions because of the widow's economic vulnerability; the other pertains to all social interactions because of the widow's emotional vulnerability.

Between these two extremes of economic and emotional interaction, there is an intermediate factor that we have often discussed: the human dimension of our market activities. The Torah touches upon this in a third mandate which is like a hybrid of the other two. The Torah warns us not to demand a pawn (collateral) from a widow before the loan is due. "Do not distort the judgment of a stranger or an orphan, and do not repossess the garment of a widow."[28] The Talmud concludes that this commandment, despite its economic nature, applies even to a wealthy widow.[29] The explanation is that a demand of this kind, despite its economic nature, can be demeaning or distressing beyond its economic impact.

This commandment is relevant to your situation. A person is always allowed to collect money for services rendered, but even legitimate collection actions sometimes have a way of declining into adversarial confrontations that do not dignify either side. If a widow is involved, we should be especially careful to make sure all collection actions or legal actions are carried out in a businesslike fashion.

The Torah's attitude toward widows teaches that we should display special consideration toward anyone who is financially or emotionally vulnerable.[30] When we interact with the vulnerable, even our economic interactions should display an extra measure of human thoughtfulness.

ENDNOTES

1. Deuteronomy 1:17
2. Deuteronomy 24:12
3. Deuteronomy 24:17
4. Deuteronomy 24:19
5. Bava Metzia 30b
6. Shulhan Arukh, Yoreh Deah 250:1 in Rema.
7. Shulhan Arukh, Hoshen Mishpat 337:20
8. Deuteronomy 24:15
9. Bava Metzia 83a
10. Bava Metzia 76a
11. Genesis 47:19–26
12. II Kings 4:1
13. Shulhan Arukh, Hoshen Mishpat 17:10
14. Bava Metzia 30b
15. Shulhan Arukh, Yoreh Deah 250:1.
16. See Shulhan Arukh, Hoshen Mishpat 312
17. Leviticus 25:14–17
18. Bava Metzia 56a
19. Bava Metzia 101b
20. Exodus 23:8
21. Ketubbot 105b
22. Sanhedrin 7b–8a
23. Maimonides, Teshuvah 4:4
24. Shulhan Arukh, Yoreh Deah 248:7
25. Shulhan Arukh, Yoreh Deah 248:1
26. Deuteronomy 24:19; see also 4:29, 16:11, 16:14, 24:20–21, 26:12–13
27. Exodus 22:21
28. Deuteronomy 24:17
29. Bava Metzia 115:1
30. See the Sema commentary on Hoshen Mishpat 97:22

HIGH FINANCE

Introduction

How Far Is Wall Street from Las Vegas Boulevard?

Speculative Activity

Introduction

Any investment involves a bet of some kind. A person who opens a restaurant is most of all providing a valuable service in return for payment. But he is also betting that people will continue to eat out and that they will find his establishment attractive enough to keep him in business.

Some other investments do not involve any active involvement in the business; indeed, sometimes investors have no idea what it is "their" companies do. This kind of "numbers game" raises the question of where we draw the line between investing and "playing the market."

The attitude of Jewish tradition to investment and speculation is lenient but not indulgent. Overall, investment is not regarded as suspicious or sinister, and a person has a right to a fair return on a business investment. But our sages were aware of the possibility of excesses that are a danger to society as a whole as well as to the speculator individually.

As we find so often, the main concern of Jewish tradition is not economic but humanistic. The ethical question our sages asked was not whether speculation contributes to the wealth of society but what its impact is on human relations. The concern, as the columns in this chapter show, was that the investor or speculator might be alienated from the work ethic of the ordinary working person, and ultimately might even become hostile to it. In the end, the speculator suffers from a distorted view of human relations, and the public may suffer from speculators abusing their economic influence through conspiracy or exploitation.

While investing is an accepted and honored activity in Judaism, the investor has to make sure that he is not led to inhumane excesses.

How Far Is Wall Street from Las Vegas Boulevard?

IS IT ETHICAL TO "PLAY THE MARKET"?

Trading on the stock market is not so different from gambling in a casino. One trader bets long, another bets short; then the wheel of the Dow (or the Nasdaq) goes round and round, and depending on where it stops the chips get reshuffled. Despite this, many people who would never go to a casino have no problem playing the market. The following discussion clarifies the moral distinction between the two activities, based on Jewish sources that discuss the ethical objection to gambling.

Q Gambling involves many ethical problems. Isn't playing the stock market just another form of the same vice?

A Most economists would probably insist that there is no connection between the dissipative activity of gambling and the vital constructive role of stock markets in the allocation of society's productive capital. These markets provide a needed way for individuals to invest their savings in productive assets.

However, this view is not quite unanimous. In 1935, the great English economist John Maynard Keynes looked at Wall Street and wrote that the capital development of the United States had become "the by-product of the activities of a casino," and added, "It is usually agreed that casinos should, in the public interest, be inaccessible and expensive. And perhaps the same is true of stock exchanges."[1] Despite the indignant protests of some orthodox economists, it is pretty unlikely that the experience of the intervening seventy years would have done much to persuade Keynes to change his mind. Plenty of stock market investors pay scant attention to capital development and continue just taking a ride on the stock-market roller-coaster.

However, before we draw any ethical conclusions from Keynes's observation, we should recall that the main objective of the Torah is not the efficiency of capital markets but individual spiritual development.

From this point of view, there is still a vast difference between the two kinds of speculation.

The Talmud points out two ethical problems with gambling. The Mishnah states that a habitual gambler is disqualified from giving testimony.[2] The Talmud then asks, What is it that a gambler has done wrong? The passage proceeds as follows: "Rami bar Hama said, Because it is a conditional commitment, and a conditional commitment is not binding. Rav Sheshet said, This is not considered a conditional commitment. Rather, he is not occupied with settling the world."[3]

According to Rami bar Hama, the problem with gambling is that the winner often takes unfair advantage of the loser, who is not always fully aware of the adverse odds he faces. The professional gambler is generally a hustler who preys on the ignorance and weakness of the amateur.

According to Rav Sheshet, habitual gambling leads to an easy-come, easy-go attitude toward money and an anti-social, underworld mentality of contempt for productive work. The gambler is unmoved by the ethical and legal sanctions against lying in court, because his whole life is just a game and a gamble.

These are both valid ethical considerations that we need to keep in mind. One can easily see these elements at work in a casino, where many bettors are in over their heads and there is a general environment of vice and immodesty.

What about the stock market? Unquestionably, there are some excesses, as occasional media exposés about the securities business reveal. But on the whole these vices do not seem to be endemic in the financial markets.

Let us first examine the problem of exploitation. While there are many unfortunate cases where unscrupulous brokers or business executives take advantage of investors, the vast majority of trades are undertaken by individuals who are well informed about their investments.

If we turn to the social issue, we can see that most people who participate in the financial markets are assiduous individuals whose commitment to social stability is no different than that of workers in other professions.

Every profession has unique ethical challenges, and workers in the financial markets need to exercise special care to escape the maelstrom of greed that has so strong a hold on their line of work. (Regular Torah study would be a highly effective antidote). But there is nothing inherently unethical or problematic about their work.

Speculative Activity

IS SPECULATION ANTI-SOCIAL?

When speculators buy assets, they hope to profit from a rise in prices that may harm others. Economists tell us that speculators perform a vital economic function, but popular opinion views them with suspicion. Jewish tradition reveals that while speculation is not inherently unethical, there are genuine ethical considerations behind the popular sentiment.

Q Some people make a lot of money by speculating. Is it really ethical to make money without producing anything, just by guessing which way prices are going to move?

A Fundamentally, speculating is an economically productive activity. But it most certainly does present some ethical challenges.

The economic importance of speculation is that it encourages the efficient allocation of resources. For instance, when speculators hoard a commodity in anticipation of a future shortage, the result is that adequate stockpiles will be available when the supply shortfall occurs. In the framework of modern competitive markets, speculation contributes to the effective exploitation of scarce resources.

Given this obvious economic function, it may seem surprising that the sages of the Talmud looked suspiciously on this phenomenon and subjected it to various restrictions. For example, they limited hoarding to producers and forbade the participation of professional speculators.[4] Why did our rabbis want to regulate such an important economic activity?

One obvious reason is economic. While speculation is efficient in competitive markets, one must acknowledge that markets are not always competitive and impartial. Sometimes speculators collude, cornering markets and creating artificial shortages in order to inflate prices. Even economists recognize that in this case speculation is extremely harmful; instead of alleviating hunger it will create hunger.

But there is also another, more profound, reason for the restrictions on speculation. In marketplace regulation as in so many other aspects of Jewish law, economic considerations were not in the forefront of the thinking of our sages. Most often, they put human considerations first. This principle applies to the restrictions on hoarding, as we can see from the source of the regulations.

The Talmud's censure of hoarding[5] is based in the context of the following prophetic passage from the book of Amos: "Hear this, you who would swallow the needy and destroy the downtrodden of the land; who say, When will the month pass so that we may sell grain, and the Sabbatical year so that we may open our granaries?...so that we may buy the poor for money and the needy for a pair of shoes."[6]

What worried the prophet above all was not the economic consequences of hoarding but the tragic human consequences, for it destroys the solidarity of society. The speculators, instead of sharing the general interest in relief, now have a private interest in continued distress, which will enrich them. They ask, "When will the month pass?" Rashi explains that they are waiting impatiently for the harvest season to pass, because then there will be a shortage of grain in the market and prices will rise.

Beyond this, the speculators are enticed to go beyond their desire for monetary enrichment, which is justifiable within bounds, and are seeking dominance over others: "So that we may buy the poor for money." This is a tendency that the Torah repeatedly condemns, since we are all servants of God. "For the children of Israel are slaves to Me"[7] slaves to Him, and not to other human beings.[8] This ethical problem with speculation is very similar to Rav Sheshet's concern about gambling discussed in the preceding column. The speculator becomes alienated from the concerns of working people, who depend on reasonable prices for commodities. The first result is that the common people are exploited, and the ultimate result is that they may be abused and enslaved.

It is a fundamental ethical idea that we should try to ally our economic and human interests so that our desire for gain does not lead us into betraying our ideals. A simple example illustrates this concept: Imagine a member of a football team just before the Super Bowl. If his team wins, he will earn a huge sum of money; if they lose, his earnings will be far less. Economic theory states that in order to hedge his risks, the player ought to bet against his own team. But human nature would view such a bet as a shocking betrayal of loyalty, even if it were so small that it is not an incentive to throw the game.

Likewise, our sages were concerned that one particular kind of speculation–namely, betting on disaster–may sometimes have a negative effect on the solidarity of our society.

Most kinds of speculation are not regulated by Jewish law and are considered perfectly acceptable. However, each individual speculator should occasionally make sure that he has not created a situation where he is "betting against the home team" and subtly alienating himself from the community.

ENDNOTES

1. *General Theory of Employment, Interest, and Money*, book IV, chapter 12, section vi
2. Mishnah Sanhedrin 3:3
3. Sanhedrin 24b
4. Shulhan Arukh, Hoshen Mishpat 231:4.
5. Bava Batra 90b
6. Amos 8:4–6
7. Leviticus 25:42
8. Kiddushin 22b

HUMAN RESOURCES

Introduction

Most people go to work primarily in order to earn a living. This is the consequence of the "curse of Adam," which decreed: "By the sweat of your brow shall you eat bread."[1] At the same time, most of us spend more time interacting with our colleagues at work than with family or friends, which highlights the need to pay attention to the human side of human resources.

Examining the Jewish sources, we can distinguish three prominent themes regarding employer/employee relations, or what is known today as "human resources."

One theme is the fundamental interdependence of the two sides, and the responsibility of employer and employee alike to fulfill their side of the employment bargain in a responsible fashion. Maimonides writes, "Just as the employer is warned not to steal the wage of the [employee] and not to delay it, so the [employee] is warned not to steal the work of the employer and idle a little here and a little there."[2]

Alongside this consideration is the recognition that despite the ostensibly equal status of employer and employee in the bargain, the hired employee is never quite the equal of the boss. Since the employee is more vulnerable, a large body of laws and customs provide him with special rights that make his subordinate status less extreme and also more tolerable. For example, the Torah warns the employer to pay wages promptly.[3]

Finally, we find a consistent emphasis on the human side of human resources—the need to supplement ethical behavior in the *monetary* aspects of work with thoughtful conduct in *interpersonal* relations in the workplace. For example, the Torah tells us not to lord it over our servants,[4] and Jewish tradition urges us to apply the same standards to ordinary worker relations.[5]

The columns in this chapter will elaborate these aspects in more detail.

Monitoring Workers

HOW INTRUSIVE MAY EMPLOYERS BE IN MONITORING
WORKERS?

Q May firms monitor worker e-mails?

A There is no doubt that it is proper and even vital to keep an eye on
workers to make sure they are doing their job. The Talmud suggests
ironically that someone who inherits a lot of money and wants to lose it
quickly should hire workers and fail to supervise them.[6] It also assures
us that someone who personally surveys his affairs each day, including
the behavior of workers, is guaranteed to benefit.[7]

However, intrusive monitoring can violate a worker's privacy. The
fact that someone is at work doesn't make his or her every move the
concern of the employer. Employers have an ethical responsibility to
monitor in a responsible way. This responsibility has two aspects, the
"what" and the "how":

1. Not to have an excessive amount of monitoring;
2. Not to use the information gleaned from monitoring in an
   inequitable or otherwise improper way.

We can get some idea of where to draw the line from a fascinating
insight of the renowned seventeenth century legal authority, Rabbi
Yaakov Hagiz. Noting that gossip is strictly forbidden in Jewish law,
according to the verse, "Don't go about as a talebearer",[8] Rabbi Hagiz
concludes that just as it is forbidden to disclose private information
to others by gossiping, so is it forbidden to reveal such information
to ourselves by prying. "It is forbidden to pursue and seek the private
affairs of one's fellow, for what is the difference between gossiping to
others or to oneself?"[9]

We can complete the picture by presenting the basic ethical principle regarding gossip or slander: Only information that is essential to

preventing substantive damage may be disclosed to the vulnerable party and only if the information will be used in a responsible way.

For example, if I happen to know that a fellow worker is using drugs, I am allowed to reveal this to the employer only if the worker's drug problem is likely to damage his work and only if revealing the information is the only way to forestall such damage. Furthermore, I must be certain that the employer's reaction will be equitable. Sending the worker for treatment or suspending him temporarily after providing a fair hearing is a measured response; but immediate dismissal or legal action would often be considered excessive.

Applying the criterion of Rabbi Hagiz, we would conclude that an intrusive drug-use monitoring program could be justified only if two conditions are fulfilled:

1. There is a reasonable presumption that this monitoring will uncover drug use that has a measurable impact on the company;
2. Results from the monitoring will be used in a measured and responsible fashion.

Employees need to know about the monitoring and be given a fair hearing if it seems to turn up damaging information.

Employers have every right to take reasonable steps to protect themselves from harm from malicious or careless workers. But this doesn't give them the right to be some kind of corporate "Big Brother." Any monitoring system should be designed to obtain only information vital for the company's protection, and needs to be accompanied by transparent and equitable procedures for using the information in a constructive way.

360-Degree Feedback

THE PITFALLS OF WORK EVALUATIONS FROM COLLEAGUES
AND SUBORDINATES.

Q Many workplaces are instituting 360-degree evaluations. Is this
innovation ethically justified?

A The "360-degree" evaluation involves input not only from a worker's
supervisor, but also from colleagues and even from subordinates.

The practical advantage of this approach is clear: it has the potential to provide invaluable information to management, since most of a person's work is done with colleagues or subordinates, rather than with superiors. The practical disadvantage is also obvious: the need to consult many individuals adds considerable time and expense to performance evaluations.

But we also need to pay attention to the ethical dimensions of this practice. In one sense allowing input from colleagues and subordinates adds accountability and empowers lower-downs to provide significant input to management. Yet this empowerment is inherently asymmetrical, since ultimately only upper management has access to evaluations and is authorized to act upon them. This asymmetry results in a number of troublesome ethical pitfalls.

One problem is the difficulty of getting objective input. Co-workers not only cooperate but also compete – for promotions, bonuses, even for attention. Enabling them to evaluate their colleagues places them in an uncomfortable position: a positive evaluation jeopardizes the evaluator's own status; a negative one puts him or her in the position of "ratting" on a colleague. The need to prevent mutual recrimination means that 360-degree evaluations are typically anonymous; this further erodes the reliability of these reports.

A closely related idea is found in the classic book on slander, Hafetz Hayyim.[10] Rabbi Yisrael Meir HaKohen writes that a person should never solicit an opinion on someone from a competitor; it's impossible for someone's competitor to be impartial and therefore the question itself is unfair.

The very knowledge that a person is likely to be evaluated by a colleague can harm worker solidarity and effective teamwork; workers are that much more likely to hide difficulties instead of soliciting friendly help in overcoming them. We find that Jewish tradition legitimizes "guilds" of skilled tradespeople, even though they limit competition;[11] one reason may be that these guilds encourage feelings of solidarity among those who could otherwise be divided by competition and suspicion.

These evaluations are a bit reminiscent of "piece-work" methods of the last century. Paying workers by the piece was supposed to "empower" workers by giving them a share of any productivity improvements. But workers were not made into true partners, and they soon perceived that any improvement in performance translated rapidly into increased demands from management. Thus piece-work resulted in a counterproductive dynamic whereby effective workers were ostracized by colleagues as "rate-busters."

Some current trends towards worker empowerment, including 360-degree feedback, suffer from the same problem of partial empowerment, which ultimately empowers the worker to his or her own detriment. In today's knowledge-driven workplace, workers are being provided with more knowledge and authority and are being asked to provide more knowledge to upper management, but ultimately it is the upper ranks who maintain the power to hire and fire.

That doesn't mean that there is no place for increased worker empowerment and input; it just means that it can't easily be ethically introduced as an "add-on" in a traditional hierarchical workplace. It requires a genuine commitment to make the worker part of the team. "Quality circles," where worker input is solicited in improving factory procedures, have been most successful in the large Japanese companies with policies of lifetime employment, promotions from the shop floor, and small worker-supervisor pay differentials. Thus worker-management solidarity is genuine, and workers truly expect to enjoy the benefits of increased productivity.

This reality is not easily transferred to the bottom-line driven orientation of Israeli and North American business. On the whole firms recognize this and tend to use this technique primarily among senior managers who have proven commitment to the company.

360-degree feedback and other elements of worker empowerment can make a valuable contribution to business effectiveness and to the ethical standing of business. But in order to be effective, this empowerment must be genuine. If the empowerment is bogus and asymmetrical, with all true authority remaining in the upper echelons, then it is likely to create more problems than it solves.

Discharge Dilemma

CAN I FIRE A DEVOTED BUT INEPT EMPLOYEE?

Employers sometimes find it necessary to fire workers who do not measure up. Since our workplace relationships are also human relationships, this step involves many complex feelings. The termination process should take account of human feelings, but a process that minimizes unpleasant emotions for the employer may unintentionally maximize them for the worker.

Q A few months ago I hired someone who is a very nice and good person, but just hasn't mastered the work. He costs me more than he is worth. Now that business has slowed, can I take this opportunity to "trim" the workforce and lay him off?

A It is generally ethical to fire someone for any reason related to his or her ongoing job performance. It isn't necessary to wait for a slowdown. A business downturn may be helpful for your feelings, because you will feel you have a stronger basis for the firing, but it is not necessarily helpful for the worker. On the contrary, when times are bad it may be more difficult for him to find another position.

Jewish law does state that even an underperforming worker should not be fired peremptorily. Instead he should be given a reasonable opportunity to improve his performance. The ideal way to achieve this goal is to undertake regular and equitable performance evaluations, giving workers ongoing feedback about what is expected of them and how they are living up to expectations. The Talmud tells us that only in selected professions, where there is a low tolerance for error, may workers be dismissed without warning.[12]

This rule can be viewed as a natural extension of the Torah commandment to give gentle reproof. "Do not hate your brother in your heart; surely reprove your fellow man, and do not sin toward him."[13] When someone acts improperly, there is a natural human tendency to withdrawal or even hostility. The Torah, with its emphasis on the perfectibility of mankind, tells us to resist this tendency. Instead of becoming hostile toward others we should reach out to them, gently explaining the basis for our concern.

In the context of workplace relationships, this means that if a worker is not performing as well as he should, the employer should not silently wait for the most expedient opportunity to dismiss him. He should meet with the worker and offer constructive advice about his shortcomings, thereby giving him a chance to improve. Or perhaps the worker will be able to explain that his work is not as deficient as it seems.

What if it turns out that the worker cannot do the work and cannot improve? Keeping a person on in this case is seldom doing a favor to anybody. You the employer need to find a worker better suited to your requirements; the worker needs to find a situation better suited to his abilities.

An employer who needs to dismiss an underachiever may find it easier to avoid criticizing the worker, saying, for example, that he is trimming the workforce. But here, too, the principle of gentle reproof applies. It would be more helpful for the employee if the employer gently indicates what his deficiencies were, so that he can learn from his experience and seek work better suited to his talents.[14] While doing this may be difficult, omit it only if you are afraid that candor will greatly offend the employee or may harm you by provoking hostility or even litigation.

Another Torah principle directly applicable to the dismissal process is the prohibition against causing unnecessary anguish. Experts on worker relations have composed a list of recommendations that minimize the negative impact of being fired. These include conducting an exit interview, not firing a person right before a weekend, and avoiding public scenes. Following these recommendations will enable you to be thoughtful and sensitive to the emotions of the dismissed worker.

A SENIOR EMPLOYEE

The approach outlined above would suit a new employee who never really fit into the firm's needs. But it is not ideal for an older worker who has contributed to the firm for a very long time but eventually becomes less able to perform. In this case, you should make a reasonable effort to see if the old-timer can be kept on the payroll. Jewish tradition is profoundly sensitive to the dignity of the older person, including the older worker.

For example, the Mishnah tells us that we should be reluctant to discharge an elderly servant who has served the family faithfully over many years because loyal servants are "the honor of the household."[15] By the same token, if there is an older worker who has served the firm faithfully over a long period, he is the honor of the firm, and you should be reluctant to let him go.

Short Notice

CAN I HIDE MY INTENTION TO QUIT?

The flip side of firing ethics is quitting ethics. Here, too, Jewish law provides some principles of thoughtful behavior that balance the needs of the departing worker with those of the dependent employer.

Q I've decided to leave my current job to work in a different field. If I give my boss only two weeks notice, as the contract requires, he'll be in a really tight spot. But I'm afraid that if I let him know, too, far in advance, I won't be assigned to any interesting projects and may even be discharged.

A The considerations that apply to a worker who is leaving an employer are similar to those for an employer who is dismissing a worker. A worker is allowed to quit for any reason he deems suitable, but his separation from the firm should be carried out thoughtfully and considerately. One aspect of this is that you should never just suddenly disappear, and you should make suitable arrangements to ensure an orderly transition when this is appropriate.

We can learn this principle from two laws. There is a general principle in Jewish law that a worker who quits suddenly, thus making it more expensive for the employer to find a replacement, is not responsible for the employer's extra expenditure. But there are two exceptions. One is if the worker's departure causes an actual loss to the employer because he was relying on the worker to fulfill the work agreement. The other is when the worker has no objection to the current job but is taking another job simply in order to improve his income. It is perfectly permissible for him to do this, but he bears some responsibility for making sure that finding a replacement is not overly burdensome.[16]

Since there is an explicit agreement that you only have to give two weeks notice, these laws do not, strictly speaking, apply to you. But implicit in these laws is an ethical principle: the worker should not leave the employer suddenly short-handed unless there is a compelling reason.

If you have a relationship of trust with your employer, you can explain that you are giving early notice in order to help him, and ask that he reciprocate by continuing to give you challenging and responsible work.

Another possible solution is to delay starting your new job. Instead of fixing a starting date for your new position, ask your new employer to give you a few weeks to finish off at your current workplace. Then you can give flexible notice, notifying your boss that you would like to leave in two weeks but are willing to stay on a little longer in order to enable him to find a replacement and provide a smooth transition.

While you are probably anxious to start your new job as soon as possible so as to make a good impression on your new employer, nothing will impress him more than seeing that you are a responsible, thoughtful worker who refuses to leave his employer in the lurch.

THE EXIT INTERVIEW

Just like the employer, an employee has to take steps to ensure that the departure process is dignified and thoughtful. Avoid using your resignation statement or letter to express anger toward the boss or to slander fellow employees. Such outbursts are not only unethical, they will give you a bad reputation that you may find hard to live down.

If there are serious lapses in the workplace that you feel a responsibility to report, it is a good idea to inform your employer, for his own benefit. But it may be best to wait until a few weeks after you quit, when both of you will be less excited and more objective. If you are asking for a reference, then it is certainly prudent to wait until after one has been provided.

When God commanded Jacob to return to his homeland, putting an end to his employment by his father-in-law, Jacob hid what he was doing because he was afraid that Laban would prevent him from leaving. Although this fear was confirmed by Laban's subsequent hot pursuit of Jacob and his family, the Torah describes Jacob's plan as a deception, indicating that in normal circumstances we should avoid this approach.[17]

No Such Thing as a Free Lunch?

ARE DELI WORKERS ENTITLED TO A CUT?

There are two cherished ideals of the enlightened workplace. One is that the worker has a meaningful connection of some kind with what he produces; he is not just a cog in the wheel but a partner with the employer in the production process. The other is that workplace conditions should reflect stability. The following question examines what happens when the employer's steps seem to undermine these ideals.

Q For years, the kitchen where I work has provided free meals to employees. But recently we got a new boss who has discontinued this policy. Now we're not even allowed to take leftovers. The new policy has created much hardship and resentment for employees. Some have even continued to take food surreptitiously. Does the employer have to keep giving us food? What steps can we take?

A It does seem a bit heartless to make a person work in the midst of food and not let him have any. Perhaps it is this sentiment which underlies the Torah's mandate to allow field workers to eat from the crops they gather in: "When you go into your neighbor's vineyard [as a hired worker], you may eat your fill of grapes."[18] Indeed, the great Medieval commentary Sefer HaHinnukh explains, "Being grudging towards the worker, by forbidding him to eat what he is working with at the very moment when he toils, especially with crops which [particularly] gladden a person with God's blessing, reveals stinginess and narrow-mindedness."

But this principle must have limits. The end of the same verse states, "But you may not put any into your container," and the next verse warns not to harvest any standing grain for personal use. Let us examine the laws and ethical principles that circumscribe the limits of this ideal.

The Jewish legal tradition states that this permission is limited to agricultural workers, specifically the field workers who first bring the crops to a state where they are edible and accessible. The Torah imposes a special degree of generosity on the reward from agricultural activity;

the most notable is tithes. But this requirement is limited specifically to growing food. As Sefer ha-Hinnukh points out, the divine contribution to productivity is so keenly evident in agriculture, where we truly seem to obtain "something from nothing."[19] Another limitation is that this permission applies only to unfinished produce; for example, workers can "nip" a few grapes but shouldn't drink from the wine.

These principles don't seem so compelling in an industrial kitchen. If you and your co-workers were actually making the cold cuts, the idea behind this mitzvah might be more applicable; but you are really working with ready-to-eat food. And you must admit that your employer's directive is understandable. Allowing restaurant workers to eat from the restaurant food, especially in a kosher delicatessen where very expensive food is sold, can be an immense burden on a place of business.

The explanation of Sefer ha-Hinnukh seems more applicable to left-overs. There does seem to be an element of stinginess in prohibiting eating them. Yet here also we should understand the justification for this rule. This policy, while unfortunate, is an extremely common one, which employers feel is necessary to protect themselves from liability as well as from conflicts of interest (employees might intentionally waste food in order to eat it or give it to charity).

CHANGE IN WORKING CONDITIONS

The real problem here is not with the prohibition per se, but with the fact that in the past the employees were entitled to this benefit. If it was always customary for employees to receive meals, then the meals would be considered part of the salary. Taking away this entitlement would be permitted only under the same circumstances that would legitimate a cut in pay. The Mishnah[20] sets forth a very basic principle of Jewish labor law: all work agreements are considered to be according to established custom unless otherwise stipulated:

> When workers are hired, the employer cannot compel them to come earlier or stay later than local custom. If the custom is to feed them, he must feed them; [if it is] to give them condiments, he must give them condiments. Everything is according to local custom.

So, for instance, the boss cannot come in one day when you have already started work and tell you that from now on there is no lunch. But he is allowed to announce a change in pay and conditions as part of a new contract when the currently operative one ends. If you have no contract, there may be local laws or customs providing that notice must be given before discharging an employee or changing the conditions of work.

At any rate, in most cases the employer would be entitled to announce a change in working conditions on relatively short notice. An employee who is dissatisfied is entitled to consider himself fired, but not to help himself to the perquisites he previously enjoyed.

It may be that the most equitable solution would be for the employer to allow employees to buy meals at a reduced rate, perhaps even slightly subsidized. This will help solve the workers' problem of what to eat for lunch, at the same time that it protects the employer from having workers eat him out of house and home. Maybe you could suggest this to your new boss.

We can obtain a fascinating insight into your situation from the continuation of the above passage from tractate Bava Metzia:

> Rabbi Yohanan ben Matya once told his son to hire some day laborers. He [the son] went and stipulated that they would get a meal. When he came back, his father told him, "My son, even if you give them a meal fit for King Solomon in his greatness, you will not have fulfilled your condition, for they are the sons of Abraham, Isaac, and Jacob. Before they start, tell them that they will receive only bread and beans."

Since local custom already guaranteed the workers a basic meal, the additional stipulation could have been interpreted as promising a truly sumptuous meal. We recognize that free human beings naturally deserve the finest fare, such as a deli meal. But we also have to face up to economic reality and make clear to the workers that, despite our best wishes, we cannot always provide conditions fit for a king.

Hard Work: Demanding or Demeaning?

HOW HARD CAN I DRIVE MY WORKERS?

Overwork has always been a central concern of business ethics. But in today's workplace this issue has a new spin. In the past, the concern was that the lowly laborer was being exploited by the business owner, but today it is the managers who are most often asked to put superhuman effort into their work.

A challenging environment, whether for managers or workers, is not inherently bad. Any successful business has to make demands on its employees, and many employees thrive in demanding workplaces because they are able to maximize their performance and obtain compensation commensurate with their abilities. The fact remains, however, that a workplace may become inhumane, and a demanding boss may turn into a slave-driver. Jewish law gives some innovative insights into what makes for a humane workplace: it is not enough to focus on the demands placed on the worker; we must also take into account the motivation for the demands.

Q My business is in an extremely competitive industry. Is there anything wrong with demanding long hours and hard work from my employees?

A Hard work is in itself an admirable trait. It is true that the decree to the first man, "By the sweat of your brow shall you eat bread," is presented as a curse, but the sages of the Talmud[21] explain that it also contains a blessing:

> Rabbi Yehoshua ben Levi said, When the Holy One, blessed be He, said to Adam, "Thorns and nettles shall it [the earth] bring forth,"[22] his eyes flowed with tears. He said to Him, "Master of the universe, will I eat from the same trough as my donkey?" But when He said to him, "By the sweat of your brow shall you eat bread,"[23] he was consoled.

Untamed nature is hostile to man and reduces him to a beast, eating the same food as a donkey. But man has the ability to perform directed work that refines and improves nature. Through hard physical work as well as intellectual labor (thus "the sweat of your brow"), complex human cultivation and processing of wheat makes it into bread. Our lifestyle based on the highly developed products of human labor distinguishes us from the beasts.

We see, too, that Jacob was proud of the dedicated service he gave his father-in-law, telling his wives, "I served your father with all my might."[24]

But we must admit that this fine trait can be overdone. The Torah is concerned that man may be reduced to a mere working machine. To this end, the Ten Commandments specifically gives the Sabbath day as a day of rest for everyone–ourselves, our animals, and our servants.[25] The Torah further tells us that we are not to give our servants "crushing work,"[26] and this ethical principle applies to ordinary workers as well.[27]

Where do we draw the line between admirable and excessive work? According to Jewish law, this distinction is not based primarily on how much exertion is involved. The *nature* of the work is just as important. In particular, we have to be careful not to assign work that is gratuitous or demeaning.

GRATUITOUS LABOR

Rashi's commentary on the Torah explains that the definition of crushing work is "work which is unnecessary, in order to dominate him. [For instance,] Don't tell him, 'Warm this cup', when you do not need it." It goes without saying that open busy-work (demanding unneeded tasks) is demeaning, but Rashi goes on to explain that it is improper even when the servant does not know the work is unnecessary.

The average employer probably does not need to be told that giving busy-work is not the best way to show respect to employees, but many modern workplaces, especially the 24/7 variety, exhibit various kinds of hidden busy-work. These can violate the spirit of Jewish law and also can be counterproductive. This kind of overtime can encourages employees to take "undertime." This is the term coined by Tara Parker-Pope of the

Wall Street Journal for all of the tricks employees use to pretend they are on the job when they're really taking care of personal affairs.

For example, in large corporations in one country, it used to be the custom that in the early evening the managers would all leave the office. But they didn't head home to their families; instead they went together to a local bar. And woe betide any aspiring manager who dared skip this nightly ritual! It goes without saying that not much work was accomplished on these jaunts, but an employee who did not participate was nearly sure to be passed over for advancement.

While this is an extreme example, employers in high-pressure workplaces would do well to review the demands they make on their workers. Most of what the workers do is probably needed, and it's certainly legitimate to cultivate a professional and collegial atmosphere. For instance, face time, dress codes, and occasional company social gatherings are certainly not gratuitous.

But if there is an ongoing pattern of norms that exist only to display assiduousness, then there is a good chance that you are imposing "crushing work" on your employees. An example would be if employees are ashamed to be the first to leave the office, even if they have finished their work satisfactorily.

Human beings naturally have a limited ability for effective work. Anyone can stay in the office for twenty-four hours, but few can accomplish more than ten or twelve hours of genuinely productive activity. So if the employer is careful not to demand gratuitous sacrifices from employees, the other aspects of a balanced workplace, including providing adequate opportunities for family life and personal development, will often take care of themselves.

INTRUSIVE DEMANDS

Many managers today do not really work very hard. They're usually no more than ten hours a day in the office, and they're home by seven-thirty, or at the latest eight. Of course, sometimes, they have to make one or two phone calls in the evening, but that's not a major demand. Of course, they can enjoy a leisurely game of golf on Sunday (with a client); but is it really such a burden to glance at your e-mail on your personal digital assistant between holes? That's dead time anyway.

The result of all of these demands is that while the actual amount of work is no more than fifty or sixty hours a week, the employee is effectively on call for twenty-four hours a day.

Jewish law and tradition strongly emphasize the need to have part of the week, and part of each day, which are completely inviolable. Each week has Shabbat, when we are not allowed to do work or even talk about it. The prophet Isaiah tells us that we will be worthy of delighting in God's blessing if we observe the Sabbath appropriately: "If you turn away due to the Sabbath from doing your business on My holy day, and you call the Sabbath a delight, and honor what is holy to the LORD; to dignify it by refraining from your customary ways, pursuing your business and speaking of it." It is not enough to avoid actual work; one day a week we need to refrain completely from all business pursuits and speech.

And each day needs to have fixed times set aside for prayer and study, when no other considerations are allowed to intrude. The Shulhan Arukh states, "A person should establish a time for study, and this time should be rigid, so that he will not miss it even if he thinks he can make a great profit."[28]

We find in Jewish law that an indentured servant is exempt from most positive time-bound commandments. He does not have to sit in the sukkah, for instance, even if he has the time to do so.[29] The condition of servitude is intimately bound up with the idea that your time is not your own; it belongs to the master. An employer should take steps to make sure that his employees are not reduced to slaves, with no time to call their own. The workplace routine should ensure that each employee has a reasonable amount of time each day and each week that is completely free of workday intrusions.

Disciplining Workers

CAN I MAKE A WORKER COMPENSATE ME FOR HIS CARELESSNESS?

The easiest part of ethics is to know what to do in the first place. The more difficult part is knowing what to do when someone has been negligently remiss. Employees are supposed to work diligently, but it is only natural that they are sometimes careless. Jewish tradition can help us decide how to divide the cost between employer and employee.

Q I have just discovered that an employee recorded transactions in a careless way. Can I make him go back and do the work properly on his own time? He claims that I have no right to ask him to work without pay.

A It's easy to understand your frustration. A manager expects his workers to be careful and assiduous. Jewish law, as codified in the Shulhan Arukh,[30] states that employees have a responsibility to work to the best of their ability:

> The worker is warned not to idle a little here and a little there, but to be conscientious about time. ...He should also work with all his strength, for the righteous Jacob said, "I have worked for your father with all my strength."[31] Therefore he received a reward in both this world and the next.

And the employer has every right to dismiss a worker who under-performs after being given a reasonable opportunity to meet company standards.[32]

But it's a long way from your right to let the worker go, to having the right to compel him to work without pay.

An employee who causes actual damage to your firm can be compelled to either repair the damage or pay for it, just as a non-employee can. Employees may also have additional responsibilities, especially if they are specifically charged with responsibility for company property or are given authority to represent the firm.[33] But practically speaking, Jewish law discourages the practice of imposing sanctions on workers for damage caused by normal carelessness. The Talmud tells us that the scholar Rabbah bar Bar Hana hired porters to move some wine barrels. Due to carelessness as well as the difficulty of the task, one of the barrels broke. Rabbah bar Bar Hana seized their coats as collateral and sued them for the value of the barrel. The porters complained to Rav, the supreme rabbinical authority at that time. Rav told Rabbah bar Bar Hana that while technically he might have the right to damages, the fair and equitable thing to do was to withdraw his claim and even to pay the poor workers the wage which they so desperately needed.[34]

In your situation there is an additional consideration. Doing careless paperwork is not the same as causing damage. You are no worse off than if the work had not been done at all. Given that the employee was at the workplace busy with his tasks, you cannot even dock his pay. The only thing you can do is decide not to keep him on.

It may seem unfair to ask you to pay for work that was never done, but remember that an employee is not like a contractor. A contractor is hired to get a specific job done; an employee is hired to carry out orders to the best of his ability. It just is not fair to the worker to impose such a heavy responsibility on him.

An additional problem with sanctions is that very often they are a way to make the worker pay for mistakes really caused by managerial shortcomings. Where were you, the manager, all the months that these transactions were improperly recorded? An employee is not just a machine that you can wind up and let go; he needs appropriate guidance, encouragement, and supervision.

If the nature of your business dictates a need to impose monetary sanctions for worker carelessness, then you will have to carefully craft a compensation system that will achieve this goal. For example, you can compensate workers with a base salary and a bonus, where it is understood that the bonus is paid only for exemplary work, and egregious errors will lead to deductions. But the average salaried worker should not have to pay out of his own pocket, or his own private hours, for work of inferior quality as long as he was present during his scheduled work time and busy with his assigned tasks.

The Talmud offers the following ironic advice: "Someone who has inherited a lot of money and wants to lose it...should hire workers without supervising them."[35] The employer has to acknowledge his own share of responsibility for losses caused by a worker who worked without adequate oversight.

Poaching Workers

CAN I HIRE AN EMPLOYEE AWAY FROM MY CLEANING
SERVICE?

Workers certainly do not belong to their employers, but there are bonds
of commitment and loyalty. Jewish law provides valuable insights into
the appropriate extent of such bonds.

Q I am disappointed with many aspects of the cleaning service I've
been using, but I am very satisfied with the young woman who
has been coming to clean. Can I just cut out the middleman and hire
her directly?

A The issue of poaching workers is an ancient one, which is extensively
discussed in Jewish law and tradition. The Jewish approach to this
question displays concern for all three parties involved: the poaching
employer, the worker, and the current employer.

In any business relationship, Jewish law shows its concern for fairness and stability by placing ethical limitations on those who want to
alter the status quo. If two sides have begun good-faith negotiations,
fairness demands that we ask ourselves two questions before trying to
lure one of them away: (1) How difficult would it be for the other side
to find a replacement? (2) How difficult would it be for me to find
someone else?[36] The same principles apply to an ongoing employment
relationship as long as there is no long-term agreement. (Encouraging
someone to breach a contract is a much more serious matter.)

In our case, we ask first of all, how difficult would it be for the cleaning service to find another worker? And second, how difficult would it
be for me to find another suitable cleaner?

At one extreme, we may imagine a situation where you could easily find some other worker, the original employer would have difficulty
replacing her, and the worker is not significantly better off in your employ. In this case poaching would cause significant harm to the service
with only minimal benefit for yourself and the worker. Hiring away the
worker in this case displays a lack of thoughtfulness.

At the other extreme is the case where the worker is vital for your needs, whereas the current employer can easily find a replacement. In this case, your benefit is at least as great as that of the current employer, and there is no reason not to offer the worker a choice. For this reason, Jewish law holds that it is not unethical to hire away a worker from a competitor if the worker has unique qualities that you require – even if your competitor also appreciates these qualities.

In your case, it sounds as if you have had trouble finding someone suitable to clean your apartment. If you think the cleaning service can find other workers without difficulty, then these basic conditions would allow you to offer her a job.

And finally, we must add an important caveat. Sometimes there are legal, contractual, or customary limitations on such "temp to perm" arrangements. Very often, for example, the temporary employer (you) has to pay a placement fee or provide some advance notice to the agency before taking on a temp on a permanent basis. These arrangements are justified because the employer makes significant investment in the worker. There are training costs, screening, obtaining permits, even advertising costs. The cleaner found a job in your home partially through these efforts on the part of the employer; it's not really fair to take a free ride on this expense. The employer deserves a grace period during which he can recoup his investment, or perhaps a fee to compensate for it.

Sometimes the contract forbids the worker to take private jobs as long as he or she remains with the agency. (Among other things, this prevents "skimming"–accepting the best customers privately and booking the worst ones through the agency.) Make sure your hiring arrangement does not fall afoul of any law or any agreements that you and the worker have made with the agency.

Because these situations are remarkably common, agencies and services should clearly spell out their policy on these matters. If you don't want your workers and customers to take a free ride on your expenses, spell out your expectations in a contract. In my opinion a placement fee is the fairest arrangement since it protects the employer without limiting the freedom of the worker, but the most important thing is not which specific arrangement you choose but rather that expectations are clearly expressed.

Exorbitant Execs

DO SENIOR EXECUTIVES REALLY DESERVE EXORBITANT
SALARIES?

Many studies show that in the last decade the compensation of the highest executives has soared to levels many times what used to be commonplace, even as worker salaries have stagnated. At the same time, executive performance does not seem to have improved. Behind the instinctive reaction of ethical indignation, we should recognize that there are actually a number of distinct ethical issues involved here: Is lavish compensation ethical in and of itself? Is the compensation *process* fair? And what is the proper relationship between executive and worker salaries? In the following discussion we will try to unravel the various strands of this divisive ethical challenge.

Q Is it ethical for top executives to be getting the eight-figure salaries that have become commonplace?

A The public recoils from stratospheric salaries for senior executives for a number of reasons, some more justified than others.

We should be cautious of condemning these salaries simply because of their magnitude. Begrudging others their good fortune is not ethics; it is just small-mindedness. Such an attitude is foreign to our tradition. The Mishnah states: "Anyone who has these three qualities is a student of our father Abraham...a benevolent eye, a modest spirit, and a humble bearing."[37] The Mishnah goes on to say by contrast that a grudging attitude characterizes the followers of the wicked Balaam, whose unenviable livelihood was earned by cursing others.[38]

The Book of Proverbs[39] says, "Do not deny a benefit from one to whom it is due." The Talmud says that this admonition applies to an overly zealous agent who saves his employer's money by scrimping on workers' pay when he is fully authorized to give them more.[40] This should teach us that if the shareholders are satisfied with the managers' performance and are satisfied to pay them generously, then it is small-minded to object on the grounds that the sums may be immodest.

The real question is not whether executive salaries are outrageous per se, but whether they are fair compensation for the services provided. What is a "fair" price for top executive talent? Three criteria will help us judge: performance, consent, and equity. Performance: Is the work these individuals do really worth such large sums? Consent: Do the shareholders genuinely consent to the salary program, or is it the result of management's power to evade and deceive them? And equity: Is it equitable for a few employees to be earning tens of millions of dollars when the average employee is struggling to make ends meet?

PERFORMANCE

It is beyond question that highly gifted managers can make immense contributions to company value. News of the arrival or departure of a CEO is sometimes accompanied by stock movements indicating that markets value his contribution in the hundreds of millions of dollars. In other words, there may be a reasonable justification for high salaries, and the shareholders may not object to paying them. We may recall the indignation over the run-up in athletes' pay a generation ago. At first the public was scandalized by the gigantic salaries demanded by top stars, but eventually the players convinced the fans that, after all, it is their efforts and talents which create value in the sports business.

At the same time, studies tend to confirm investor instinct: today's managers seem to perform no better than those of a generation ago who earned only a small fraction of current salaries. Each case needs to be examined in isolation, but on the whole investors feel justified in asking highly paid business leaders, "Where's the beef?"

CONSENT

The consent issue arises because managers often set their own pay scales. Technically, the board of directors may be responsible for supervising the compensation of top executives. But practically speaking, the directors often defer these decisions to the executives, because of time constraints or because of their own dependence on management. (In some countries, particularly the United States, it is common for the CEO, who is the top manager, to function also as chairman of the board, thus making him responsible for overseeing his own performance!)

This situation creates an obvious conflict of interest. As a loyal *employee*, the manager is responsible for keeping salaries at a reasonable level. But the manager's *personal* objective is to obtain a very high salary. There does not seem to be a very effective firewall between these two functions. In a great many cases, it is hard to believe that the managers would agree to pay other, comparably qualified candidates the same extravagant amounts they pay themselves.

Sometimes managers add insult to injury by taking time away from their managerial responsibilities in order to craft increasingly lucrative and underhanded compensation schemes for themselves. Not only are executives hoodwinking shareholders, they are doing so at shareholder expense! A compensation package in a public company cannot be ethical if it lacks adequate transparency.

Jewish law states that if an agent exceeds his authority and offers to pay workers more than the going rate, the employer is not obligated to pay the inflated salary, and the agent himself must bear the loss.[41] The application to executive salaries is clear. Since managers are the agents of the stockholders, they may pay themselves only a salary commensurate with their level of ability. Any salary agreement beyond this is illegitimate.

EQUITY

The equity issue arises because the manager is also a worker, and an equitable policy toward workers means that there should be some kind of rationality in the relative pay scales. While a gifted manager does add immense value to the firm, he or she doesn't do it alone. Workers at every level contribute to this value. As mentioned above, market value is greatly influenced by turnovers in top management. But a massive turnover of lower-level workers would probably have an even greater impact on value. Executive pay scales need to reflect the manager's contribution, but the same criterion applies to other employees as well! Many prominent executive pay schemes defy every reasonable measure of rationality.

An ethical compensation package is one that gives due recognition to the special contribution of executives without allowing them to take unfair advantage of their positions. We can benefit from the example of the Garmu family, which had a unique secret for making the show-bread in the Holy Temple. The Talmud[42] tells us that they were able to negotiate a very high pay level for themselves because of their special knowledge; this shows that Jewish tradition does not condemn tenacious negotiations to realize our full value. But the Talmud also tells us that despite their lavish salaries, the members of the Garmu family never ate white bread, so that they would never be suspected of obtaining unjustified benefit from their position.

It is ethical for managers to get a competitive return for their unique talents. However, when they have a say in determining their own compensation, they are obligated to evaluate impartially the value they bring to the company and its relation to the contributions of others – just as they would evaluate salary offers for hiring some other individual with a similar background.

Referrals and Letters of Reference

CAN I BE FRANK IN A LETTER OF REFERENCE?

When called upon to give a reference, we want to be helpful to the prospective employer without maligning the former employee. Everyone benefits when prospective employers have access to adequate information about new hires, including references from previous employers. Even so, we need to exercise great care in providing this information so as not to be unfair to the employee. Jewish law gives very explicit and useful guidelines to help us through this moral minefield.

Q I was just asked to give a reference for a former employee. I want to give the prospective employer as much information as possible, but I don't wish to bad-mouth my former hire.

A The tension you describe is very real for employers, and for this reason many consider giving references a nightmare. Supervisors frequently evade the issue by writing perfunctory letters that only give verifiable data, but if we delve into Jewish tradition we will find that it is possible to fulfill our obligations to both the job seeker and the prospective employer.

A degree of frankness in referrals is ethically appropriate, because accurate information is an immeasurable aid to the prospective employer. An inappropriate hire is frustrating for employer and employee alike. There may even be a third victim: another, more suitable applicant who was not hired and remains out of a job.

Yet there is a significant danger that the information you provide may be improper, or may be improperly used. The ethical responsibility to avoid slander is a primary concern.

The Torah emphasizes the need to balance our ethical obligations to the recipient and to the subject of negative information by mentioning the two considerations in a single verse: "Do not go about as a talebearer among your people, and do not stand idly by the blood of your fellow man; I am the LORD."[43]

The first half of the verse warns us against slander, but the continuation of the verse tells us not to stand idly when we have the ability to come to the aid of our fellow man. The final expression, "I am the LORD," reassures us that we have the God-given ability to fulfill both obligations in a responsible way.

Sefer ha-Hinnukh, an important medieval commentary on the commandments, explains:

> We are forbidden to gossip, as it is written, "Do not go about as a talebearer."[44] This means that if we hear someone say something negative about his fellow, we should not tell the victim that "So-and-so said such a thing" unless our intention is to prevent harm and avoid a dispute.

Here we see that what is forbidden is gratuitous slander, but if we have appropriate intentions and exercise due prudence, disclosure is proper and may be an obligation.

The Sefer ha-Hinnukh continues: "We may not avoid saving our fellow Jew when we see that he is in danger of death or loss, if we have the ability to save him in some way." This verse, with its legal interpretation, gives us two complementary principles regarding the spreading of negative information:

- "First do no harm": we must first of all be careful not to arbitrarily spread damaging information, even when it is true.

- Subject to this restriction, we should reveal information when it will help protect someone else from harm.

These guidelines are an excellent start, but it is necessary to elaborate the specific criteria that will enable us to stick to them. A renowned and saintly scholar, Rabbi Yisrael Meir ha-Kohen, devoted meticulous and painstaking effort to elucidating the exact criteria for disclosure. He came up with a list of practical rules set down in his classic work Hafetz Hayyim.[45] As an aid to memory, we have arranged these rules in an alphabetical list.

- *Accuracy.* It is forbidden to exaggerate or embellish.

- *Benefit.* Revealing information must be the only way to obtain some constructive benefit.

- *Certainty.* We must be sure the information is reliable.

- *Desire.* The informant's intention must be constructive, not vindictive.

- *Equity.* Revealing the information must not cause undeserved harm to the subject. It is not equitable to protect one person at the expense of another.

It is amazing how valuable these five rules are. They are adequate in virtually any situation where we are considering passing along damaging information.

Let's see how the five conditions of the Hafetz Hayyim apply to letters of reference.

- *Accuracy.* A letter of reference is not a literary creation, and colorful language is out of place. For example, if a person has a brusque, overly businesslike manner with clients, it may be justified to reveal this, but do not use words like "rude" or "offensive."

- *Benefit.* This is probably the trickiest area. If we have information that can protect someone from harm, careful thought and some creativity are required to see whether the harm could be avoided without disclosure.

  For example, suppose you think the applicant might be unable to stand up to the pressure in a high-stress workplace. Putting your reservations in writing could be very damaging. It might be better to be less specific: "This individual is an excellent worker, but could have problems adapting to your work environment."

  Often the best solution is to turn directly to the applicant.

Explain why you think this particular vacancy might be a mismatch. The applicant may solve the problem by persuading you that you are mistaken or by withdrawing the application; if not, you can ask his permission to be frank since your reference may be critical. In this way slander is avoided, and learning and growth have taken place.

- *Certainty.* An employer may develop suspicions about an employee over the course of time. These may even play a role in the individual's termination. But as long as they are not verified, they should not be transmitted to anyone else.

- *Desire.* Your employee's negative traits may have caused a reservoir of resentment. Don't look on your reference as an opportunity to open up the floodgates of this reservoir. Be businesslike and focus on the needs of the prospective employer. Vindictive motives in this area are a common pitfall.

- *Equity.* Even if you feel that the information you intend to transmit is reliable, precise, helpful, and necessary, do not give it to the prospective employer until you have considered any ways in which it could cause unjustified harm.

  For example, perhaps the applicant has a disability. While the prospective employer would certainly be interested in knowing this, you never know where the information may go once you have put it in writing. The recipient of the letter may use the information in an unjustified way; for example, a prospective employer who is honest and equitable may pass the information along to another party who is not so scrupulous. It is justified for the prospective employer to know this, but it is inequitable for this information to get passed along.

Another case of unjustified harm is where revealing information about one individual will have negative repercussions on someone else.

What is the solution? You may be able to give a verbal explanation where your evaluation is transmitted by your tone of voice and not your words, so that the recipient will be able to make inferences but will be unlikely to transmit them to others. Or you may have to decide that however much you would like to help the prospective employer, you cannot do so without risking undeserved harm to the subject.

It goes without saying that you should never give references unless you can verify that the individual or firm asking for them is a bona fide potential employer. Posing as a prospective employer is one way unscrupulous individuals acquire information they should not have. For example, the recipient could be a creditor, a litigant, or a personal enemy who would use the information for a damaging and inappropriate purpose.

Because of the many cases where reference letters have been abused, by the former or new employer, most large firms today have strict standards about what kind of information may be included in these letters and how they may be used. Having equitable and transparent standards is the best solution, because then all parties concerned know exactly what to expect. The criteria we have mentioned can serve as an excellent basis for such a policy.

ENDNOTES

1. Genesis 3:19
2. Maimonides, Sekhirut 13:7
3. Deuteronomy 24:15
4. Leviticus 25:43
5. Sefer ha-Hinnukh 346.
6. Bava Metzia 29b
7. Chullin 105a
8. Leviticus 19:16
9. Responsa Halakhot Ketanot 1:276
10. Hafetz Hayyim 1:4:11 in note
11. Bava Batra 8b, Shulhan Arukh, Hoshen Mishpat 231:28
12. Bava Metzia 109a
13. Leviticus 19:17
14. Leviticus 19:17
15. Ketubbot 79b
16. Shulhan Arukh, Hoshen Mishpat 333
17. Genesis 31:20
18. Deuteronomy 23:25
19. See Responsa Havvot Yair 224
20. Bava Metzia 7:1
21. Pesahim 118a

22. Genesis 3:18
23. Genesis 3:19
24. Genesis 31:6
25. Deuteronomy 5:14
26. Leviticus 25:43
27. Sefer ha-Hinnukh 346
28. Shulhan Arukh, Orah Hayyim 155
29. Maimonides, Shofar 6:1
30. Shulhan Arukh, Hoshen Mishpat 337:20
31. Genesis 30:43
32. Shulhan Arukh, Hoshen Mishpat 306:8
33. Bava Metzia 73b and commentaries; Pithei Hoshen, Pikadon 12:14–15
34. Bava Metzia 83a
35. Bava Metzia 29b
36. Shulhan Arukh, Hoshen Mishpat 237:2
37. Avot 5:19
38. Numbers 22
39. Proverbs 3:27
40. Bava Metzia 76a
41. Shulhan Arukh, Hoshen Mishpat 333
42. Yoma 38a
43. Leviticus 19:16
44. Leviticus 19:16
45. Hafetz Hayyim Sec. 11, chap. 9:2

JEWISH
INTERNET ETHICS

Introduction

As an Internet column launched in the days of the Internet revolution, it is only natural that the Jewish Ethicist has responded to a number of questions on Internet ethics. Readers have asked about the ethical use of chat rooms, e-mail, file-swapping, and other commonplaces of cyberspace that were unimagined only a few short years ago.

Fundamentally, all the ethical questions of the Internet have parallels in the ordinary "bricks and mortar" world. Yet reviewing the many questions, one characteristic emerges as the special ethical challenge of the Internet: anonymity.

The highest level of human interaction is the face-to-face encounter, and when this degree of rapport is created, the sense of empathy and the ethical motivation are highest. When we look into the face of a fellow human being, we sense the common human element we share and recognize ourselves, as if looking in a mirror. "As the reflection in the water is to the face, so is the heart of man to man."[1] Empathy opens our hearts and makes them as one.

As the Torah tells us, Esau was determined to take vengeance on Jacob, but he relented when the anonymous meeting of armed camps turned into a face-to-face meeting of the twin brothers; at that moment Esau ran toward his brother and hugged and kissed him.[2] Similarly, Joseph was unable to keep up his carefully planned act of haughty aloofness with his brothers after several face-to-face meetings; his emotions overcame him and he revealed himself to them.[3]

As the individual element of communication is diminished, so is the psychic connection between individuals. This idea has entered common discourse in the expression a "bare-faced lie." The highest level of insolence is to lie to someone to their face; when the face is hidden, our ethical scruples tend to be diminished.

Once other people become depersonalized in our minds, we lose sight of our ethical obligations to them. In a face-to-face encounter, we actually see the person; if we talk from room to room, we at least hear their voice. A telephone conversation is held over a distance, but at any rate we hear the voice's reproduction in real time; even a letter bears the sender's personal imprint through his or her unique handwriting. In traditional communication, "the medium is the message"–the tokens of individuality are an inherent part of the encounter.

But the Internet strips our communications of all personal embellishments apart from the actual words of the sender. The factors of distance and anonymity increase the opportunity as well as the temptation for deceit.

This anonymity plays some role in all of the Internet questions. Two questions pertain to using false identities, which is much easier in the chat rooms of cyberspace than in the physical world. Another relates to sending copies of e-mails without obtaining the permission of their authors and primary recipients or informing them that there are now many other readers peeking into the correspondence–a further exploitation of the Internet's potential for creating anonymity. Others pertain to the great anonymous ease with which we can copy material protected by copyright or snoop on our employees.

The key to Internet ethics is to remember that there is a real, live human being at the other end of the connection, a person with feelings and rights. We need to be sensitive to the feelings and expectations of other chat room members, of e-mail recipients, of artists, and of employees.

The ultimate face-to-face encounter is with the Creator. Judaism's sources on ethics tell us that when we live up to the ethical challenges we face, we can, in a certain sense, "look God in the face" without being ashamed of our behavior. The prophet Isaiah tells us that at the time of the future redemption, when all our human relations will be repaired, we will see God "eye to eye."[4] If we conduct ourselves in the anonymity of cyberspace just as we would in a personal encounter with a fellow human being, then we will be worthy of the divine glance and of God's special providence.

Chat Room Charades

CAN I RECOMMEND MY COMPANY'S PRODUCT IN A CHAT ROOM?

It is a basic principle of business ethics that salespeople may not lie about their products. But Jewish tradition can make us sensitive to other, more subtle ways in which we may be misleading a customer.

Q Companies sometimes advertise their products by paying someone to enter an Internet chat room under a false name and praise the product as if he or she were an ordinary customer. The representatives view this as a service to the consumer. Is this an acceptable practice?

A The Torah tells us, "Distance yourself from any lie."⁵ Wouldn't it be enough to just command, "Thou shalt not lie"? Perhaps because it's so easy to deceive *without* telling an outright lie that a simple prohibition on lying is not enough. Therefore the Torah warns us to distance ourselves from falsehood of any kind.

In the case mentioned in the question, it may seem as if no one is lying. Using a fake name is a common practice in chat rooms and certainly does not fool anybody. And the recommendations being made are sincere. The words are true–but the message is a lie.

By using this strategy, the company is trying to communicate the notion that satisfied customers all over cyberspace are buzzing about their product. If the salespeople were to say this outright, they would certainly be lying; "telling" people the same thing through an elaborate charade only adds insult to injury by wasting people's time–and bandwidth–with bogus endorsements.

The Torah forbids us to "put a stumbling block before the blind."⁶ This includes misleading anyone who is blind to what is really happening. The sages give an example almost identical to the situation you describe. In his commentary on this verse, Rashi says, "Do not advise someone that it is in his interest to sell his field in order to buy a donkey, when your real intention is to buy the field from him." Here, too, the person is giving advice, perhaps even sincere advice, but his counsel is misleading because he hides his own interest in the outcome.

In addition to being unethical, this practice is unprofessional. The code of ethics of the American Marketing Association, to take just one example, requires "avoidance of sales promotions that use deception or manipulation." Many chat rooms also have their own by-laws regarding commercial promotions, and participants must observe these.

The problem here is not sincerity but transparency. Since the identical endorsement will have vastly different meanings for the consumer depending on whether it comes from a disinterested fellow consumer or from an incentivized salesperson, hiding the personal stake in the outcome is definitely a form of deceit.

Aside from the business ethics issue, there is also a problem here of personal ethics. You present yourself to this online community as someone who is interested in forming a human connection with other members, yet your real interest is commercial. This is an unfair exploitation of the norms of these communities.

Commerce is a positive area of human endeavor. Not only does it provide us with goods and services, it also stimulates human relations, because we need to reach out to others to meet our needs. The marketplace is also a meeting place, and in cyberspace as well people enjoy the fellowship of chat rooms and newsgroups. Jewish tradition explains that our material desires have an important role to play in encouraging us to form human connections. But we should never put the cart before the horse and make profits the end and human relationships only a means.

It is wonderful to exploit selling in order to generate friendships, but it is shameful to exploit friendships in order to generate sales.

Chat Room Charades II: Internet Fantasy

SHOULD YOUNGSTERS ADOPT FANTASY "CYBERSELVES"
FOR ONLINE CHAT?

As we pointed out in the introduction to this chapter, the most salient ethical characteristic of the Internet is its extreme anonymity. When we enter the world of cyberspace, we can hide our true identity and assume a new cyberself of our own choosing. These fantasies seem innocent enough, but it's worth asking if they are really healthy for our individual development.

Q Some of my friends love to prowl Internet chat rooms using fabricated identities. Their Internet identity may change their age, gender, and background. Is there any ethical problem with this?

A Making up a fantasy identity for the Internet sounds very innocent, and many times it is. However, this practice can sometimes involve two kinds of ethical challenges. In some circumstances such a fake identity may unfairly harm others; just as seriously, sometimes we may be hurting ourselves.

In the previous column, we pointed out that joining a chat room or other online group should be done with sincere intentions to be a good citizen of the on-line community. You should not pass yourself off as a fellow hi-fi buff if your true intention is to hawk a particular brand of speakers. Occasionally, the same problem can arise in a personal context. It would certainly be improper to participate in a dating forum, for example, if there is no genuine interest (How would you feel if you discovered that that charming, athletic thirty-ish bachelor was really a sixty-year-old granny in disguise? Or vice versa?)

The Torah includes many commandments teaching us to adhere to our unique identity. For instance, the Torah warns women not to wear men's clothing and vice versa,[7] and it tells the Jewish people not to adopt the customs of the surrounding nations.[8] Even if there is nothing inherently improper about other people's customs, they need to be avoided if they will cause us to forget who we are.

What is true of a nation is also true of the individual. These commandments convey a universal educational message: each of use should be secure in our own identity and not be carried away by efforts to escape it.

Of course, this does not mean that we should not experiment within our identities. Our identities are not simply given to us; we have to shape them. But we shape them within certain God-given restraints, including age and gender.

This idea can be explained by a simple analogy. Teenagers often decide to adopt a distinctive signature. They spend hours experimenting with different options: Script or print, large or small, initials or full name, florid or stark, and so on–the possibilities are endless. Yet one characteristic unites all of these efforts: they are all the person's own name. This exercise is a normal and healthy part of growing up.

But it would be surprising, and dismaying, to find a teenager experimenting with a variety of different names, especially names completely inappropriate to the youngster's background.

When the Torah tells us to love our fellow man, it uses a very precise expression: "Love your neighbor as yourself."[9] In order to love and respect others, we have to know how to love and respect ourselves. If you become absorbed in an alternative identity on the Internet, you are probably not guilty of fooling anyone else. But you may be guilty of fooling yourself, and if so, you are your own worst victim.

E-mail Ethics

IS IT ETHICAL TO SEND HIDDEN COPIES OF E-MAIL?

Good etiquette requires a delicate balance between openness and discretion, and Internet etiquette is no exception. The sending of hidden copies of e-mails is a good illustration of the problem.

Q Is it unethical to send a "BCC" of an e-mail? I'm worried that this could be deceptive.

A While the ethics and etiquette of e-mail are still evolving, the basic principles of thoughtful behavior are always applicable.

For those unacquainted to e-mail, "BCC" stands for "blind carbon copy." Once upon a time, copies of correspondence were made by putting two or three sheets of paper in the typewriter with a sheet or two of carbon paper sandwiched in between. Usually the writer added a "CC to" list at the end of the letter, indicating that carbon copies were being sent to other people. But occasionally a "blind" carbon copy was made and the recipient was not informed. Today, our e-mail programs do the same thing by sending a copy of an electronic letter to the BCC recipient without the knowledge of the original recipient. The e-mail puts this information at the front of the letter; it seems that in our generation form is gaining in importance at the expense of content.

There are many reasons for wanting to keep the additional recipient hidden, some of them good and others not so good.

A not-so-good reason for this is when you conceal the other recipient because you know the addressee would not want the message known. The message you send may reveal some private information about the recipient and the nature of your relationship, and if recipients want this information kept private their wishes should be respected. If you feel you have a very good reason to disclose the information, then at the very least you should inform the recipients that the content is known by making the copy a CC instead of a BCC.

The problem is far worse when the message you send contains a copy of the letter you originally received—the usual case in the world of e-mail. Letters you receive should generally be kept in the strictest confidence, and Jewish law protects them in a variety of ways. Consider that revealing the content of a letter is often a form of gossip; in addition, the ancient decree of Rabbenu Gershom prohibits reading someone else's mail without their permission. (Forwarding of e-mails involves the same problem and should be done judiciously; when appropriate the sender should be informed that the letter is being forwarded.)

However, there are some valid reasons to take advantage of the BCC feature. One good reason to keep someone hidden is to protect his privacy. Using the CC line not only reveals that the letter has been sent to others, it also discloses their identity and their e-mail addresses. This can be ethically problematic, as demonstrated by the following true story:

Not long ago there was a very unfortunate incident in which a man who ran a small-scale meeting service (*shadchan*) wanted to send a message to all his clients. He wrote a message and put each one on the CC list. Being a neophyte in the new-fangled world of e-mail, he probably didn't realize that this would disclose the identities of his customers. Many were embarrassed at having it widely known that they were using a match-making service. Using the BCC would have saved his customers from this discomfort and the business from suffering significant ill will.

In other cases, people do not mind having their identities revealed, but they do not want their e-mail addresses publicized, since this can lead to unwanted mail, which may be annoying, offensive, or even threatening.

Another good reason for using BCC instead of CC is when the letter is being sent to large numbers of people; it can be annoying to wade through a gigantic list of recipients before you get to the letter itself. In this case the olden days were really better, since the CC list was at the end of the letter.

Another possibility is that the CC is being sent to an innocuous individual, but the recipient does not know that the recipient of the copy is trustworthy. Sending an ordinary CC may cause the recipient unnecessary worry that confidence has been breached. For example, on some sites queries sent to the Jewish Ethicist are first received by the host site, which then forwards them to me. When I reply to the questioner, I often send a copy of my answer to the host site as a courtesy, because they are often curious to know how I will respond. This does not breach any confidence, because the host site's representative has already seen the letter. But if the letter had a CC, the recipient would be understandably concerned, because he or she probably does not know that the other recipient is already in the loop. So I generally use a BCC for these replies.

In these cases, it is appropriate to use a BCC rather than a CC. But we may still encounter the problem mentioned above: the recipient may be misled into thinking the communication is private. There are two solutions to this problem.

First, you can mention in the body of the letter that a copy is being sent to someone else. Perhaps in the future I will add to my replies the line "I am sending a copy of this reply to the editor of the host Web site."

An even better solution, when practical, is to avoid the BCC shortcut altogether. Instead of sending an exact copy of the letter with a BCC, prepare a sanitized copy that eliminates any problematic details, and send it as a separate e-mail to someone who needs to know about the correspondence but does not need to know the identity of the correspondent.

Remember that there are many reasons why your recipient might not want details of your correspondence to be known to others. Perhaps the personal details revealed by your letter are unflattering; perhaps they are confidential. Even positive information can have negative consequences if it is, too, widely known. The Book of Proverbs tells us, "When someone blesses his friend in a loud voice early in the morning, it is considered like a curse."[10]

Therefore, you should think carefully before routinely forwarding e-mail or sending copies. At the very least, you should inform the recipient about the disclosure, except when the message is not really private or when the disclosure could cause unjustified worry. Even in these cases there are often better solutions than the BCC, which should be used sparingly.

Copies and Rights

CAN I TRADE SONGS OVER THE NET?

Copying copyrighted music has always involved an ethical question. But in the past the practice caused relatively little harm, since it was only possible to copy tapes from the limited selection available in a friend's collection, and copying entailed a sacrifice of both time and quality. But in the Internet age, it is easier to copy than to buy, there is no loss of quality, and the available selection is virtually unlimited. As a result, there is a much greater temptation for wrongdoing.

Q Is there anything wrong with downloading MP3 songs from the Internet, using anonymous peer-to-peer networks?

A Recorded songs are similar to other public goods like bridges or roads; they cost a lot to create, but once they exist, many people can enjoy them at low cost. In a way it seems unfair to pay a high toll to cross a bridge even though your trip contributes only a tiny amount to the cost of maintaining the bridge; yet we all recognize that the bridge has to be paid for somehow, or no more bridges will be built.

It may seem likewise unfair to demand a large fee to buy or download a song since your copy doesn't cost anything to the copyright owner. But remember that music production is an expensive business, which has to be paid for somehow; otherwise the recording industry won't be able to maintain the scope of music production that we now enjoy.

Just as the government supports bridges and highways by giving builders a concession to collect tolls, so it supports music production by granting a copyright that enables the artist to collect payment from listeners.

While it is not automatically true that what is legal is ethical and what is illegal is unethical, there is a general ethical obligation to be law-abiding. Above and beyond our civic duty to obey the law, Jewish law states that there is a specific religious obligation to uphold any legitimate law that is in the public interest[11]. Interestingly, paying tolls is the primary example cited by the Talmud for the application of this principle.[12] Our sages teach that we should avoid even the appearance of evading such payment.[13] Fostering the conditions that will encourage an adequate supply of valuable public goods is one of government's most important functions, and we should certainly respect laws, such as copyright regulations, that create these conditions.

Copying a song from the Internet is like taking a detour around the toll booth. Even if you don't get a ticket, you've taken an unfair free ride on someone else's efforts.

Internet Privacy

WHAT CUSTOMER INFORMATION CAN WE COLLECT AND SELL?

Collecting and selling information about customers' characteristics and buying habits of customers has become a sensitive and widespread ethical question. Many vendors claim that customers don't mind if they store and use such information, since ultimately the customer benefits from the marketing this information enables. Even if this is true, Jewish tradition can sensitize us to two additional issues. First, perhaps customers *would* mind if they were adequately informed about the uses and value of the information they provide. Second, perhaps customers *should* mind. The very fact that people do not care what others know about them is itself an ethical problem, a symptom of the excessive openness of our society.

Q Our firm collects private information about our customers. For instance, we have the measurements and style preferences of garment purchases. Can we sell this information to other vendors?

A Giving personal information to other vendors does have some advantages for the customer. Such information enables the seller to concentrate his ad budget on consumers who are likely to be interested in his message, so the consumer is presented with more advertisements for products and services that interest him and – theoretically – fewer messages that he finds annoying and irrelevant.

At the same time, the collection of personal information raises immense privacy dilemmas. Most people would shudder at the very thought that neighbors, creditors, competitors, or even distant busybodies might have easy access to all of their buying and browsing habits.

The topic of disclosing private information has two aspects: consent and modesty. Consent means that information should be disclosed only with the full agreement of the subject; modesty dictates that some information should not be made public at all.

INFORMED CONSENT IN DATA SHARING

It is widely accepted that data should not be disclosed without the agreement of the subject, but there are many views regarding how much agreement is needed. Some are satisfied with an "opt-out" policy, in which all information is considered public unless the user explicitly expresses a desire to keep it private; others demand an "opt-in" policy in which service providers may collect information only when explicitly permitted by the user.

Many advocates are concerned that even an opt-in policy may lack adequate consent. Perhaps the consumer does not have enough information about the policy to give truly informed consent, or perhaps there is a degree of coercion because withholding consent has negative consequences, such as limited access to service.

Jewish tradition has a definite viewpoint on the consent issue. Consider the following passage from the Talmud:[14]

> Where can we learn that anytime someone says something to his fellow it is subject to "'Don't say" until the person says "Go ahead and say"? [From the biblical verses where] it is written, "the LORD spoke to him from the tent of meeting to say."[15]

This passage points out that in the Torah, God explicitly tells Moses when His words are to be transmitted to the people. When God does not do so, Moses understands that the prophecy is intended for him alone. From this we learn that in general it is proper to refrain from repeating to others what we have been told unless the speaker explicitly consents.

This source seems to support opt-in over opt-out; information should generally be considered private unless there is explicit consent to disclose.

The issue of *informed* consent is also prominent in Jewish sources. Regarding someone who waives his rights to something without a full understanding of its extent or value, the Talmud states: "A mistaken waiver is no waiver at all."[16] We can extrapolate to the situation of Internet privacy, where the consumer seldom fully appreciates the value of the information he is allowing the collector to use–a value that can easily reach hundreds of dollars.

One major danger to informed consent is the phenomenon of "data mining," sophisticated accumulation and analysis of seemingly innocent data. This practice can be likened to examining someone's rubbish. If someone sees me throw out a soda can, they have learned little about my lifestyle. But if someone were to carefully scrutinize every scrap of garbage that left my home, they would know practically everything about my private affairs. If I give someone permission to rummage through my garbage can for something useful, I do not have in mind that he may prepare a detailed catalogue of every item I discard. Likewise, a person who gives consent to reveal some particular bit of information may not have in mind that this datum will be pooled with vast amounts of other private information.

Thus consent is unlikely to be truly informed and complete unless the subject has adequate knowledge of two facts:

- The approximate value of the information he is giving up.

- The scope of the use he is permitting, including the potential for pooling this information with other data.

We see that the Jewish ethical tradition is quite stringent about the protection of private information and sets a very high standard of consent for valid agreements. While accepted custom does have a certain weight, these principles definitely favor an Internet privacy standard based on opt-in revelation, and require the information collector to provide adequate information about the value of the information being gathered and the full extent of the permitted use.

PRIVACY VS. MODESTY

Up to now we have examined the issue of Internet privacy from the standpoint of informed consent. But Jewish tradition does more than guide us within this conventional approach to the issue of privacy; it helps us to look beyond it. A Torah perspective calls upon us to consider not only formal requirements of privacy and consent, but also social ideals of modesty and discretion.

Here, "privacy" refers to what a person would prefer to keep hidden, and "modesty" to what normatively ought to remain hidden. Jewish tradition affirms that a certain part of our being can flourish only in protected seclusion, and warns against a life lived in the public eye even if a person might be persuaded to consent to such exposure. Forcing someone to reveal intimate details of his or her private life is an invasion of privacy; but a person who readily reveals these details to others is guilty of indiscretion.

Modesty is a paramount value in Jewish tradition. In the Torah, Balaam comments, "How goodly are your tents, O Jacob."[17] Rashi explains that the tents of the Jewish people are goodly because they are carefully arranged so that no one can see into his neighbor's dwelling. And Jewish law asks us to avert our gaze if we see someone engaging in a private activity, even an innocent activity that is not being concealed. Eighteenth-century authority Rav Shneur Zalman of Lyady writes, "Neighbors need to be as careful as possible not to look at one other's activities in their common courtyard."[18]

Modesty is one of the most important foundations of a Torah personality. Modesty means there are some things that we should keep to ourselves or within a small circle of friends. In order to develop a healthy personality, we need a clear demarcation between ourselves and others; we need to know that there are some things that belong only to ourselves, secrets between the individual and the Creator.

One way of expressing the idea of modesty is through modesty in dress; men and women alike are encouraged to avoid clothing that is revealing, provocative, or flaunts the anatomy. The identical principle applies to one's character; Jewish tradition discourages being, too, open with private information. Our sages state, for instance, that a person should not flaunt his achievements; conversely, someone who has a shortcoming should be discreet about that, too.[19]

A related consideration is that scrutiny damages our sense of dignity and restraint. Research studies on prisoners and others who lack privacy confirm this effect. In some cultures penitents are encouraged to "open up" and confess their sins in front of a group, but our tradition discourages this. Thus the Talmudic sage Rava Kahana, citing the verse "Happy is the one whose transgressions are borne and whose sins are covered,"[20] says that it is impudent to enumerate one's sins out loud.[21] (An exception is made for sins against another person, which we need to reveal in order to obtain forgiveness.)[22]

Of course there is a difference between statistical information about a person's purchases and browsing behavior, on the one hand, and gossip about his personal habits, on the other. The sources do not categorically condemn the collection of personal information about Internet usage, especially given the great commercial value of this information. But by impressing on us the human problems inherent in situations of surveillance, they introduce a new and valuable dimension to the discussion. Merchants and consumers alike should ask themselves: Is this disclosure really necessary?

We began by discussing data-sharing from the point of view of consent, focusing on what human beings want. But a Torah perspective reminds us that we must also concern ourselves with who human beings are. The character of the individual and of society as a whole requires the shelter of modesty for its development, and an environment of constant surveillance and information gathering has the potential to undermine this shelter. While Internet information-gathering certainly has commercial value, we must be mindful of its humanistic and spiritual costs.

Spam Jam

CAN I ADVERTISE MY PRODUCT THROUGH MASS MAILING?

Q My firm provides a unique product that could be of interest to many individuals. Someone has offered to make a pitch through a "spam" mailing to millions of individuals. Can we take advantage of this offer?

A In principle, Jewish tradition does not frown on promotion. It is legitimate for a seller to try and make his product known to potential buyers, and to inform them of the benefits of his wares. For example, the Mishnah states that a storeowner is allowed to give free gifts to buyers in order to induce them to come to his store.[23] And our ancient sages, too,k special steps to encourage door-to-door salesmen who sold important products, such as cosmetics, which were not available in stores.[24]

However, we must take care that selling doesn't turn into harassment. We can learn this principle from two laws of commerce that relate to buyers, and apply them to sellers as well.

The Mishnah states that a buyer shouldn't waste the time of a seller by feigning interest in a purchase.[25] This is considered a violation of the Torah prohibition of causing gratuitous torment to others. The seller devotes his energy to the customer believing he is being given a fair chance to make a sale; if in fact the "customer" has no interest, then the seller is being imposed upon. The customer should take the time of the seller only if he has some minimal interest in buying.

By the same token, a seller shouldn't waste the customer's time by an offering when there is no particular basis for thinking that the customer might be interested. There should be some rational basis for assuming that the e-mail (or junk mail) recipients may have some interest in your product or service. Otherwise, you are imposing on the recipient.

There is another, complementary law which provides a complementary insight. One of the Ten Commandments is "Don't covet" what belongs to our neighbor.[26] But we must admit that giving a hard and fast definition of "coveting" is not so easy. Our tradition tells us that the red line is definitely crossed when our desire is so great that we try to convince the owner to sell us a personal possession that he really has no interest in parting with.[27] Such uninvited approaches are again really just a form of harassment.

This law, too, can be extrapolated from buyer to seller. Someone who tries to convince someone to buy a product that he has shown no interest in acquiring is engaging in exactly the same kind of harassment.[28] This is completely different from a salesperson trying to persuade a customer who has intentionally come into the store or who has agreed to listen to a salesperson's pitch.

It's hard to provide a clear definition of when targeted marketing turns into spam. But the two sources from Jewish law can help provide some context. In both cases, the criterion that makes the approach permissible is not a desire to make a deal per se but rather the existence of a basic interest. A customer who has some interest in making a purchase is not wasting the salesperson's time, and a person who has expressed even a possible interest in selling his property may be approached by someone with an interesting offer.

By the same token, a recipient considers an e-mail to be "spam" not because he doesn't want to buy the product but rather because he is not interested in even learning about the product. It's not only a waste of his time to read the message; it's even a waste of time to go to the trouble of deleting it.

Based on this criterion, a mass mailing would be problematic if it is for something that relatively few people are interested in learning about and no efforts are made to target specifically those individuals who would express interest.

It goes without saying that the message should not be misleading, tricking the recipient into reading the message by camouflaging it as a message which is of interest, such as a business or personal communication, winning a contest, etc. This violates the prohibition of "geneivat da'at" or misleading others.

It also goes without saying that the mailing should not violate the law. Very often middlemen of the kind you mention use illegal techniques to evade anti-spam efforts of Internet service providers. For example, they use a false return address. When you use the services of such an agent, Jewish law views you as an accomplice to the crime.

Targeted mailings, when carried out in a legal fashion, are a legitimate selling technique according to the principles of Judaism. But these mailings turn into unethical harassment when no effort is made to target individuals who would be expected to have some interest in learning about your product, or if the message is misleading.

ENDNOTES

1. Proverbs 27:19
2. Genesis 33:4
3. Genesis 45:1–2
4. Isaiah 52:8
5. Exodus 23:7
6. Leviticus 19:14
7. Deuteronomy 22:5
8. Leviticus 18:3
9. Leviticus 19:18
10. Proverbs 27:14
11. Bava Kamma 113a
12. Sukkah 30a
13. Eruvin 53b
14. Yoma 4b
15. Leviticus 1:1
16. Bava Metzia 66b
17. Numbers 24:5
18. Shulhan Arukh ha-Rav, Nizkei Mammon
19. Bava Metzia 23b, Shabbat 53b
20. Psalms 32:1
21. Berakhot 34b
22. Yoma 86b
23. Mishnah, end of fourth chapter of Bava Metzia
24. Bava Batra 22a
25. Mishnah, end of fourth chapter of Bava Metzia
26. Exodus 20:14
27. Mechilta on Exodus 20:14
28. Rabbi Yaakov Bloi, Pitchei Hoshen Geneiva 30 note 26

MARKETING
AND SELLING

Introduction

It is ironic that marketing, which specializes in creating images, seems to suffer from the worst image of all business specialties. Many people identify marketing with manipulation and exploitation. Yet marketing people are often astonished at this reputation. From their point of view, their profession is the most ethical of all areas of business, for it is the marketer, more than anybody else, who is trained to be pro-active in anticipating and accommodating the wants and needs of the customer.

Each point of view has an element of truth. If ethics is about care, the marketer, more than anyone else in the business establishment, cares about the customer's point of view. Yet for this very reason the marketer faces the greatest temptation to try and manipulate the customer's view to the seller's advantage.

One might say that marketing takes business ethics to new highs and new lows. Why to new highs? As we explain in the very first colum of the book, part of the divine purpose of business is to create new areas for human cooperation. God could have created a world where everyone provided only for himself and his own family, but instead He designed a world where each of us has much to gain from others. The marketing profession is uniquely dedicated to this end, determining exactly what it is that the customer wants, and how to provide it while creating mutual gain.

Why to new lows? Because in the normal course of business, the worst an unethical business person can do is deprive you of your money. But a manipulative or pandering marketer can erode not only your budget but your character. The most disgraceful marketing campaigns induce us to buy, not by offering ways we can improve ourselves, but by deepening and indulging our negative characteristics, such as envy or lust.

The ethical marketer is attentive to the customer and works together with the target audience to find ways to improve our moral standards along with the material aspects of our life.

The columns in this chapter relate mainly to two aspect of marketing and selling. One is the problem of misleading customers. Jewish law takes a very strict view of the obligation to be candid about flaws in merchandise. The second is that of taking responsibility for any dishonest use the customer may make of the merchandise. Judaism firmly rejects a "buyer-beware" approach.

It is remarkable that in Judaism the merchant's responsibility is not limited to the customer's material well-being; it extends, as well, to the customer's ethical well-being. Thus the merchant must not sell items that he knows will be used unscrupulously.

Marketing "Lite" Degrees

ARE NON-ACCREDITED DEGREE PROGRAMS PARTIES TO
DECEPTION?

Good business ethics always means taking responsibility for the customer's material well-being and satisfaction with the product. Jewish law takes this responsibility one step further and forbids selling products that may encourage the customer to mislead others.

Q I'm a telephone seller for a college which gives non-accredited degrees based on our courses, standard exams, and life-experience evaluations. Our students are informed that our bachelor's, master's, and doctoral degrees are not recognized, but I am concerned that graduates may be using these degrees to deceive their employers or clients. Do I need to worry?

A Your concern is well placed, because the seller's responsibility does not end with the customer. In the chapter of the Mishnah that deals with the ethics of selling, we learn: "Someone whose wine became diluted should not sell it in his store unless he informs the customer. And not to a merchant even if he does inform him, since it is liable to mislead."[1]

The first half of this passage is perfectly understandable. The Torah rejects a buyer-beware approach that places all responsibility on the buyer, and therefore makes the seller responsible for creating an informed trade. But why should the wholesaler not sell diluted wine to a merchant? The wholesaler has a cogent excuse: "Informing the retail customer is his responsibility, not mine; furthermore, if he wants to sell diluted wine, he doesn't need my help."

The Mishnah conveys the profound ethical insight that one of the main contributors to ethical lapses is the dilution of responsibility. The greater the number of people involved in unethical activities, the less responsibility each one feels. Each participant says to himself that he personally is not responsible; most of the wrongdoing was carried out by others. In addition, when there are many participants, each one tells himself that the activity must be perfectly acceptable, otherwise the others would not be engaging in it.

What this means is that a person who would never dilute the wine he sells his customers might be tempted to sell such wine if he obtained it from someone else. The Mishnah's message states that every participant in a deal has to tell himself, "The buck stops here"–I must take responsibility for preventing wrongdoing. If the original seller passes the wine along to someone else, he bears some responsibility for helping the store owner to hoodwink his clientele.

Likewise, selling a "diluted" degree even to an informed customer is wrong if you are helping him go ahead and try to "sell" his degree to employers or clients as a prestigious accredited credential. You cannot tell yourself that any deception is the responsibility of the college that gives the degrees, or of the students who obtain them, or of the employers who should have checked to see if there is accreditation; you have to tell yourself "the buck stops here," and take personal responsibility for any lapses.

The main ethical question for you is how likely this is to take place. Is the abuse you fear an occasional lapse in a system that is basically on the up-and-up? Or is it a significant factor in the market for degrees?

While it is hard to give an authoritative answer to this question, here are some relevant considerations.

The same passage in the Mishnah explains that there is no problem about mixing water with wine if it is customary to sell "lite" wine in that locale. This may be a good description of some non-accredited degrees. Many institutions grant "lite" degrees, and there are legitimate reasons why people value them. If the school is reputable, its diploma testifies to a certain level of academic achievement and life experience, and this is worth something to an employer. Additionally, such a diploma can have a positive effect on the self-esteem of someone who has learned a lot over the course of life without much formal schooling. And in some newly developing fields, there may as yet be no accredited course of study.

At least as often, however, unaccredited degrees are part of a cynical web of lies. The student is led to believe that the degree is more valuable than it really is, or easier to obtain, or less expensive; furthermore, the institution hints that the student can benefit from the degree by misleading others.

Two major danger signs are if the diploma doesn't give any hint that the program is non-accredited, or the institution actively tells students that the degree will help their career. These signs suggest intentional connivance in hoodwinking employers. Conversely, fully transparent advertising and documentation are encouraging signs of responsibility.

Just as we have to avoid the unethical dilution of wine, so we need to eschew the dilution of ethical responsibility. Everyone in the system has to ask himself whether the activity is ultimately justified by providing a beneficial and moral good or service at a reasonable price.

Unwarranted Warranty

CAN I PUSH EXTENDED WARRANTIES THAT MOST
CUSTOMERS DON'T NEED?

An effective salesperson may be persuasive and even forceful, but should never be aggressive or manipulative. The goal of business is to create mutual understanding and benefit; this can only be achieved when the customer has enough information and reflection to make an informed decision. This attitude must be maintained even in the face of pressure from employers to push merchandise. Care is called for in selling pricey extended warranties that most people do not need.

Q Markups on home appliances are not so high lately, so our employer is encouraging the salesmen to make up some of the slack by pushing "extended service warranties." The problem is that these warranties are very expensive and most customers do not really need them. How far can I go in encouraging these purchases?

A The fact that something is very expensive and may not suit every customer does not automatically mean that it is unethical to offer it. But it is true that selling such a service involves many ethical pitfalls.

In Jewish law, a very high markup is not inherently unethical. If you provide a valuable service that the informed customer is willing to pay for, you do not have to suffer because your outlays are low. However, there are two things to watch out for.

First, the customer has the right to assume that your prices are "in the ballpark." Some price variation among merchants is normal, due to the differences between them in such matters as service, location, and specialty items. (Businesses often have low prices on high-volume items and high prices on less popular ones; but different merchants will do their volume business in different products.) Nonetheless, if your place of business charges a price well above what competitors charge for a virtually identical product, the customer should be informed. We learn this from the biblical verse, "And when you sell to your fellow or buy from your fellow, let not each man oppress his brother."[2]

Interestingly, the word the Torah uses here is *ona'ah*, which does not really mean "overcharging" but instead denotes "oppression" or "distress." The emphasis in Jewish tradition is not on the monetary aspect of over-charging but on the human side: when we take advantage of someone's trust, we cause them distress.

The Torah law of *ona'ah* does not apply to personal services. One reason is that services, unlike goods, are never really standardized, since every individual is unique. But the service you are selling is completely standardized, and to be an ethical seller you should make sure that you do not charge substantially more than the accepted price without informing the customer. (Twenty percent is the usual guideline for "substantially more.")

It's also worth remembering that ethics aside, charging way beyond what others get is a surefire way to alienate your customers.

The second pitfall is that, while it is not improper to sell something for a high markup, it is wrong to describe an overpriced item as a bargain or as low-priced. When you call something a bargain, you are clearly signaling the consumer that your price is quite low; you must stand by your word.

What about the fact that such warranties are not advantageous for most customers? This does not prevent you from pointing out the benefits of the service for those customers who may really benefit. There are always a few worriers out there who greatly value the peace of mind derived from knowing that they will have no repair bills for a period of years. But here again there are two pitfalls.

A salesperson is permitted to give a sales pitch that emphasizes the positive aspects of his merchandise. If the merchandise does not suit everyone, then it is up to the salesperson to make out the best case for the item and up to the customer to decide whether the pitch is convincing. (Of course, if the merchandise has a defect of some kind, the salesperson must reveal this to the customer. A defective product is different from one that is of good quality but may not fit the needs of every prospective buyer.)

But a salesperson is not permitted to give partial advice. A salesperson is not expected to be objective and impartial, and the customer knows that the product description, even if accurate, will also be one-sided. But a salesperson who says something like "I advise you to take out this plan" or "This plan really suits your needs" is putting on the hat of the expert adviser; such advice needs to be completely objective. We learn this from the verse, "Do not put a stumbling block before the blind."[3] Rashi explains that this refers to someone who is "blind" to the bias of the adviser: "Do not advise someone to sell his field and buy a donkey if your true intention is to acquire the field for yourself."

In general, salespeople need to avoid giving advice. Aside from the fact that it is almost impossible to maintain the proper objectivity, salespeople are not always experts on the merchandise they sell, and often they are not really qualified to provide advice.

The second pitfall here is misleading the customer. Marketers often try to "repackage" a familiar product in an innovative way. There is nothing inherently wrong with this, and sometimes it shows the customer a new way to benefit from your product. But the repackaging has to be consistent and honest.

For example, insurance salesmen sometimes say that they're not selling insurance–they're selling "peace of mind." In other words, a customer who purchases the policy can rest easy knowing that whatever happens, the insurance will take care of it. In our case, there is nothing wrong with pointing out to the customer that paying an extra hundred dollars for a service contract could save him thousands of dollars in future repairs, and so he's really buying peace of mind. But you need to be consistent. For example, if the service contract does not cover every possible kind of breakdown, then the customer is not getting peace of mind at all – only an ordinary insurance policy with an inflated price tag and a limited value.

Another misleading tactic that is sadly common with warranties is selling protection that is already provided by law or by the ordinary warranty. This is definitely misleading and unethical.

It goes without saying that high-pressure tactics are always improper, no matter what is being sold.

Here is an interesting analogy: the salesman is like a lawyer, but the customer is the judge. The salesman is allowed to be an enthusiastic advocate for his point of view, but needs to maintain professionalism. The most important thing is constant deference to the authority and judgment of the magistrate – your customer!

Pyramid Puzzle

WHAT ARE THE CHALLENGES OF MULTI-LEVEL MARKETING?

Marketers are always looking for innovative ways to get out the news about their products. There's nothing wrong with seeking new angles to get the customer's attention, but some marketing systems require very high ethical standards to avoid the temptation to mislead consumers. This applies in particular to multi-level marketing.

Q A neighbor tried to sell me some cosmetics, and suggested that I if I like the product I could also make money by selling to others. Is this selling scheme ethical?

A The phenomenon you describe is called "multi-level marketing." The idea is to create a kind of pyramid where each customer has the opportunity to become a salesperson, thereby creating a new level in the marketing pyramid. The many salespersons in the scheme obtain earnings from the sales beneath them in the pyramid: their own customers, their customers' customers, and so on.

Multi-level marketing is not inherently unethical, but it presents a number of difficult ethical challenges which are not easily overcome. It is worth considering these challenges carefully before joining such a network. This complex question presents two really distinct issues: neighborhood selling, and multi-level selling. Although these issues are independent, they often go together.

NEIGHBORHOOD SELLING

One problem with multi-level marketing is not unique to the "pyramid" selling idea but is found in all kinds of "neighbor to neighbor" selling or even incentive schemes like "bring a friend and get a discount." The problem is that the seller is often trying to mask the salesperson's financial interest in the transaction. As we have pointed out in the previous column, this violates the Torah prohibition of "putting a stumbling block before the blind;"[4] this prohibition, according to our tradition, includes giving advice to someone who is blind to the adviser's conflict of interest. Rashi gives the example of advising someone to sell a field and buy a donkey while hiding your own interest in acquiring the field.

There is nothing wrong with a neighbor giving a friendly recommendation for a product he or she enjoyed. There is also nothing wrong with a salesperson giving a glowing but honest account of the advantages of his or her merchandise. But problems may arise when we mix these two kinds of endorsements. In particular, it is misleading for the salesperson to somehow imply that the sales pitch is really an impartial endorsement.

Therefore, one prerequisite for this selling is that the sales pitch be professional and not build on neighborly trust, which it will ultimately undermine. It's a shame to damage relations of trust carefully built up over years just for a few dollars earned from a marketing campaign.

A related problem with neighbor selling is that it often pressures people into buying items that they do not really need, out of a desire to avoid saying no to a neighbor. There is nothing wrong with voluntarily buying something from a merchant out of a desire to help him make a living. Indeed, this is the highest level of charity: to help a person by doing business with him rather than through a handout. It is also permissible to give some non-pressured encouragement to people to give to a worthy charity; therefore, selling cookies and the like for youth groups is not unethical even though some people buy only in order not to seem miserly.

But this is completely different from buying something to avoid awkwardness, which is not voluntary at all but pressured. Another column discusses the similar idea of subtle pressure on a person to give a gift without true consent (see p. 159).

Neighbor-to-neighbor selling schemes can be "value-adding" if there is a real advantage to knowing the needs and habits of potential customers and if the seller's enthusiasm for the product is sincere. However, not everyone is capable of living up to the challenge of taking off the neighbor hat and putting on the seller hat for the duration of a sales presentation.

Furthermore, the basis of ethical selling is to have the full desire and consent of the customer, and neighborhood selling runs the risk of leveraging carefully nurtured good will for the purpose of making money. In order to avoid both of these problems, the neighborhood seller needs to strive for an attitude of professionalism in selling.

MULTI-LEVEL SELLING

One of the most attractive things about multi-level marketing is that it allows the little guy, the salesman in the field, the opportunity for rapid advancement. Promotion to management in a regular business organization can take years, but in a multi-level selling organization, anyone who has the ability to organize a few other individuals and get them started in selling has become an instant manager, complete with an instant raise in pay from his commission on their sales.

But this attraction implies a certain danger. The "upstream" seller in a multi-level program also has to take on the responsibilities of a manager. A good manager needs to be an expert on his firm's product, knowledgeable about market potential, and an effective motivator and enabler for salespeople. That's one reason it generally takes years to reach this status.

The problem is that the more casual structure of multi-level selling sometimes encourages managers to give unrealistic expectations to prospective salespeople. In addition, it encourages sellers to provide an unhealthy mix of selling and managing.

An ordinary salesperson tries to convince the customer that his firm's product meets the customer's needs. This is legitimate in any kind of selling structure. In multi-level selling, the salesperson may be part-seller, part-recruiter. On the one hand, he is saying to the customer, "You can benefit from this product"; at the same time he is saying, "You can persuade others that they can benefit from this product."

If the customer is fully convinced that he wants to buy the product, there is no problem. If he is genuinely interested in learning about selling the product and buys it with an informed understanding of the opportunity this may provide him in selling, this is also legitimate. But here again we encounter the problem of blurred distinctions: Multi-level marketing can sometimes create an unhealthy amalgam of these motives where someone puts out money on the product in the vague expectation that there will be some future benefit.

At its very worst, multi-level marketing can degenerate into a pyramid or Ponzi scheme, a business model named after a legendary swindler who made a quick fortune with a business that rewarded investors with high profits that were no more than the investments of the newest victims of the scheme. When the supply of new investors ran out, so did the earnings, and the investors at the bottom of the pyramid were left holding the bag, having lost even their capital, which was distributed as "profits" to earlier investors, above them in the pyramid. Ponzi's brilliant scheme earned him many years in prison, but variations of his idea are constantly reappearing. Chain letters that promise getting more than we give, "investments in charity," and other systems that seem too good to be true usually turn out to be too good to be ethical.

If the *main* inducement to customers is their own future profits, then multi-level marketing has become a pyramid scheme. The basis of any ethical business is selling a valuable product or service at an attractive price, thereby creating a satisfied customer. If the basis of the system is selling the next level the promise of profits by creating yet another layer, then someone will be left holding the bag. This is definitely a case of misleading others.

Even if you are sure the people you contact will benefit, and any future victims will be farther down the road, you are not exempt. You may not be causing your contacts a financial stumbling block, but you are presenting them with a moral obstacle instead. Like any manager, you must take responsibility for ethical lapses which occur downstream as a result of your policies. The Mishnah teaches that a wholesaler who sells diluted wine to retail merchants transgresses the Torah commandment, "Do not place a stumbling block before the blind," because it induces the retailers to cheat customers.

In order for multi-level marketing to avoid falling foul of this problem, we need at the very least two criteria:

- The main reason for participating has to be an earnest desire for the product. While it is hard to give hard-and-fast standards, if fewer than half of the buyers are interested solely in the product without participating in further marketing, this is definitely a danger sign.

- The system has to have a built-in protection against leaving someone holding the bag. Each salesperson needs to have an updated forecast of sales potential. If sales representatives at the first level are told that this product has an estimated market of 100,000 units, they cannot just parrot this figure to the next layer. By the time this layer is reached 10,000, units may already have been sold. When the market is near saturation, the game has to end, and customers have to know that all they are getting is a quality product, since extensive further sales are no longer projected.

In the ideal model of multi-level marketing, value is added by having salespeople who are knowledgeable and enthusiastic about a quality product because of their own personal experience and who are familiar with the market because of their neighborly relations, which they understand but do not exploit. But often this structure involves unethical practices, such as concealing conflicts of interest, leveraging personal relationships for business advantage, and giving promises of easy profits that are sure to be disappointed at some point; finally, there is the problem of inducing others to fall into the very same ethical pitfalls.

Before entering into one of these arrangements, you should be convinced that you have the ability to adopt a professional attitude toward selling, and that all levels of marketing are provided with accurate and up-to-date information about their prospects. Most of all, you have to be convinced that you are providing a quality product at a fair price without any connection to the possibility of future profits.

Fit Flat

DOES A RENTAL APARTMENT HAVE TO BE LIVABLE?

The landlord-tenant relationship is fraught with ethical issues. Making a rental apartment livable is one of them.

Q Is a landlord required to make sure that a rented apartment is livable?

A The civil law generally holds the landlord to an implied warranty of habitability. In other words, by the very fact of offering a property for rent, the landlord is assuring the tenant that the apartment meets the generally accepted standards for a dwelling.

Jewish law has imposed a similar requirement at least since the time of the Mishnah, about two thousand years ago. The Mishnah states: "The landlord is obligated to provide a door, a bolt, and a lock, and anything else that requires skilled labor." The Talmud adds that this includes providing windows for air and light, strengthening the roof when this is necessary, and so on. The Mishnah continues that routine maintenance which can be done by an unskilled workman is the responsibility of the tenant.

Maimonides generalizes this ruling in a broad statement: the landlord is obligated to provide everything that is a "fundamental requirement in habitation of dwellings."[5] And the renowned nineteenth-century authority Rabbi Yechiel Michal Epstein points out that this standard is dependent on what is accepted in the given time and place for ordinary dwellings: "In each place according to its custom, the landlord is required to install and repair fixed items."[6]

Rabbi Epstein emphasizes that this obligation is absolute:

Even if the tenant came to see the house before renting and saw that these items were lacking, we do not assume that he accepted what he saw. Rather, the assumption is that he did not even need to mention it, and relied on the fact that the landlord would install and repair everything that was needed and everything that the majority of householders and properties are accustomed to.

SELF-HELP

Since these basic necessities are the obligation of the landlord to the tenant, if the landlord fails to provide them the tenant will generally be able to repair them at the landlord's expense, for example by deducting the costs from the monthly rent.[7] But this course should only be a last resort, after the landlord has been given proper notification of the problem, a reasonable opportunity to take care of it, and a warning that the tenant intends to take care of it by himself.

Naturally, the application of this rule will depend on the situation. If the radiator is not working and it is summertime, there is no justification for the tenant to take responsibility for the work without giving ample time for the landlord to find the most economical solution. On the other hand, if a pipe bursts in the middle of the night and begins to cause massive damage to the apartment and to the neighbors, the tenant should not hesitate to immediately call a plumber to take care of the emergency.

As we have already pointed out, the Mishnah does not neglect the obligations of the tenant. Many kinds of routine, unskilled maintenance tasks are the responsibility of the tenant, and those who dwell in rental housing need to take this responsibility seriously. The property should be kept clean and well-tended.

The ethical approach to business relations is a balanced one. While the exact extent and breakdown of responsibility will vary according to time and place, the Mishnah implies as an unvarying principle that landlord and tenant each have obligations to take appropriate care of any problems and to make the rental arrangement successful and mutually beneficial.

Distant Danger

MUST I WARN CUSTOMERS OF MINOR HEALTH HAZARDS?

Is it ethical to sell cosmetics that pose a minor health hazard? It is unquestionably unethical to sell dangerous merchandise to an unsuspecting customer. But nowadays the situation is not always so simple. Scientists are constantly discovering new and increasingly remote health hazards in common products, while consumers are displaying increased sensitivity to these distant dangers.

Q Some of the cosmetics I sell contain ingredients that are now suspected of increasing the risk of disease. Can I continue to sell these products?

A Products that constitute a clear and present danger to health may not be sold even to a willing customer. The Torah commands us, "Be very careful of your soul,"[8] and our sages explain that this obliges us to take care of our health.[9] Another verse states that we should not place a stumbling-block before the blind,[10] which means causing another person to falter in his personal obligations.

In light of this, peddling a clearly dangerous product, like selling glue for sniffing, is categorically prohibited because it helps the customer to do something totally improper.

However, the health hazards typically discovered in common products are seldom of this nature, especially in advanced countries where personal care products are subject to regulation. It is very unusual for risks to be so great that use would actually be prohibited to an informed customer.

In this case the ethical dilemma is not the danger per se, but the chance that you may be misleading the customer. Can you let "the buyer beware," or do you have to take some responsibility for product safety that meets customer expectations?

Jewish law clearly states that merchants are responsible for providing products that meet reasonable customer expectations. They have this responsibility, not because of any particular customer need, but because a genuinely ethical exchange is one in which there is complete understanding and agreement between the sides.

As an example, the Talmud teaches that it is forbidden for a kosher butcher to sell unkosher meat to an unsuspecting non-Jew.[11] Even though non-Jews have no religious requirement for kosher meat, and even if the price is fair, the seller may not disappoint the customer's reasonable expectations—and it is certainly reasonable to assume that meat sold by a kosher butcher would be kosher.

So your dilemma boils down to the following question: Do your customers have a reasonable expectation that the products you sell are free of known hazards? This will depend on many factors, but the most important is whether you, or the manufacturer, has developed an image of purity and safety. The average customer who buys an unknown product off the shelf does not expect it to exceed regulatory requirements. If this anonymous transaction describes your relationship with your customers, then you may sell the problematic merchandise.

But if you, or the manufacturer, have sought a reputation for healthy and pure products, then you have simultaneously fostered expectations on the part of your clientele that your products go beyond the letter of the law and meet a higher standard.

You should examine your advertising and marketing materials and your sales pitch to determine whether you are communicating a message of healthfulness, purity, and responsibility over and above what the law requires. If you have cultivated these expectations in your customers, then you should not sell the problematic products to your unsuspecting clientele. You should either delicately inform them of the possible problems or else pass the products on to a more anonymous selling network, such as a drugstore.

Advertorials

ARE ADVERTORIALS LEGITIMATE?

In order to properly serve the public interest, the press needs to maintain a modicum of independence, not only from government but also from commercial interests. The editorial staff of a newspaper should not decide what is news on the basis of what the advertisers want published. This "fire wall" between the editorial and marketing staffs is a basic principle of ethical journalism. The wall is breached by camouflaging advertising to look like a feature article.

Q My publication has a major advertiser who buys space every week. For the coming week, he provided copy that reads like an objective public interest article and asked me to type-set it like a regular article. Is this ethical?

A The intense competition in the communications media is leading to the creation of innovative new media categories like infotainment and edutainment. One of the most popular categories, and also one of the most ethically problematic, is the so-called advertorial. An advertorial is an advertisement carefully written and type-set to have the look and feel of news or of an editorial opinion piece.

The ethical problem here is that the reader believes he is getting information or advice which is unbiased, while the true motive for presenting the content he sees is commercial. According to Jewish law, this practice runs afoul of the strict prohibition against concealing a conflict of interest when giving advice.

The Torah tells us, "Do not put a stumbling block before the blind."[12] According to Jewish tradition, this refers to anything that would incline a person to blindly act against his or her own best interest. Rashi's commentary to the Torah explains, "This refers to someone who is blind in the matter; do not give him advice which is not in his best interest. Don't tell him 'Sell your field and buy a donkey' when you are secretly scheming to acquire it from him."

Note that the conflict of interest per se is not the problem. It is a normal element in negotiating aimed at persuading the other party that the proposed deal is in his or her best interest. The other party considers the information you present, but also knows to take into account that it is colored by your self-interest. That is why Rashi says that the problem is the "secret scheming."

The ethical pitfall here is that the adviser is concealing his interest. There is nothing wrong with trying to advance one's own interests, as long as it is done in an ethical way. But it is wrong to pretend to be impartial when actually you are pursuing a hidden agenda.

The same is true of advertising. It is not unethical for an advertiser to make a one-sided presentation of the many advantages of a product, in order to persuade the consumer to buy (of course, the presentation must not be dishonest or misleading). But an advertisement is unethical when it masquerades as an impartial editorial piece.

Therefore, a publication that wants to run such a piece needs to clearly label it as an advertisement, to avoid fooling readers into thinking that it is an impartial statement of editorial opinion.

CREDIBILITY: A ZERO-SUM GAME

Ethical considerations aside, there are excellent professional reasons not to run advertorials. Many publications do not accept them even when they are clearly labeled. Why won't these papers run advertorials? For the very same reason the advertisers want them to: The editorial format of these ads adds credibility even when readers know they are ads, but credibility is a zero-sum game. If the newspaper format gives credibility to the ads, it surely at the same time takes the same measure of credibility away from the paper's regular articles.

Credibility is the stock in trade of any reputable publication. Before deciding to humor your sponsor and lend your paper's editorial typesetting to commercial content, you must make sure that any advertorials are clearly demarcated; and you should carefully consider whether you want to dilute your credibility in this way.

State Lotteries: Entertainment or Exploitation?

IS THE LOTTERY ETHICAL?

As governments around the world find themselves strapped for funds, and with moral opposition to gambling a less effective force than ever, more and more state and national governments are turning to state-sponsored gambling, including lotteries. The ethics of these enterprises should be a concern to all citizens and especially to the public employees who run them.

Q I work for a state lottery. Sometimes I wonder if we are taking unfair advantage of our customers' dreams of riches.

A While this question may seem simple, it is actually quite involved. What makes it complex is that lotteries, like other gambling games, mean different things to different people.

For some people, gambling is a form of entertainment. Just as some people play cards for fun and introduce stakes just to make things interesting, so some people enjoy testing their luck and look at the jackpot as a source of added excitement. They see their gambling losses as belonging to their recreation budget. This is not morally objectionable. One person who has a dollar to throw away puts four quarters into a video game; another has more fun investing in a Powerball ticket.

A few people gamble in order to lose. They want to show off how much money they have. While conspicuous consumption of this kind is certainly objectionable, the business providing the service is not necessarily to blame.

Quite a few lottery players even have charitable intentions. They know that income from state lotteries goes to worthy causes, and the possibility of winning is only a small incentive. The administrators of one popular lottery system try to draw business by advertising that the profits go to the following good causes: mass transportation in Arizona, education in Connecticut, economic development in Kansas, natural resources in Minnesota, school aid and crime control in Montana.

But unfortunately, there are a significant number of players who perceive gambling as a viable road to riches. They play the lottery because they feel they could use the money. These individuals close their eyes to the minuscule chances of winning; what they could really use is the precious few dollars they are throwing away on tickets. A significant minority are actually addicted to gambling.

The saddest part of all is that the cost of winning may be as punishing as the cost of losing. Research shows that even if they win, the longed-for jackpot is more than likely to make their lives miserable. (This is called the "sudden wealth syndrome.")

Selling tickets to these poor souls is improper. According to Jewish law, it borders on theft.[13]

So how can you tell if your lottery is an ethical business? An ethical problem exists in either of the following two situations:

- If disappointed dreamers constitute a significant fraction of your business, then you cannot ignore the detriment your business is causing them. You need to take positive steps to avoid roping in the compulsive or unsophisticated player.

- Even if only a few customers are addicted, there may still be a problem. If your advertising is deliberately directed at gambling addicts, then you are taking conscious advantage of them. You should find out what the numbers are and take a careful look at the advertising campaign for your state lottery.

At a deeper level, there is something fundamentally phony about gambling. There is nothing wrong with wealth, but there is something inherently unfulfilling about unearned wealth. One person who understood this well was the saintly Rabbi Aryeh Levine of Jerusalem. Rabbi Aryeh merited seeing many miracles performed for him, and someone once asked him why he never bought lottery tickets. He gave a surprising answer: "I'm afraid I might win." A person with a truly enlightened perspective does not even desire unearned riches; he knows that they will never bring contentment. On the contrary, as the Mishnah states, "The more possessions, the more worry."[14]

Defect Disclosure

CAN I DELAY DISCLOSURE OF MINOR DEFECTS?

It is certainly unethical for over-zealous salespeople to withhold information the customer needs. But Jewish tradition acknowledges the right of the salesperson, within ethical limits, to present the positive aspects of the purchase item and make a good impression.

Q If I tell a customer the whole story when he first comes to look at a property, he may lose interest before he becomes aware of its advantages. How far can I put off disclosing some details?

A One thing is certain: any flaws in a purchase item must be made known to the customer before the agreement is closed. The Talmud teaches explicitly that any attribute of the item that is material to the seller must be made known to him, and the seller needs to take the initiative in disclosing this information. Maimonides writes: "It is forbidden to cheat people in commerce or to mislead them. ...If he knows of any defect in the sale item, he must disclose it to the buyer."[15]

Thus Jewish law categorically rejects the norm of caveat emptor, "let the buyer beware," which places all responsibility for a satisfactory purchase on the buyer. The seller has to volunteer information that he knows is material for the buyer.

But Jewish law also avoids the opposite extreme of placing the entire burden on the seller. The seller is not expected to be a fiduciary or agent for the buyer; it is perfectly legitimate for him to promote his own interest by trying to persuade the buyer to buy. While he may not mislead the customer into thinking that the product has qualities that it really lacks, the seller does have the right to present the genuine characteristics of the merchandise in a flattering way that maximizes its appeal to the customer.

One way the merchant can do this is by giving the merchandise an attractive appearance. The Mishnah states that it is forbidden to paint old utensils so that the buyer is misled into thinking that they are new, but by the same token, painting them to make them more attractive, without passing them off as new, is permissible.[16] So painting a house before putting it up for sale is okay, as long as the paint is not used to disguise decay or other defects.

Another legitimate selling tactic is to give the product an attractive name. The Talmud tells of an unusual case where the kosher butchers in a certain city had only non-kosher meat to sell. Since customers would normally assume that the meat they were offering was kosher, the defect had to be revealed to all customers, even non-Jewish ones, to avoid misleading them. However, the butchers were not required to bluntly announce that the meat was treif, meaning "carrion." They were permitted to use an elegant circumlocution, stating that this was "meat for the soldiers."[17] Any reasonable buyer would get the hint. When dealers sell "pre-owned cars" or computer sellers market "out-of-the-box" items, they are taking advantage of this leniency. These expressions are more elegant than "used," but they definitely get the message across.

Finally, the seller is allowed to use some judgment in deciding *when* to reveal defects. The Talmud tells of a certain man whose father was a non-Jew. Although he was fully Jewish, some people were reluctant to make a match with him because of his family background. The leading sage Rav advised him to go to another city where his background would not be known. As a consequence, people would not prejudge him as a marriage prospect based on this one characteristic. In other words, it was permissible for him to put off disclosure until the "buyer" had a chance to evaluate his positive qualities.[18]

So if you are selling a beautiful property but some of the plumbing needs replacement, you do not have to disclose this fact immediately. You can allow the customer to be impressed by the positive aspects of the home first, and disclose the flaws afterwards when the customer will be able to consider them in the total context of the property's characteristics.

However, you must be careful not to cross the line into bargaining in bad faith. If you wait until the closing to disclose the property's flaws, then you are taking advantage of the fact that the customer has already invested time and money in pursuing this home; to some extent you have him over a barrel. This is a misleading and exploitative sales tactic. You must advise the customer of any material disadvantages as soon as you feel that he has obtained a fair impression of the property's advantages.

The ethical approach to selling is based on respect for the customer. On the one hand, respect for the customer obligates us to inform him of any significant problems with the merchandise, so that he can make a rational decision about whether to buy. But respect for the customer also means that we recognize that he is able to decide for himself whether the merchandise suits his needs and tastes; he does not need the seller to do this for him. The seller should present his wares in an accurate and attractive way; the buyer then has the responsibility to make an informed decision.

ENDNOTES

1. Bava Metzia 4:11
2. Leviticus 25:14
3. Leviticus 19:14
4. Leviticus 19:14
5. Maimonides, Sekhirut 6:3
6. Arukh ha-Shulhan, Hoshen Mishpat 314
7. Shulhan Arukh, Hoshen Mishpat 375
8. Deuteronomy 4:15
9. Berakhot 32b
10. Leviticus 19:14
11. Hullin 94b
12. Leviticus 19:14
13. Shulhan Arukh, Hoshen Mishpat 34:16
14. Avot 2:7
15. Maimonides, Mekhirah 18:1
16. Bava Metzia 4:12
17. Hullin 94b
18. Yevamot 45a

SCHOOLYARD ETHICS

Introduction

People today spend more of their lives than ever in educational institutions. Almost everyone in the industrialized countries obtains at least twelve years of formal education; many obtain far more. Our school years are the most formative stage of our life. It is at this time that our ethical values are crystallized; a person who leaves college with solid values is far less likely to be corrupted afterwards, whereas a person who is already corrupt when he begins his working life will find it difficult to internalize more enlightened standards of behavior.

The most important aspect of Jewish education, perhaps of Jewish life as a whole, is Torah study. Countless passages of the Talmud deal with the appropriate conditions for Torah education, including the elementary school, or "Talmud Torah," for younger students, as well as the yeshiva or beit midrash for older students, including mature scholars. These institutions of Torah study, no less than the family, are viewed as the forge in which character is shaped. In the time of the Talmud, and sometimes today as well, even young teenagers are boarded far from home and have the yeshiva as their main social environment.

Professional education is also highly valued. The Talmud states that it is a mitzvah to teach your child a profession,[1] and this mitzvah is so important that it is permissible to discuss arrangements for such education even on Shabbat, when livelihood considerations are normally unmentionable.[2] Passages in the Talmud discuss the high degree of respect a pupil owes to his teacher in professional studies[3] and the importance of finding an instructor of good moral qualities.[4]

The main ethical challenges in the school environment are for students to maintain the proper degree of respect for their instructors and fellow students, and for faculty members to respect their students and remain always aware of their heavy responsibility as role models and examples. The questions discussed below relate to certain unique ethical rules that apply to academia, such as the importance of regular attendance and the special severity of cheating and plagiarism.

Tattling

CAN I "TATTLE" ON A CLASSMATE?

Most people, and especially children, have a natural aversion to "telling on" their peers. Jewish tradition legitimizes this instinct and the respect for social solidarity and individual responsibility that underlies it. Even so, the restriction has its limits. Sometimes it is necessary to turn to authority figures for the good of the community as a whole or even for the good of the wrongdoer. Jewish law gives very specific and useful guidelines for knowing when to speak up.

Q Two students in my class are always being disciplined for misbehavior. Recently, I heard them whispering that they were afraid they would be caught for cheating on an exam. Should I tell the teacher?

A Cheating on an exam is certainly a serious ethical lapse. But you have to be careful not to compound the problem by unnecessarily denigrating others.

This is a good time to review the criteria for talking about someone's faults or misdeeds. According to the classic Hafetz Hayyim by Rabbi Yisrael Meir ha-Kohen of Radin,[5] there are basically five guidelines. Only if all five are met may we speak negatively of someone. As an aid to memory, we can arrange them according to the letters of the alphabet:

- *Accuracy*. It is forbidden to exaggerate or embellish.

- *Benefit*. Revealing the information must be the only way to obtain some constructive benefit.

- *Certainty*. The information must be reliable.

- *Desire*. Your reason for telling must be constructive, not vindictive.

- *Equity.* Revealing the information must not cause undeserved harm to the subject. It is not equitable to protect one person at the expense of another.

Let us examine these criteria one by one as they apply to your situation. We will discuss them in the order in which they present themselves, rather than in the alphabetical order of our list.

- The *accuracy* criterion is critical here. You do not know that your classmates actually cheated. Therefore, even if all the other criteria are met, the most you may tell the teacher is the content of the conversation you overheard: that the girls expressed fear that they could be caught cheating. To state unambiguously that the girls cheated would be an unwarranted embellishment.

  If you relate the story accurately, the certainty criterion is now not a problem. You are not certain that your classmates cheated, but you personally overheard the conversation in which they discussed their behavior. The certainty criterion would be problematic if there was a persistent rumor that these youngsters cheated.

- The *equity* criterion will depend on the likely reaction of the teacher. The equitable way for the teacher to deal with your information is to take it as one possible indicator of wrongdoing on the part of the pupils. Perhaps she could take a closer look at the exams of the "culprits" to see if there are signs of cheating; other possibilities include giving some oral questions to verify that they did the work or giving a make-up exam. If you think that this will be her reaction, then equity is attained. But if you think that the teacher will accept your report as conclusive evidence that your classmates acted improperly and take immediate disciplinary action against them, then the response will not be equitable. In this case it would be unethical to disclose the conversation you overheard.

- The *desire* criterion needs to be evaluated through introspection. If the reason you want to inform the teacher is to make sure that everyone in the class is graded fairly or because you think that the teacher will take action that will help the misbehaving students to attain a higher level of personal conduct, then your desire is legitimate. But if your intention is vindictive, because you want them to "get what's coming to them," then you may not inform on them even if the other criteria are fulfilled. Your negative intention makes your act unethical even if the practical consequence is positive.

- But the main problem here is *benefit.* What constructive objective is achieved by telling on these youngsters? Let us consider some candidates:

Harm to classmates. If one student cheats, then in some cases this will have a significant impact on the grades of others. It may be permissible for someone to protect his own grade by letting the teacher know that someone else's grade is undeserved. But ask yourself if this is really applicable here. The undeserved grades of these two students will probably have a negligible effect on the grades of the rest of the class.

Discipline. Often, revealing someone's misbehavior is doing him or her a favor. Discipline from a teacher or parent, especially if applied in an understanding way, may be just what a person needs as a motivation to improve behavior. But in your case the students involved are already discipline problems; ask yourself if one more rebuke from the teacher or principal will really have an impact.

Deceit. Someone who cheats on a qualifying exam, such as certification for a professional degree, is defrauding future employers and clients by misrepresenting his or her qualifications,[6] so it is appropriate to report cheating of this nature But a routine quiz in middle school is not likely to result in an undeserved job or even school admission for your classmates.

Here is another consideration: As we have just pointed out, the teacher is not allowed to act without checking the facts. If the teacher will be unable to verify that cheating, too,k place, then nothing is to be gained by telling on these young people. Ask yourself why the teacher should believe your story. Perhaps telling will only create an atmosphere of ill will. The bottom line is that the benefit criterion may not really be fulfilled in your case, and if so, it may well be that there is nothing to be gained by telling.

When we are tempted to tell on peers, whether in the classroom or the workplace, we should ask ourselves if this is the most constructive way to deal with the problem. Perhaps there is some other approach. Let us take your case as an example. Maybe the next time there is an exam you can approach your classmates and offer to help them study. That's probably the most constructive thing you can do to reduce the cheating problem, and it will contribute to an atmosphere of cooperation, not of retaliation.

Now let us see how these exact same criteria play themselves out in a slightly different situation. Suppose that a questioner said, "I'm almost sure that a certain person stole from a classmate. Should I tell the teacher?"

Whenever we weigh disclosing potentially damaging information, we apply the five criteria of the Hafetz Hayyim. Here is how they apply in the stealing case:

- *Accuracy, Certainty.* Since you are not sure that the person stole, you must be careful not to make your knowledge sound more certain than it really is. If you do decide to inform, you must clearly state that you have only circumstantial evidence.

- *Benefit.* Is telling the teacher (or the victim) likely to help the victim recover the stolen object? If not, then informing is of doubtful benefit.

- *Desire.* Make sure your intention is to help the victim, not to harm the wrongdoer.

- *Equity.* If the teacher, or the victimized classmate, will act in an undeservedly harsh way against the suspect, then you should not tell. Example: if they will consider it a certainty that he stole when there is only a suspicion, or if they will impose an unduly harsh punishment on him if the story is corroborated.

If all these criteria are fulfilled, it is not only permissible but even desirable to transmit the information. But if you are not sure whether the criteria are fulfilled, then you should just live with your doubts. It is better for one crook to go unpunished than to unwittingly contribute to an environment of suspicion and mistrust.

What's It All About, Hafetz Hayyim?

Many people are surprised by the cautious attitude of Jewish tradition about informing on others. If previous generations, too,k an ultra-conservative view toward authority, condemning informing under virtually all circumstances, nowadays attitudes have changed, and often an ultra-permissive view is adopted in which informing is encouraged and praised. It is true that a few whistle-blowers have displayed admirable courage in some high-profile cases, but this does not mean that a culture of informing is the best route to an ethical workplace or schoolyard.

Let us provide a little more explanation of the ethical importance of the old saw, "If you cannot say anything nice about someone, do not say anything at all."

There are a number of reasons for being extra careful before making accusations.

- *Enlightened objectivity.* The most obvious reason is the objective need to be conservative until we have all the facts. Maybe what we think we see is not really the whole truth. As Hillel stated in the Mishnah,[7] "Don't judge your fellow until you have reached his place"–until you have seen things from his point of view. There are many remarkable stories about people who were condemned for terrible crimes based on circumstantial evidence which later turned out to be misleading.

  As long as we are withholding judgment, we should assume that a person is free of wrongdoing. In the eyes of the secular law, everyone is presumed innocent until proven guilty. In Jewish law, this principle applies not only to the courtroom but also to what the popular author Hanoch Teller calls "the courtrooms of the mind." The basis for this approach is the fundamental belief that human beings are basically good. "God created man upright."[8]

  As long as the matter is not firmly determined, we should give the benefit of the doubt and not let loose with a careless condemnation that is easy to withhold but very difficult to retract once

268

publicized. This is an essential consideration in the requirement for certainty and accuracy.

- *Unforeseen effects.* Even when the negative information we provide is carefully checked for content and context, we lose control over it once it is disclosed. We may not exaggerate or embellish, but others may do so, whether innocently or maliciously. The first person to relate the tale bears some responsibility for the damage wrought by the carelessness of others.

  Even if your information is sound and appropriate, other people are not so careful. We must err on the cautious side to avoid creating a culture of mutual suspicion and slander, and this means that sometimes it is necessary to keep quiet even when we have something accurate and beneficial to relate.

  This concern lies behind the requirement for accuracy and equity. It is also related to the requirement for benefit, since alternative solutions may be less subject to unforeseen effects.

- *Effect on character.* Even when passing along negative information is justified, doing so can have a detrimental effect on our character. A hallmark of the Jewish approach to ethics is that "Our hearts are drawn after our actions."[9] The more we devote our words and our thoughts to the negative attributes of others, the more we are drawn, almost inexorably, toward the pole of cynicism and misanthropy.

  If we feel inclined to tell of someone's faults, we should ask ourselves not only whether he deserves it but also whether we ourselves deserve it. Is the benefit from disclosure really worth the detriment to my character?

  Of course, the opposite can also be true. Sometimes someone who refrains from disclosing wrongdoing is drawn inexorably to condoning and excusing it; and this insight is behind the commandment to protest wrongdoing. But great care is needed to examine whether silence tends to condone wrongdoing or merely to withhold judgment.

  This idea lies behind the concern for beneficial intention. From the point of view of consequence, it does not matter whether the teller has positive or negative intentions, but from the point of view of the impact on his own character, the difference is critical. Someone who slanders his fellow with vindictive motives is reinforcing his own basest character traits.

- *Educational message.* A very important and profound reason to limit negative speech is based on a basic insight into human nature: our behavior is motivated not only by incentives but perhaps even more by expectations. There is nothing novel about this insight; it is enshrined in the Bill of Rights, which forbids "cruel and unusual punishment." The founding fathers of the United States recognized that such punishment, far from deterring crime by providing frightful consequences, is likely to encourage it by reducing our basic human sensitivity, which is the surest guarantor of a humane society.

  When we inform on others and make sure they are punished, it is true that we are creating incentives to act properly. But we are also in danger of transmitting the message that bad behavior needs to be avoided because of punishment and not because it goes against our conscience. Sometimes looking the other way sends a message that wrongdoing is something unusual, something we do not expect and do not consider overly important. Ironically, when someone's misdeeds are kept quiet, it is easier for the wrongdoer to repent and straighten out.

  We can exemplify these considerations using the example of the family. Virtually all parents try to discourage their children from tattling on each other. Such informing may help the parents a bit in discipline, but they soon learn that it reinforces negative character traits in the children. Responsibility for maintaining standards is transferred from the child to the parent; vindictiveness is rewarded, while cooperation is not being taught; and the misbehaving child is reinforced in a negative image and in feeling that others are conspiring against him. This doesn't mean that silence is the solution; the solution is that problems are worked out whenever possible among peers without turning to authority, and when authority must be summoned it is exercised equitably and educationally.

If you succumbed to temptation and cheated on a test, you would probably resolve never to do it again and hope you never got caught; you should consider giving others the same treatment. (Of course another thing you should do is make sure you do not garner any advantage from your dishonest act.)

Reading Private Messages of Students

SHOULD I ACT ON INFORMATION I GOT SNOOPING ON STUDENTS?

Teachers and other authority figures often find themselves faced by a trying ethical dilemma. Even if an act seems beneficial, it may set a bad example. Those who serve as role models for others need to pay special attention to the messages they transmit through their behavior.

Q I'm a high school teacher. I recently found a student's note that showed that he was engaging in immoral and potentially self-destructive activities. Should I take action by contacting the student or his parents?

A This is a very important question which requires several layers of analysis.

The first thing to know is that it is generally forbidden to read other people's private mail without permission. A seventeenth-century authority, Rabbi Jacob Hagiz, explains that this is implicit in the Torah's prohibition on gossip. If I know private information about someone, the Torah forbids me to disclose it to someone else. In the case of mail, I do not have the information before I read the message. What difference does it make, asks Rabbi Hagiz, if I reveal people's private information to others or to myself?[10]

This prohibition was formalized in a famous ban of Rabbenu Gershom, one of the leading early medieval authorities.[11] Rabbenu Gershom's edict explicitly forbids reading someone else's mail without permission.

On the other hand, private information may sometimes be revealed if disclosing it is the only way to achieve an important benefit, as we discussed in the preceding section. One instance of this is revealing information to a parent or teacher when necessary for the youngster's moral education.[12]

So it would seem that you are permitted to act on the basis of the student's note. Despite this, you should think carefully about the wisdom of doing so. Very often an act is technically ethical but educationally damaging. For example, although Jewish law permits spanking children when necessary for discipline, our tradition warns that this method of discipline is likely to be counterproductive, especially with an older child. The Shulhan Arukh states: "One who beats an older child is worthy of being placed under a ban, as this is likely to lead [the child] astray."[13]

A high school student is certainly considered an "older child," and embarrassing a youngster by reading his private mail and revealing the contents to parents could definitely have destructive consequences. If there is no relationship of trust and understanding between the teenager and his parents, then they will be unable to influence him. If there is a relationship of trust, you have to consider the possibility that your breach of trust may damage it.

The same reasoning is enunciated by a renowned ethicist, Rabbi J. David Bleich. In Volume 2 of his *Contemporary Halakhic Problems*, he warns against reading students' correspondence:

> Procedures involving violation of privacy are likely to be counterproductive. To be successful in their efforts, educators must gain and retain the confidence and trust of their students. It is virtually impossible to impart ethical sensitivity while employing means which are themselves perceived by students as being unethical in nature.

The only exception would be if action were necessary to stave off a clear and present danger of some kind.

Truth and Truancy

IS PLAYING HOOKY UNETHICAL?

A school is a workplace, with expectations and rules, and has its own unique business ethics issues. One dilemma faced by virtually all students is the ethics of cutting classes.

Q All the kids at my high school, when they have doctor's appointments and the like, stay out a little longer for lunch or ice cream. On a "once in a while" basis, is this a real problem ethically? Are we "robbing" our parents, who pay a fortune to send us to private school?

A The issue of cutting class is a difficult ethical dilemma. On the one hand, it seems clear that cutting class occasionally is not inherently unethical. After all, you're not getting paid by the hour. Judaism considers girls over the age of twelve and boys over the age of thirteen to be adults responsible for their own decisions. Sometimes a student may make a mature decision that some other activity is more important than school attendance.

At the same time, there is no doubt that playing hooky can involve a variety of serious ethical problems. It's rare to find a conscientious individual who does not make class attendance an overriding priority, and there are plenty of students who are scrupulous never to miss class.

An examination of some of the ethical issues involved will provide a foundation for judging the boundaries of acceptable behavior.

HONORING PARENTS

Honoring parents is a very important matter. Everyone has an obligation to honor their parents; this is so important that it is one of the Ten Commandments.[14] Although this obligation does not require a child to obey every order given by a father or a mother, Jewish tradition ascribes immense value to obedience. The parents are generally in an excellent position to judge what norms and obligations are best for their children.

As long as you are living at home, you have the additional responsibility of conforming to household norms, which probably include regular school attendance.

If good attendance is very important to your parents, or if your skipping classes will reflect badly on them or on other family members, there is a good chance that you will be falling short of your responsibility toward your family if you miss class.

RESPECT FOR TEACHERS

In Jewish tradition, a student is obliged to show respect and reverence toward his teachers. This is especially true in Torah studies but applies also to secular studies.[15] Skipping class shows disrespect for teachers and for the school as a whole. In addition to the inherent problem of showing disrespect, class cutting may demoralize a school's teachers and precipitate a breakdown in the school's discipline, problems that may eventually affect the entire student body and faculty.

Another serious problem is that playing hooky may incite other students to follow your example, against their better judgment and their best interest.

HONOR CODE

If your school has an honor code, you must abide by it. An honor code is a solemn obligation that students take upon themselves, and they must be careful to live up to its standards.

But by the same token, the school's administrators should ensure that any honor code students are expected to adopt makes only reasonable demands. If the code's requirements are excessive, then it invites cynicism and educates towards expediency. Jewish law specifies that sons and daughters have a strict responsibility to obey when their parents ask for help, but balances this with a stern warning that parents must not make excessive and unreasonable demands.[16]

TEMPTATION TO COVER UP

The act of cutting class has very serious ethical ramifications because a student who cuts may be strongly tempted to misbehave in other ways. If he is caught, he is tempted to lie; having missed class, he may be tempted to copy homework or cheat on an exam. The Mishnah tells us that "one transgression drags along another,"[17] and this is certainly true of playing hooky.

Jewish tradition warns us against putting our values to the test in this way. A short prayer which is part of the morning service begs God to save us from "temptation and disgrace," which all, too, often go together.

CONCLUSION

Mature teenagers are beginning to take on adult responsibility. This means that they can begin to establish their own priorities, which are not necessarily identical to the expectations others have of them. Perhaps there are times when serious and important commitments should have priority over school attendance.

On the other hand, attaining a sense of responsibility means that the students should be able to appreciate the immense importance of a good education and of a positive attitude toward the schools they attend and the norms that apply in school. A student who carefully takes account of all these considerations will very likely conclude that skipping class is seldom a good idea.

The best solution is to obtain permission in advance for any valid absence from class, thus avoiding the problems of cynicism and disrespect.

Paper Mill

CAN I SELL TERM PAPERS TO A COMMERCIAL SITE?

Many people who would never dream of committing wrongful acts find ready excuses when it comes to helping others transgress. Some of these excuses may be valid, but Jewish law helps us look at the entire picture. In this section we discuss the ethical aspects of contributing material to a term-paper archive.

Q I'm a good student. Sometimes I make a little extra money by selling my term papers to a Web site that maintains a kind of archive of papers on various topics. Of course, I would never use one of these services, but is it unethical to contribute to them as well?

A It's a good thing that you do not use these services to submit bogus term papers. The very foundation of academia is that students are judged equitably on their own work; this foundation is completely undermined by plagiarism of any kind.

Copying term papers is a kind of lying, of misleading others. When you put your name on a paper, you are making a statement that the work is yours. The Torah tells us, "Distance yourself from any falsehood."[18]

The late Rabbi Moshe Feinstein points out that copying in school does not simply mislead the school; in many instances it constitutes a kind of stealing. The reason is simple. A prospective employer or client will naturally assume that an applicant has actually attained the level of training attested by his diploma or professional certification. If the applicant cheated and thus obtained the diploma fraudulently, any payment he receives from the employer or client is, in effect, stolen.[19]

Apart from this universal ethical problem, there is the simpler problem that all college students are bound by the academic rules of their institutions and these invariably prohibit plagiarism. Even if the scourge of plagiarism were not inherently unethical, it would still be wrong to go against this basic agreement to abide by the rules.

Finally, there is the problem that the true author is not acknowledged. Jewish tradition is profoundly sensitive to the pedigree of ideas.

This is especially true in Torah study, where we find that the sages of the Talmud displayed incredible self-sacrifice to carefully recall the exact chain of transmission of various laws. The Talmud tells us that we should strive to cite our sources even in mundane matters. It notes that the miracle of the Purim holiday, as related in the biblical book of Esther, began when the king was informed about Mordecai's aid in uncovering the murderous plot of Bigthan and Teresh. This was possible because Esther carefully specified that the information came from Mordecai. Based on this story, the Talmud states, "Anyone who cites a quotation in the name of its author brings redemption to the world."[20]

But your question is more subtle. You are not personally engaging in plagiarism; you are only aiding others to plagiarize. Furthermore, there are some convincing arguments in your favor.

First, many people undoubtedly use term-paper services for permissible reasons, in order to get ideas and references which they will then use as source material for their own original work (the truth is that even this is academically questionable if they fail to reference the bought term paper). You might claim that it's not your fault if unscrupulous individuals submit the paper as is.

Second, you may reason that you are really not contributing to the plagiarism problem at all. There are plenty of other papers out there, and if your paper were missing from the archive, those who wish to plagiarize would have lots of other opportunities.

These arguments have a certainly validity, but they are not sufficient to justify selling term papers. Let us explain why. Jewish law discerns three different levels of connivance with wrongdoing.

- *Enabling.* The most serious level is when you actually *enable* wrongdoing. The Torah tells us, "Do not put a stumbling block before the blind."[21] Rashi explains that this refers to a spiritual obstacle which will enable the person to sin.

  The excuses we mentioned are valid ones from this point of view. Given the current (unfortunate) state of the term-paper market, there really are lots of other people offering the same merchandise. Adding one more paper is not "enabling" the student to cheat, unless perhaps the paper is on a very unusual topic.

- *Abetting.* *Abetting* transgressions, that is, being an active participant, is less serious but also ethically condemned. Even if somebody else would help if you didn't, it is still wrong to be actively involved in helping someone transgress.

  The exact boundaries of abetting depend on many details; one important factor is the likelihood that your work will be ultimately used for a forbidden purpose.[22] And practically speaking, the chances seem overwhelming that your papers are wanted in order to mislead instructors.

  Even a cursory look at the most prominent term-paper sites shows that they are carefully targeted to meet the needs of students who want to submit the paper they purchase. One site starts out by mentioning that it cannot guarantee a grade; only afterwards does it mention in passing that you should use the paper only as a source. Another site implies that plagiarism is illegal only in some places, but in others it is permissible. Practically all the sites mention that students using their services get excellent grades, implying that other clients can do the same by submitting papers from their service.

  To make matters worse, many sites offer to "personalize" the style and structure of the paper you purchase. Having a paper written in a particular style is of absolutely no use to someone wanting to use it as reference material, but it is certainly very important to students who want to actually submit the downloaded papers.[23]

- *Condoning.* The third level of connivance is *condoning* a transgression. This is violated when you give the impression that there is nothing wrong with wrongdoing. An ethical person is not supposed to condone improper behavior; it is his responsibility to protest it. Seeming to be involved in the activity is the ultimate form of condoning. On this basis, the Talmud[24] teaches:

> Anyone who is capable of protesting the acts of his household but does not protest is liable together with the members of his household; [if he does not protest] the acts of the residents of his city, he is liable together with the people of the city; [if he

does not protest] the acts of the entire world, he is liable together
with the entire world.

This obligation devolves upon anyone who is in a position to make
an effective protest against wrongdoing. One need not be involved
in the wrongdoing to engage in protest. So, for instance, if term
papers were sold in a store, it would be ethically problematic to
go in and buy a term paper even if you wanted it for a legitimate
purpose.[25]

Practically speaking, however, term-paper sites tend to be completely anonymous. The user is not identified with the transgression
and does not give the impression of condoning it by using the service. Therefore, if you wanted to use a site for a permissible purpose,
such as to obtain ideas or source references, you could do so without
seeming to condone the more common illegitimate uses.

To sum up, there are various levels of forbidden cooperation with wrongdoing. The activity you mention, selling term papers to a site that will
sell them to students to be submitted as their own work, falls into the
category of abetting transgression. Even though you do not enable the
transgression to take place, you are an active partner in it.

HOW SHOULD THE INSTRUCTOR REACT?

The phenomenon of plagiarism demands ethical behavior from students,
but it also places demands on instructors to take reasonable steps to avoid
putting honest students at a disadvantage. Here are some useful tips:

1. Assign paper topics that are a little off the beaten track. If you
    ask students to write a paper on "The Concept of 'Nature' in
    King Lear," you are inviting trouble. Ask them instead, say, to
    compare the concepts of nature in Lear and some other, more
    obscure work that is not likely to be in anyone's term-paper
    file.
2. Do the same thing for the structure and organization of the pa-
    per. Demand the unexpected and unconventional: for example,

require some minimal number of citations from the original or the adoption of a specific analytic approach.

3. Give occasional oral quizzes to make sure the students understand what they have submitted. This may not be enough to make the students write their own papers, but at the very least it will induce them to read the papers they purchase.

ENDNOTES

1. Kiddushin 29a, 82a
2. Shabbat 105a; Shulhan Arukh, Orah Hayyim 306:6
3. Pesahim 108a, Avodah Zarah 17b
4. Avodah Zarah 15b
5. Hafetz Hayyim 1:10, 2:10
6. Responsa Iggerot Mosheh, Hoshen Mishpat 2:30
7. Avot 2:4
8. Ecclesiastes 7:29
9. Sefer ha-Hinnukh 16
10. Responsa Hilkhot Ketanot 1:276
11. See Be'er ha-Golah on Shulhan Arukh, Yoreh Deah 334:123
12. Hafetz Hayyim 1, 8:3
13. Shulhan Arukh, Yoreh Deah 240:20
14. Exodus 20:12
15. Pesahim 108a
16. Shulhan Arukh, Yoreh Deah 240:19
17. Avot 4:2
18. Exodus 23:7
19. Responsa Iggerot Moshe, Hoshen Mishpat 11:30
20. Mishnah Avot 6:6, Megillah 16a
21. Leviticus 19:14
22. Gittin 61a
23. Shulhan Arukh, Yoreh Deah 151 and commentaries
24. Shabbat 54b
25. Shulhan Arukh, Yoreh Deah 334:48 in Rema

Brief Introduction to the Sources

Most of the books cited in The Jewish Ethicist are well-known works in the public domain, which can be found in any reasonably extensive Torah library. Therefore, the footnotes are brief and don't bring much bibliographical information. However, since these works are not familiar to all English-speaking readers, especially by their Hebrew names. Following is a brief introduction to the main source works cited in The Jewish Ethicist.

THE "ORAL LAW"

Jewish law is based on two main sources. One is the written Torah, the first five books of the Bible which are also called the "Five books of Moses". Together with the text of the written Torah, Moses also transmitted the "Oral Torah", which was also part of Moses' unique prophecy. The oral Torah consists both of specific explanations and elaborations of the written commandments, and of principles by which later generations of scholars could further elucidate the text. It also came to include all of the special additions and emendations made by Rabbinic leaders over the generations, according to the responsibility given them in the Torah itself to make "by-laws" which would keep Torah observance alive and complete.

The main works of the Oral Torah are as follows:

Mishnah: Students of Torah were accustomed to summarize their learning of the Oral Law in brief "epigrams". Rabbi Judah the Prince, one of the greatest Torah as well as secular leaders of the Jewish people, redacted an extensive and authoritative collection of these legal epigrams in the second century CE. This collection is known as the Mishnah. The Mishnah is divided into tractates, chapters, and specific epigrams or "mishnahs".

Babylonian Talmud: Over the course of centuries, scholars in the great academies of Babylonia discussed and compared the laws of the Mishnah with each other and with parallel legal traditions. These discussions were written and redacted in the seventh century CE and constitute the Babylonian Talmud, which is the authoritative source for Jewish law to this day. The Talmud also contains much non-legal material, including instructive stories (Aggadah), elucidations of the Bible (Midrash), and much secular wisdom.

Page references are according to the standard pagination of the Talmud, which has been in use for hundreds of years.

Jerusalem or Palestinian Talmud: A parallel process, too,k place in the academies of Northern Israel, leading to the so-called "Jerusalem Talmud", which is briefer, earlier and less extensively redacted and therefore less authoritative than the Babylonian Talmud. Since there is no one standard version of this Talmud, references are brought by tractate, chapter and law, which are virtually identical in the varying editions.

Midrash: The Sages of the Talmud expressed many profound insights in the form of exegetical explanations of the Biblical text. These were collected sometime after the redaction of the Talmud and are known as Midrash. These also lack any accepted standard pagination or chapter division, therefore we cite the Midrash according the verse discussed.

RASHI

There are innumerable commentaries on the Bible and the Talmud, but the most important is undoubtedly that of Rashi (1040–1105), an acronym for Rabbi Shlomo Yitzchaki ("son of Yitzchak"), who lived in France. Rashi composed lucid yet inspired commentaries on the Bible and on almost the entire Talmud. The influence of these commentaries is so immense that it is almost difficult to believe. Already during Rashi's lifetime his commentaries were widely copied and studied and became standard accompaniments to Torah and Talmud study throughout Europe, spreading soon afterwards to the entire Jewish world. And to this day these commentaries remain the standard; virtually every edition of the Torah or Talmud found in any Orthodox synagogue or study hall includes Rashi's words as the main commentary.

LEGAL CODES

Mishneh Torah: The first extensive and authoritative legal code was that of Maimonides. His code is called the Mishneh Torah (Recapitulation of the Torah), and is divided into scores of individual legal topics. Citations from this work are according to topic, chapter, and specific law.

Shulchan Arukh: In the fourteenth century CE, Rabbi Jacob ben Asher wrote a new extensive code in four sections or "columns" each divided into hundreds of specific legal topics or chapters. This book is called the "Tur", the Hebrew word for column. In the sixteenth century, Rabbi Joseph Karo wrote a more up-to-date code based on the identical book and chapter division. He called his work the "Shulchan Arukh", meaning the "Laid Table". In the same generation, the Polish authority Rabbi Moses Isserles added glosses to indicate where the customs of northern European (Ashkenazi) Jewry was different. The Shulchan Arukh remains today the main authoritative code of Jewish law for virtually all Jewish communities.

The codes are accompanied by a number of authoritative commentaries, which are also frequently cited in the Jewish Ethicist.

RESPONSA

Throughout the ages leading rabbinical authorities wrote replies to queries which reached them. These replies are known as "responsa" and are another important source of legal precedent.

About the Author

Rabbi Dr. Asher Meir is Research Director at the prestigious Business Ethics Center of Jerusalem and Senior Lecturer in economics and business ethics at the Jerusalem College of Technology. He studied economics at Harvard and MIT, where he received his doctorate, and worked on the staff of the Council of Economic Advisers in the Reagan administration as well as in the private sector. He also writes a weekly business ethics column for the *Jerusalem Post*. Rabbi Meir's many lectures and columns on Jewish law and its ethical lessons are highly popular.

Rabbi Dr. Meir is also the author of *Meaning in Mitzvot*, a popular commentary providing insights into the inner meaning of the everyday laws and customs of Jewish observance.

Index